FROM THE LIBRARY OF:

Jaime Hernandez

FANTAGRAPHICS BOOKS
7563 Lake City Way NE
Seattle WA 98115

Edited by Gary Groth
Design by Jacob Covey
Production by Paul Baresh
Gary Groth and Kim Thompson, publishers

This is Volume 24 in The Complete Love and Rockets.

The material in this edition originally appeared in
Love and Rockets Vol. II #11-19.

Distributed in the U.S. by W.W. Norton and Company, Inc. (212-354-5500)
Distributed in Canada by Canadian Manda Group (416-516-0911)
Distributed in the United Kingdom by Turnaround Distribution (208-829-3009)

See the last page of this book for information on ordering more Love and Rockets work!

First printing: February, 2008
Second printing: July, 2008

ISBN: 978-1-56097-939-5

the Education of Hopey Glass

FANTAGRAPHICS BOOKS

HOPEY!

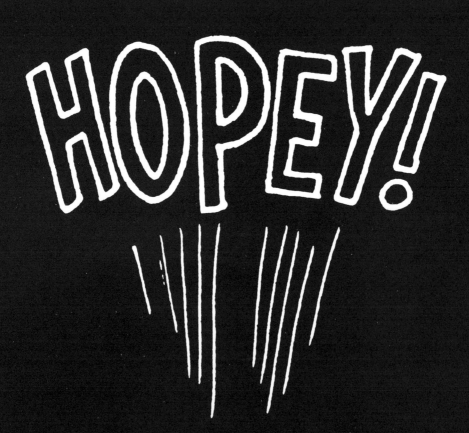

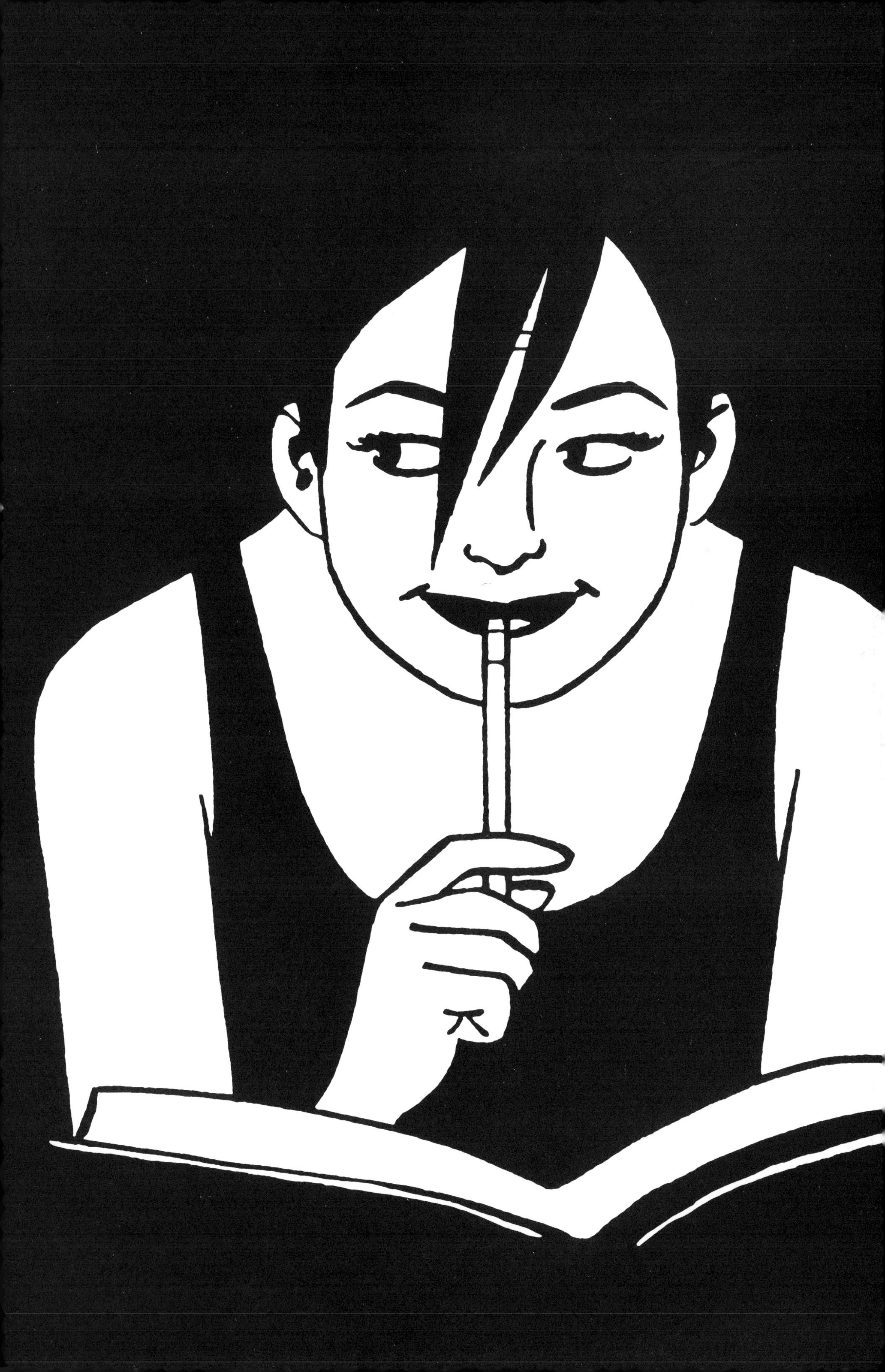

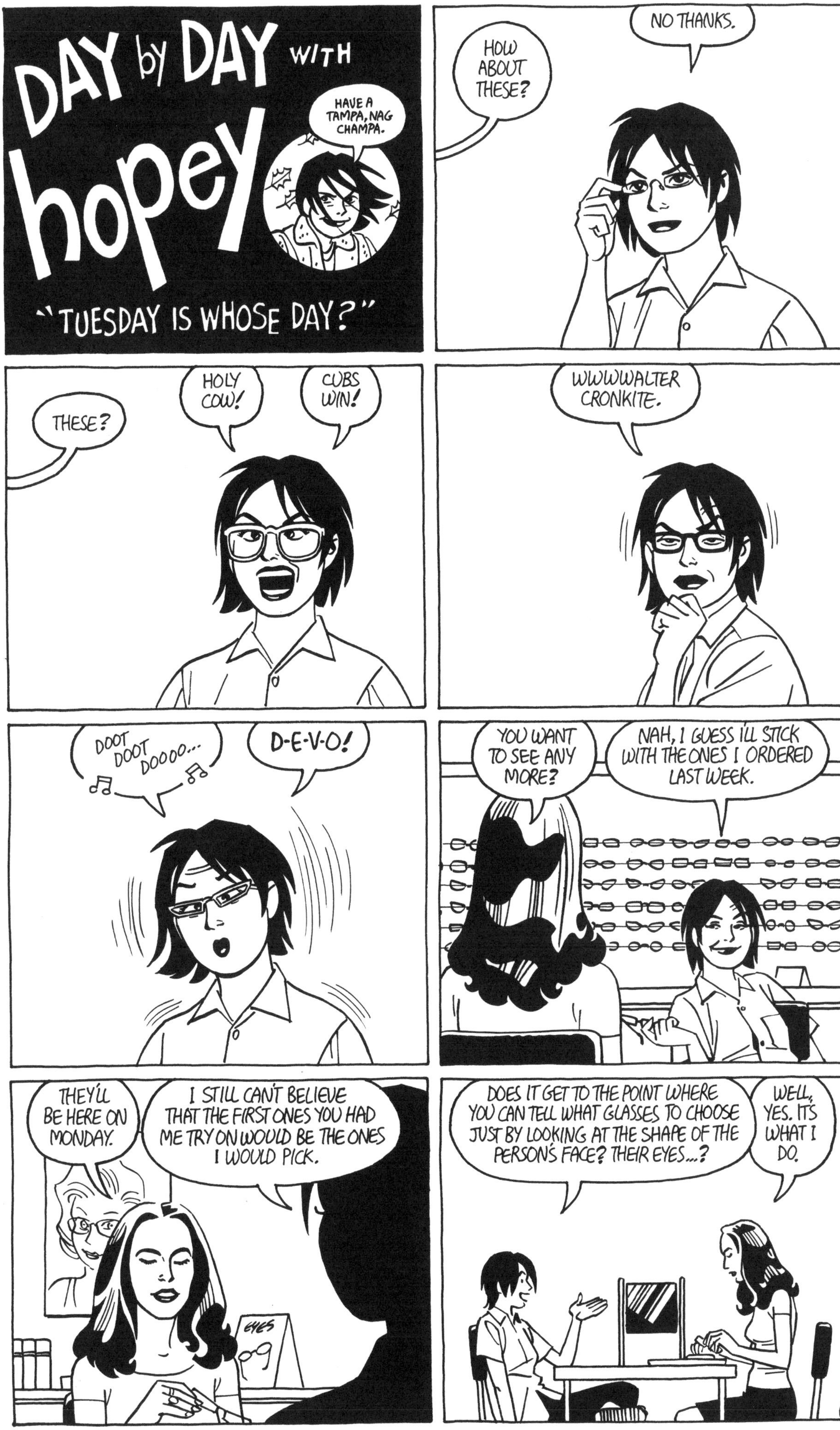
DAY by DAY WITH hopey
HAVE A TAMPA, NAG CHAMPA.
"TUESDAY IS WHOSE DAY?"
HOW ABOUT THESE?
NO THANKS.
THESE?
HOLY COW!
CUBS WIN!
WWWWALTER CRONKITE.
DOOT DOOT DOOOO...
D-E-V-O!
YOU WANT TO SEE ANY MORE?
NAH, I GUESS I'LL STICK WITH THE ONES I ORDERED LAST WEEK.
THEY'LL BE HERE ON MONDAY.
I STILL CAN'T BELIEVE THAT THE FIRST ONES YOU HAD ME TRY ON WOULD BE THE ONES I WOULD PICK.
EYES
DOES IT GET TO THE POINT WHERE YOU CAN TELL WHAT GLASSES TO CHOOSE JUST BY LOOKING AT THE SHAPE OF THE PERSON'S FACE? THEIR EYES...?
WELL, YES. ITS WHAT I DO.
1

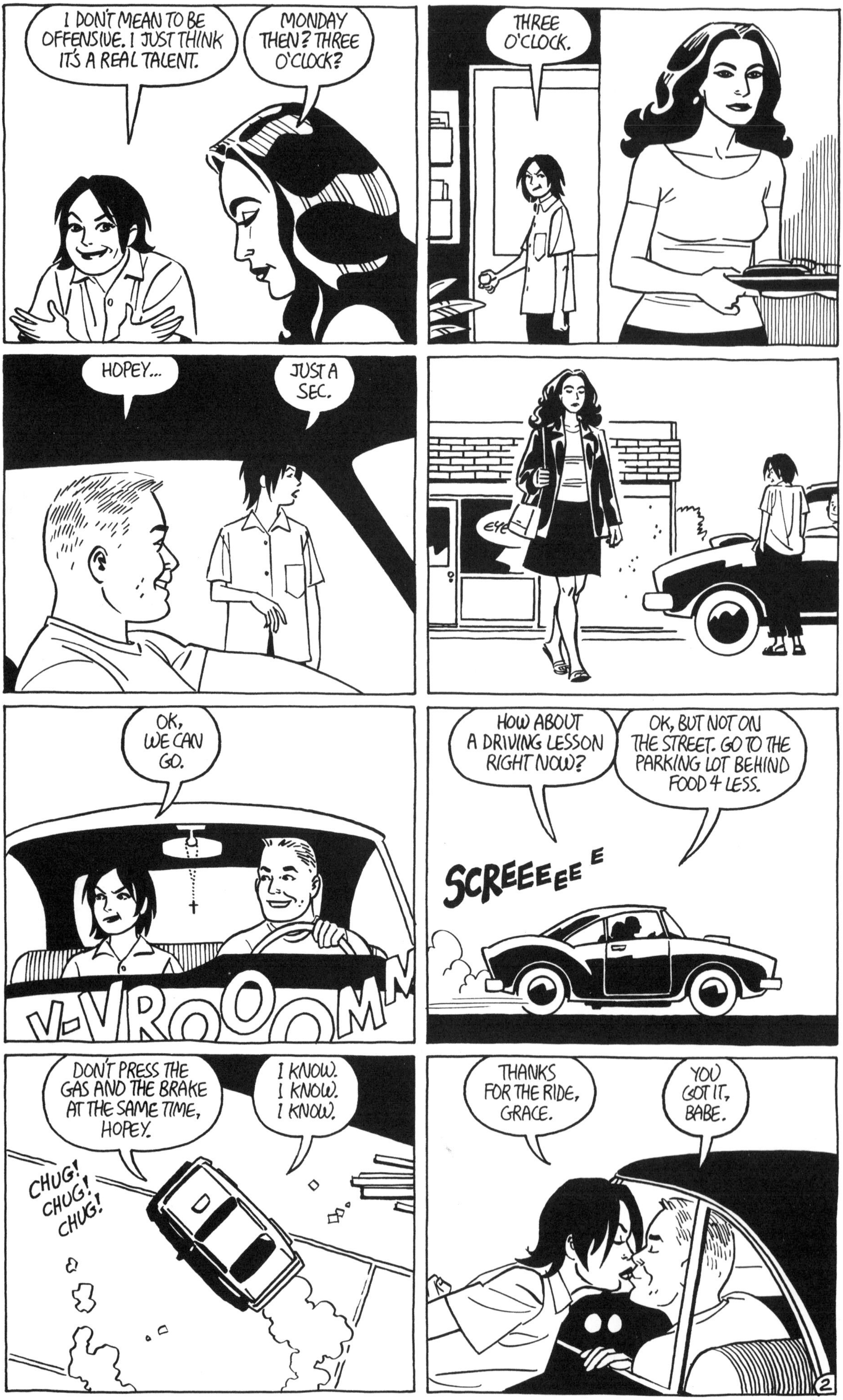
I DON'T MEAN TO BE OFFENSIVE. I JUST THINK IT'S A REAL TALENT.
MONDAY THEN? THREE O'CLOCK?
THREE O'CLOCK.
HOPEY...
JUST A SEC.
EYE
OK, WE CAN GO.
V-VROOOOMM
HOW ABOUT A DRIVING LESSON RIGHT NOW?
OK, BUT NOT ON THE STREET. GO TO THE PARKING LOT BEHIND FOOD 4 LESS.
SCREEEEEE E
DON'T PRESS THE GAS AND THE BRAKE AT THE SAME TIME, HOPEY.
I KNOW. I KNOW. I KNOW.
CHUG! CHUG! CHUG!
THANKS FOR THE RIDE, GRACE.
YOU GOT IT, BABE.
2

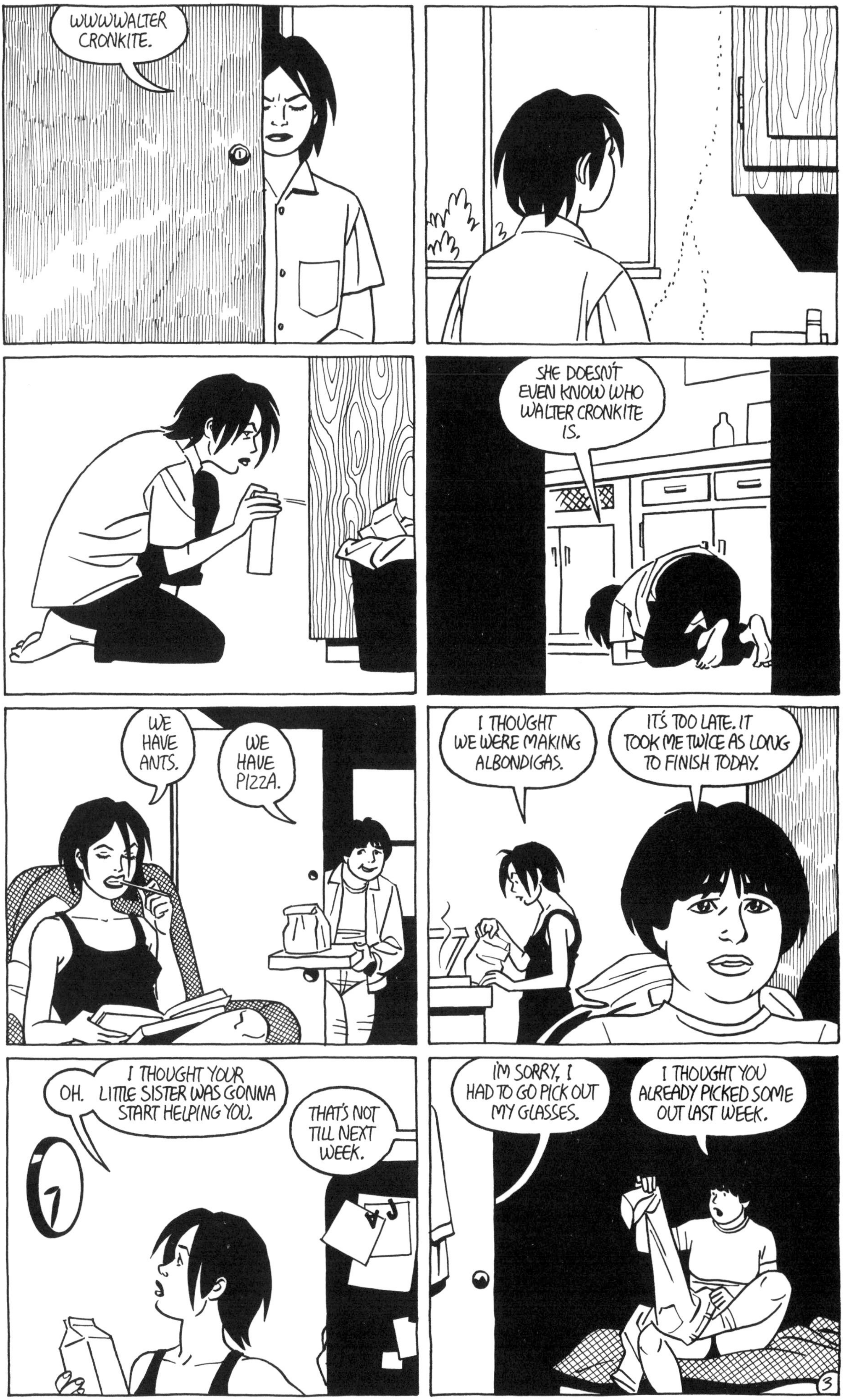
WWWWALTER CRONKITE.
SHE DOESN'T EVEN KNOW WHO WALTER CRONKITE IS.
WE HAVE ANTS.
WE HAVE PIZZA.
I THOUGHT WE WERE MAKING ALBONDIGAS.
IT'S TOO LATE. IT TOOK ME TWICE AS LONG TO FINISH TODAY.
OH.
I THOUGHT YOUR LITTLE SISTER WAS GONNA START HELPING YOU.
THAT'S NOT TILL NEXT WEEK.
I'M SORRY, I HAD TO GO PICK OUT MY GLASSES.
I THOUGHT YOU ALREADY PICKED SOME OUT LAST WEEK.
3

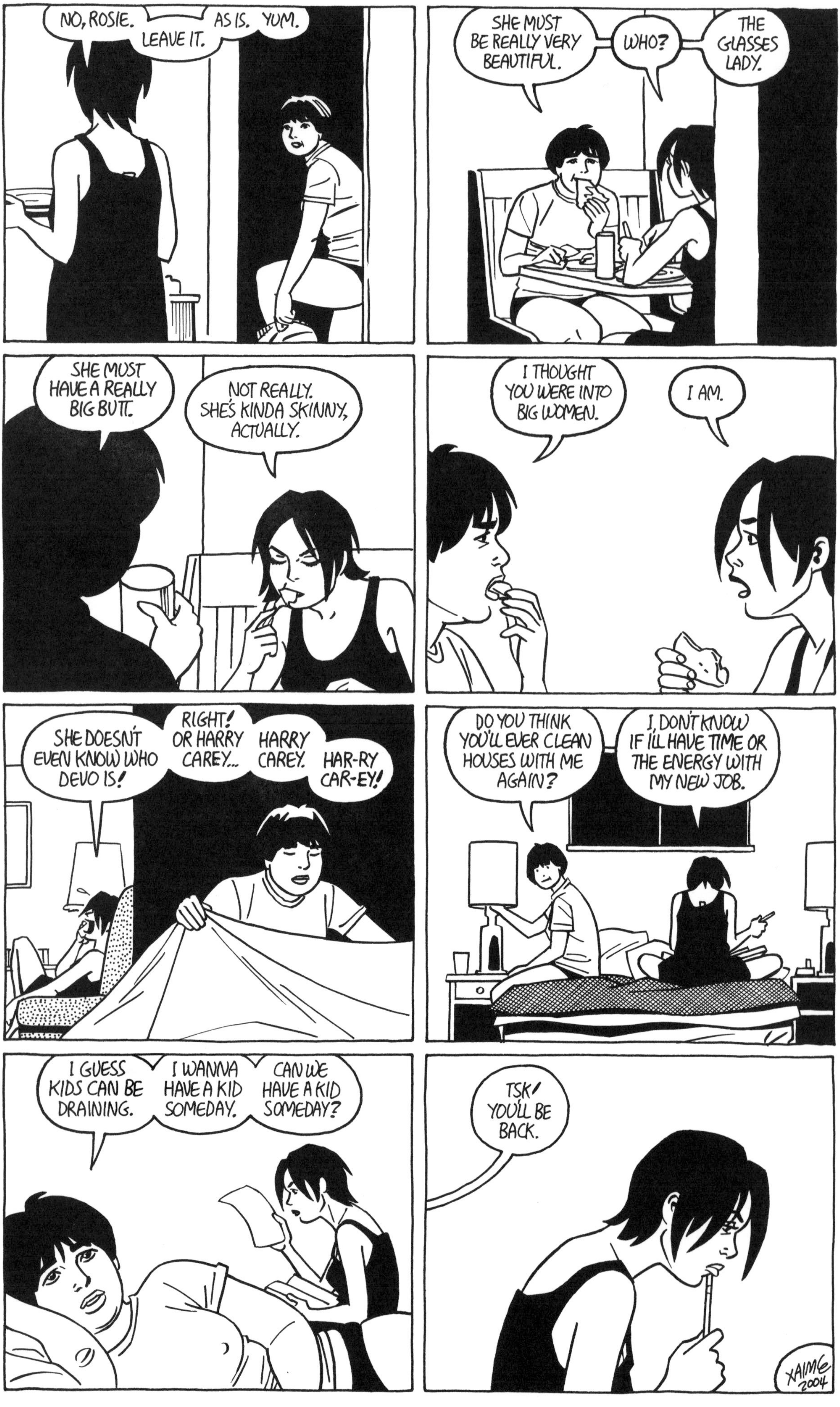

NO, ROSIE.
LEAVE IT.
AS IS.
YUM.
SHE MUST BE REALLY VERY BEAUTIFUL.
WHO?
THE GLASSES LADY.
SHE MUST HAVE A REALLY BIG BUTT.
NOT REALLY. SHE'S KINDA SKINNY, ACTUALLY.
I THOUGHT YOU WERE INTO BIG WOMEN.
I AM.
SHE DOESN'T EVEN KNOW WHO DEVO IS!
RIGHT! OR HARRY CAREY...
HARRY CAREY.
HAR-RY CAR-EY!
DO YOU THINK YOU'LL EVER CLEAN HOUSES WITH ME AGAIN?
I, DON'T KNOW IF I'LL HAVE TIME OR THE ENERGY WITH MY NEW JOB.
I GUESS KIDS CAN BE DRAINING.
I WANNA HAVE A KID SOMEDAY.
CAN WE HAVE A KID SOMEDAY?
TSK! YOU'LL BE BACK.
XAIME 2004

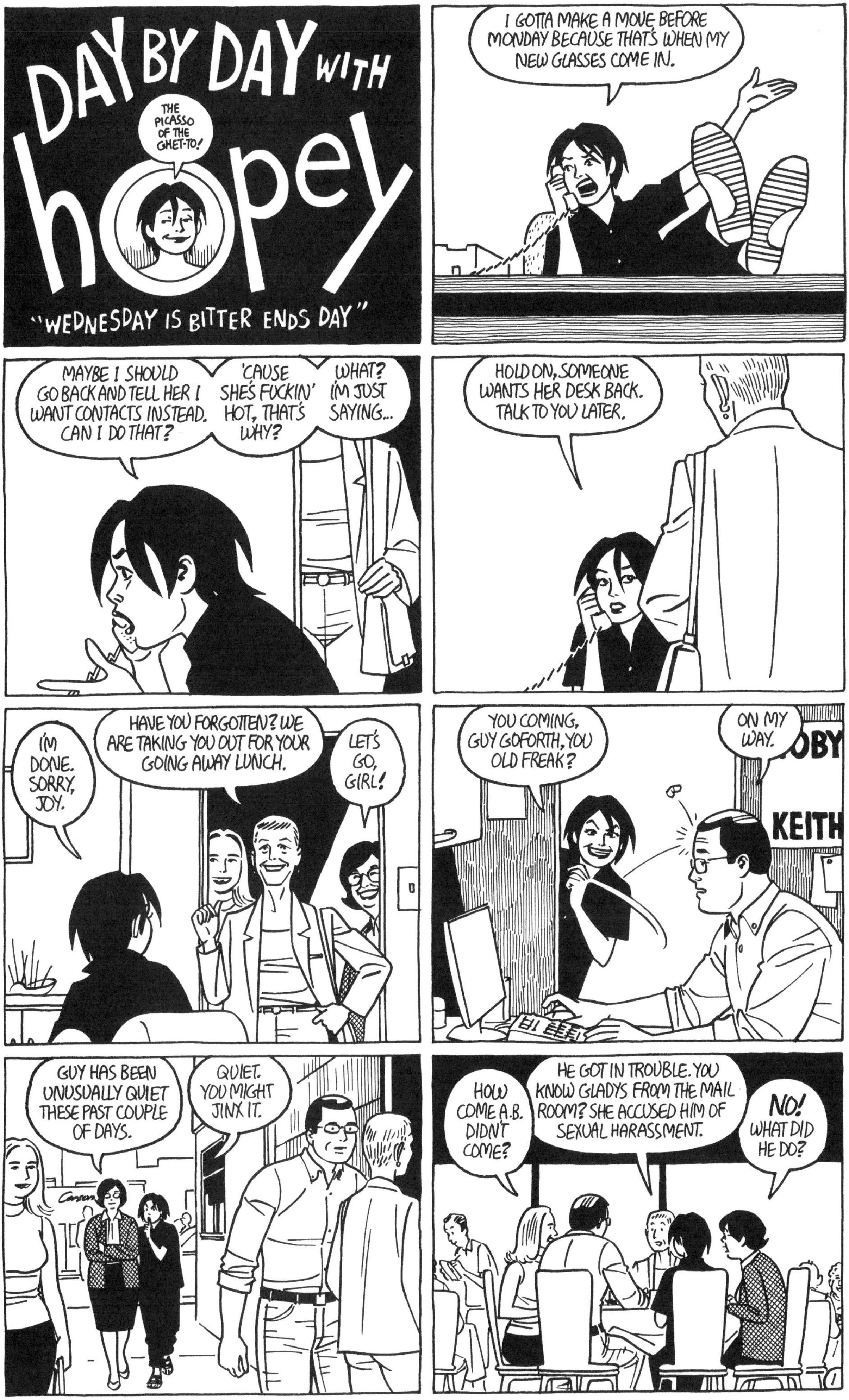
DAY BY DAY WITH hopey
THE PICASSO OF THE GHET-TO!
"WEDNESDAY IS BITTER ENDS DAY"
I GOTTA MAKE A MOVE BEFORE MONDAY BECAUSE THAT'S WHEN MY NEW GLASSES COME IN.
MAYBE I SHOULD GO BACK AND TELL HER I WANT CONTACTS INSTEAD. CAN I DO THAT?
'CAUSE SHE'S FUCKIN' HOT, THAT'S WHY?
WHAT? I'M JUST SAYING...
HOLD ON, SOMEONE WANTS HER DESK BACK. TALK TO YOU LATER.
I'M DONE. SORRY, JOY.
HAVE YOU FORGOTTEN? WE ARE TAKING YOU OUT FOR YOUR GOING AWAY LUNCH.
LET'S GO, GIRL!
YOU COMING, GUY GOFORTH, YOU OLD FREAK?
ON MY WAY.
TOBY
KEITH
GUY HAS BEEN UNUSUALLY QUIET THESE PAST COUPLE OF DAYS.
QUIET. YOU MIGHT JINX IT.
HOW COME A.B. DIDN'T COME?
HE GOT IN TROUBLE. YOU KNOW GLADYS FROM THE MAIL ROOM? SHE ACCUSED HIM OF SEXUAL HARASSMENT.
NO! WHAT DID HE DO?

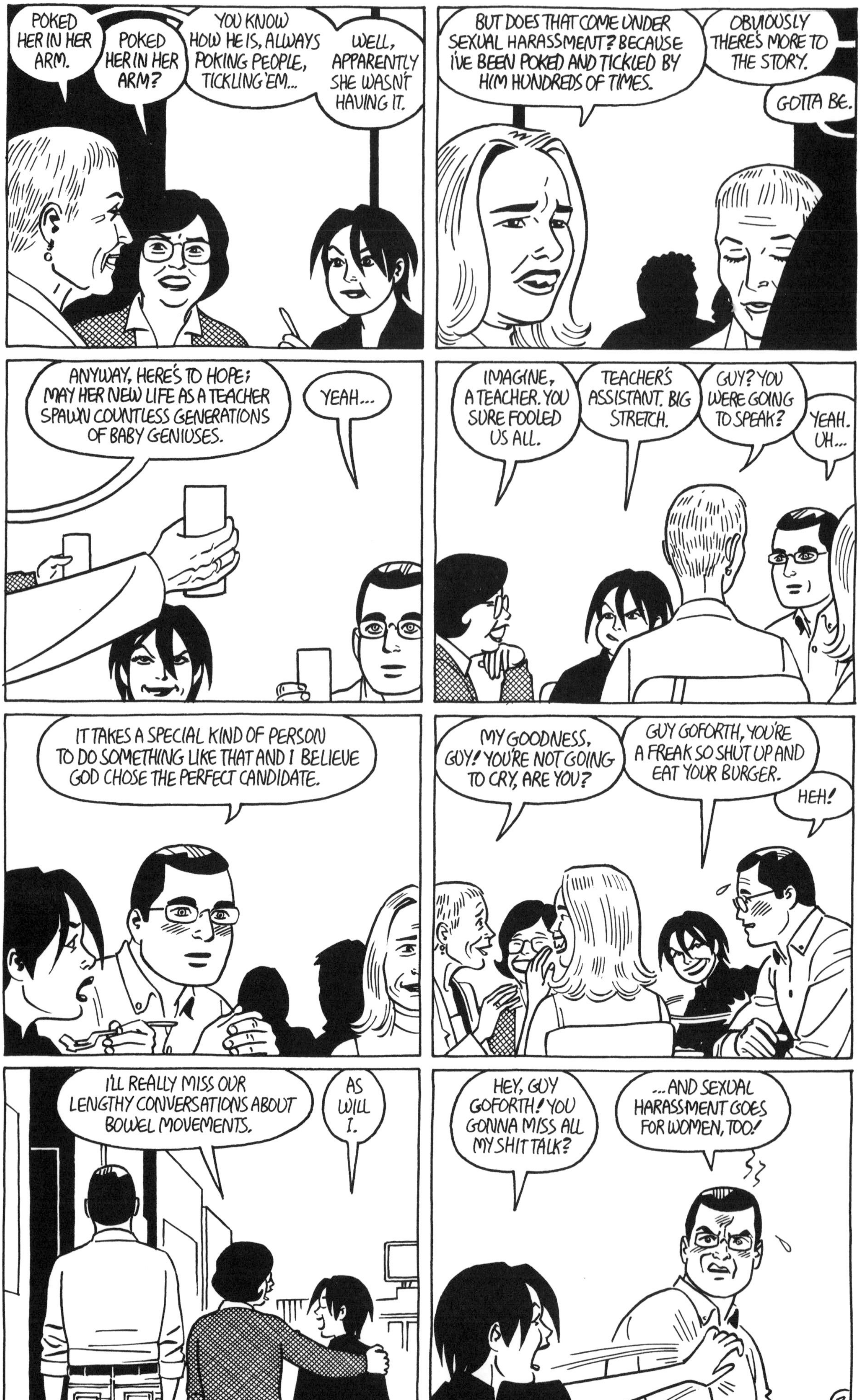
POKED HER IN HER ARM.
POKED HER IN HER ARM?
YOU KNOW HOW HE IS, ALWAYS POKING PEOPLE, TICKLING 'EM...
WELL, APPARENTLY SHE WASN'T HAVING IT.
BUT DOES THAT COME UNDER SEXUAL HARASSMENT? BECAUSE I'VE BEEN POKED AND TICKLED BY HIM HUNDREDS OF TIMES.
OBVIOUSLY THERE'S MORE TO THE STORY.
GOTTA BE.
ANYWAY, HERE'S TO HOPE; MAY HER NEW LIFE AS A TEACHER SPAWN COUNTLESS GENERATIONS OF BABY GENIUSES.
YEAH...
IMAGINE, A TEACHER. YOU SURE FOOLED US ALL.
TEACHER'S ASSISTANT. BIG STRETCH.
GUY? YOU WERE GOING TO SPEAK?
YEAH. UH...
IT TAKES A SPECIAL KIND OF PERSON TO DO SOMETHING LIKE THAT AND I BELIEVE GOD CHOSE THE PERFECT CANDIDATE.
MY GOODNESS, GUY! YOU'RE NOT GOING TO CRY, ARE YOU?
GUY GOFORTH, YOU'RE A FREAK SO SHUT UP AND EAT YOUR BURGER.
HEH!
I'LL REALLY MISS OUR LENGTHY CONVERSATIONS ABOUT BOWEL MOVEMENTS.
AS WILL I.
HEY, GUY GOFORTH! YOU GONNA MISS ALL MY SHIT TALK?
...AND SEXUAL HARASSMENT GOES FOR WOMEN, TOO!
2

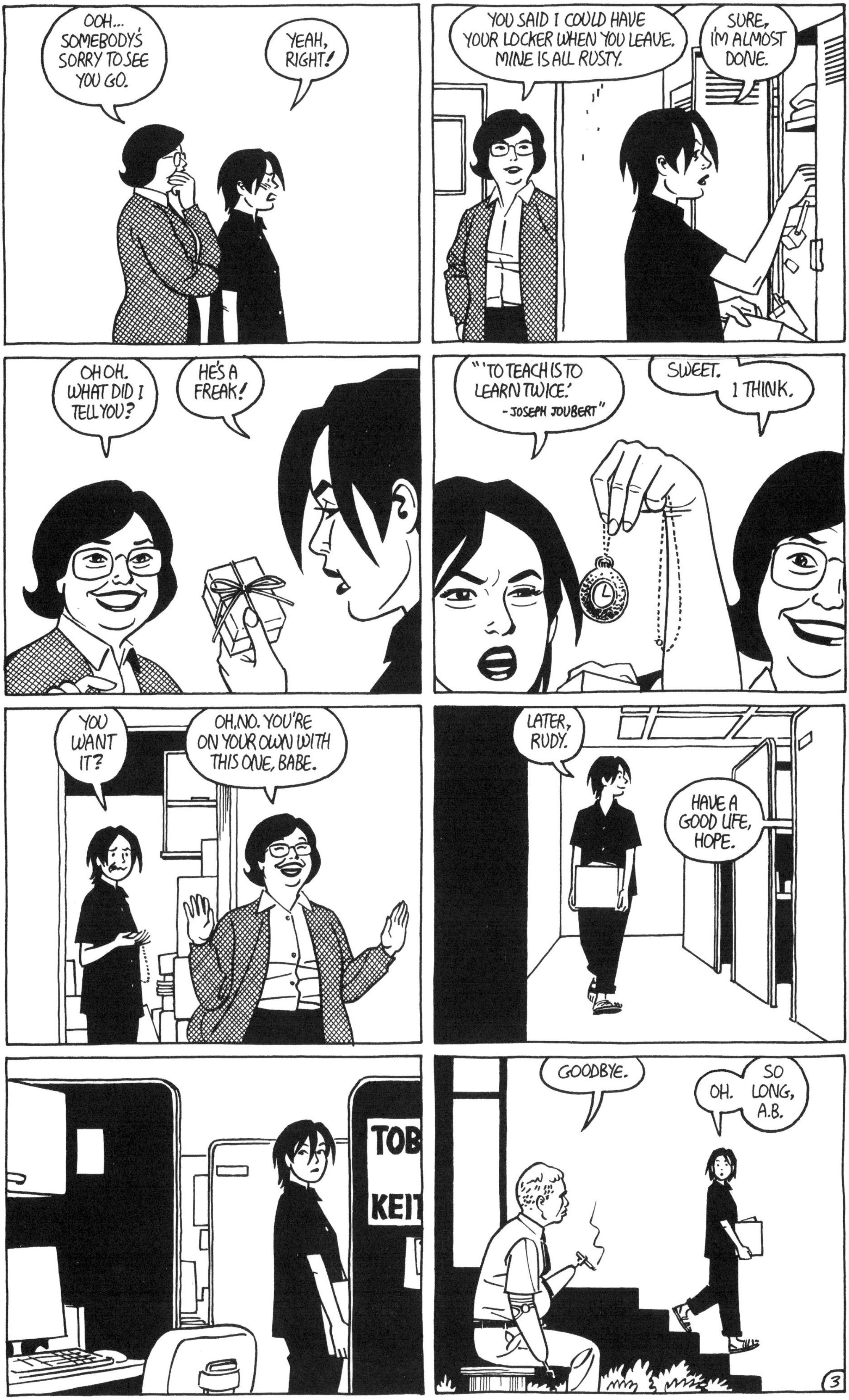
OOH... SOMEBODY'S SORRY TO SEE YOU GO.
YEAH, RIGHT!
YOU SAID I COULD HAVE YOUR LOCKER WHEN YOU LEAVE. MINE IS ALL RUSTY.
SURE, I'M ALMOST DONE.
OH OH. WHAT DID I TELL YOU?
HE'S A FREAK!
"'TO TEACH IS TO LEARN TWICE.' -JOSEPH JOUBERT"
SWEET.
I THINK.
YOU WANT IT?
OH, NO. YOU'RE ON YOUR OWN WITH THIS ONE, BABE.
LATER, RUDY.
HAVE A GOOD LIFE, HOPE.
TOB
KEIT
GOODBYE.
OH.
SO LONG, A.B.
3

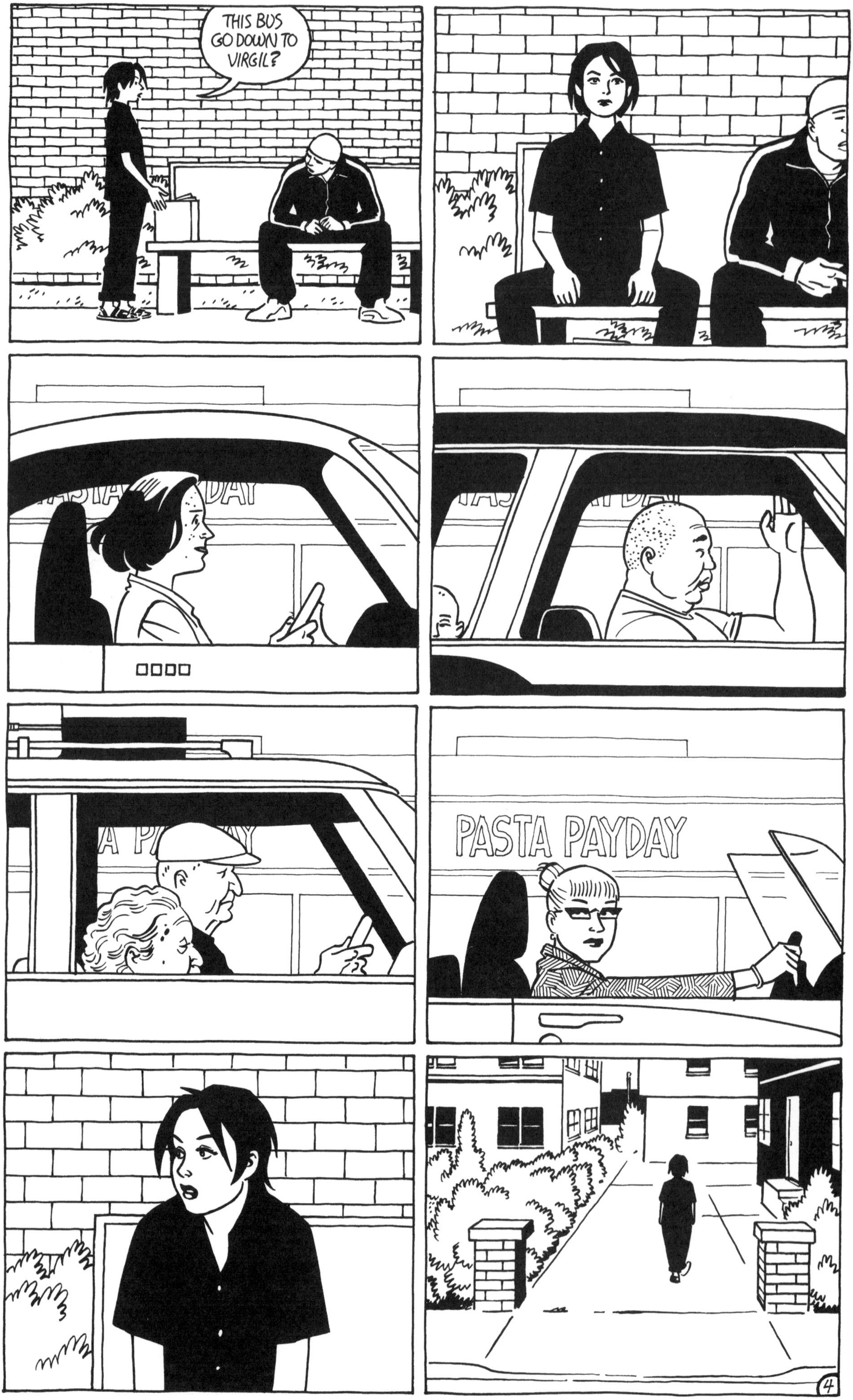
THIS BUS GO DOWN TO VIRGIL?
PASTA PAYDAY
4

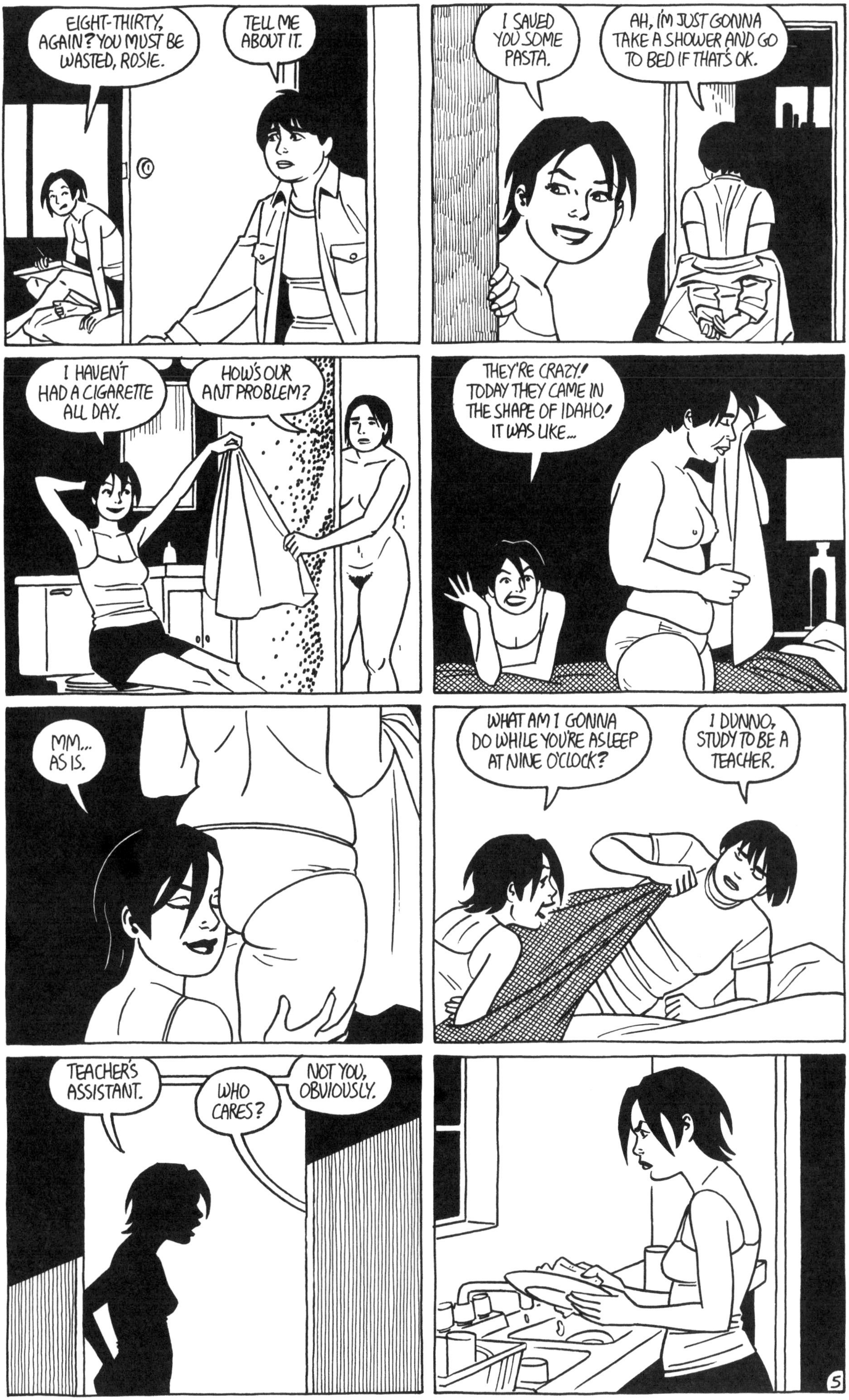
EIGHT-THIRTY, AGAIN? YOU MUST BE WASTED, ROSIE.
TELL ME ABOUT IT.
I SAVED YOU SOME PASTA.
AH, I'M JUST GONNA TAKE A SHOWER AND GO TO BED IF THAT'S OK.
I HAVEN'T HAD A CIGARETTE ALL DAY.
HOW'S OUR ANT PROBLEM?
THEY'RE CRAZY! TODAY THEY CAME IN THE SHAPE OF IDAHO! IT WAS LIKE...
MM... AS IS.
WHAT AM I GONNA DO WHILE YOU'RE ASLEEP AT NINE O'CLOCK?
I DUNNO, STUDY TO BE A TEACHER.
TEACHER'S ASSISTANT.
WHO CARES?
NOT YOU, OBVIOUSLY.
5

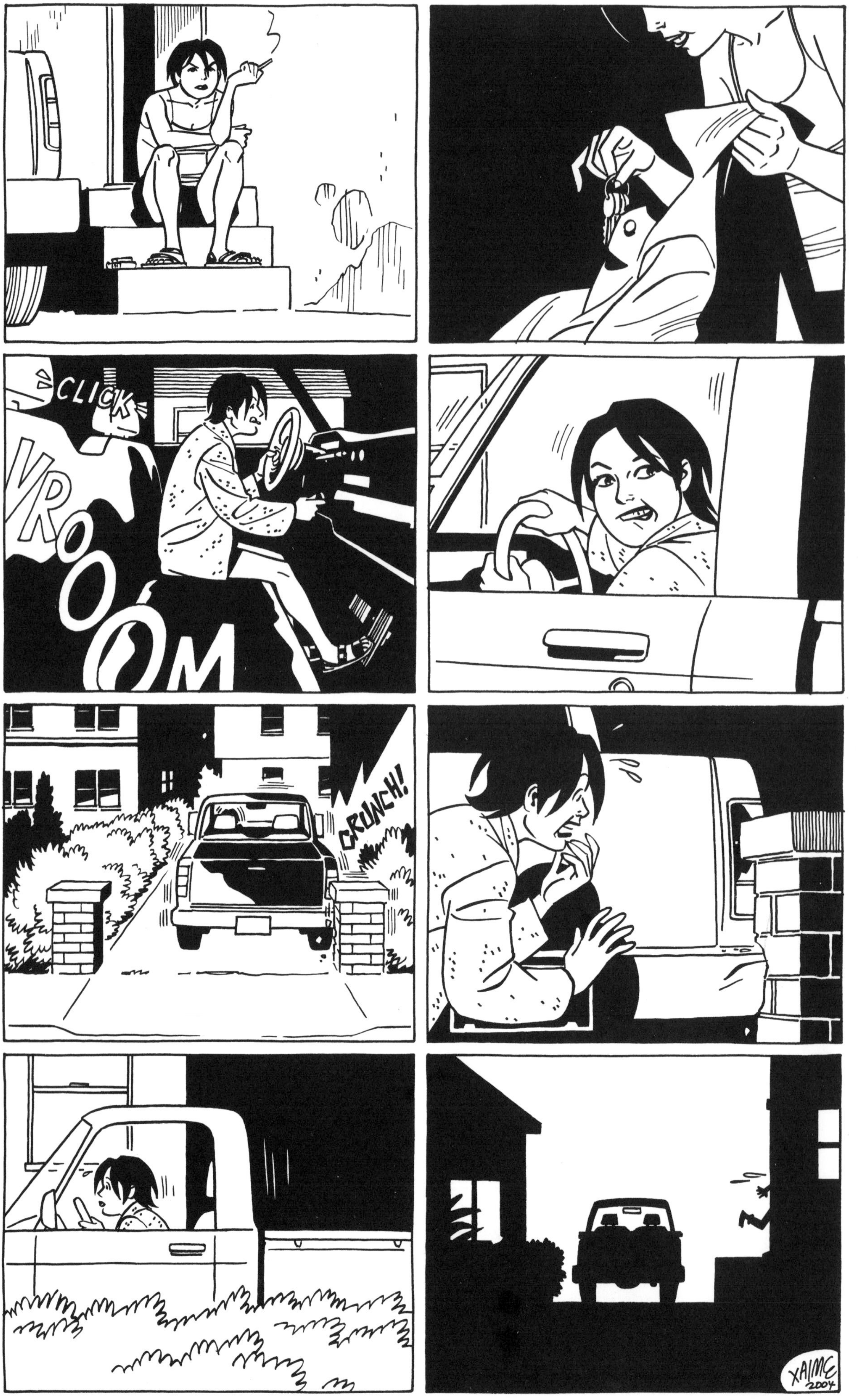
CLICK
VROOOOM
CRUNCH!
XAIME 2004

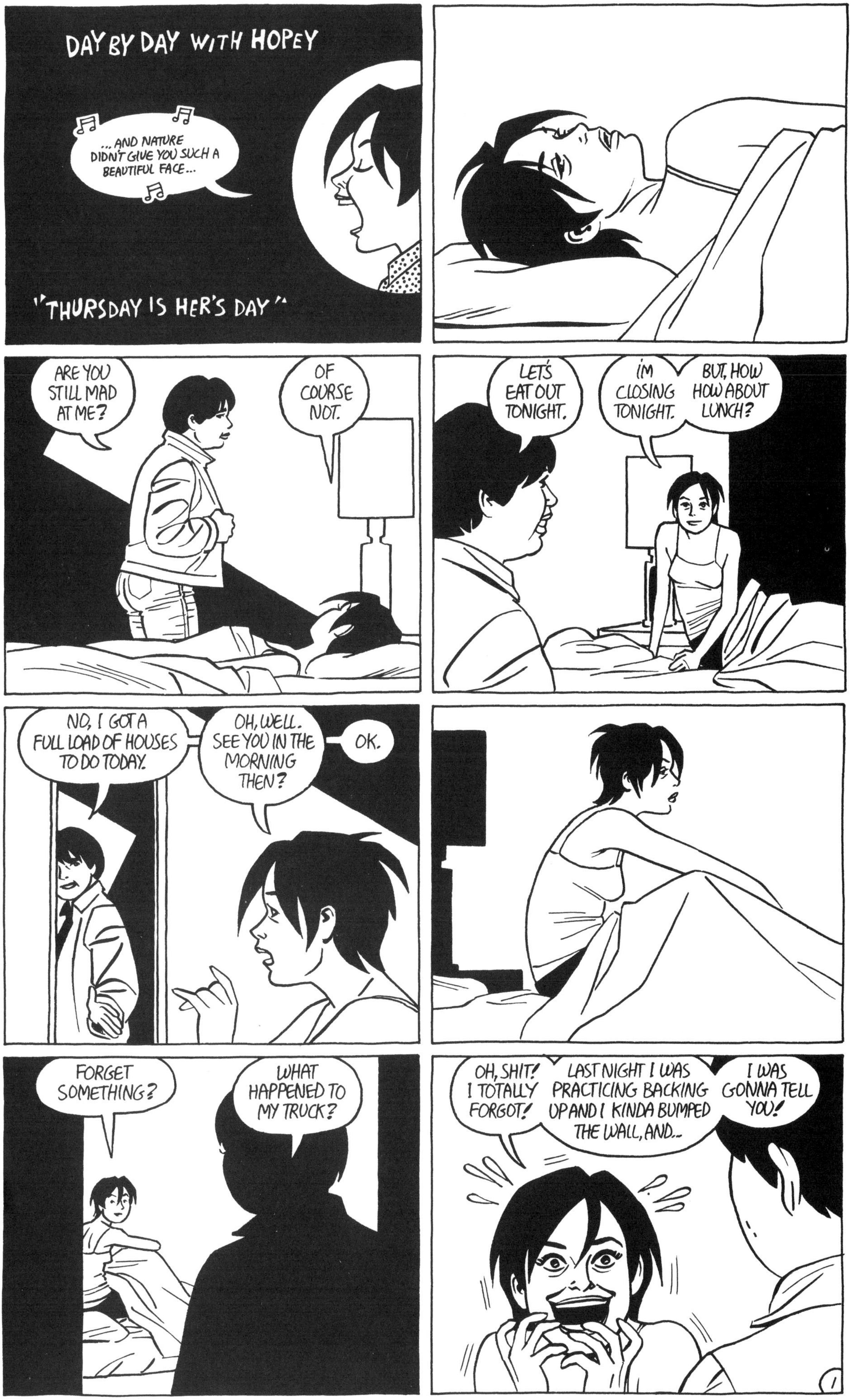
DAY BY DAY WITH HOPEY
...AND NATURE DIDN'T GIVE YOU SUCH A BEAUTIFUL FACE...
"THURSDAY IS HER'S DAY"
ARE YOU STILL MAD AT ME?
OF COURSE NOT.
LET'S EAT OUT TONIGHT.
I'M CLOSING TONIGHT.
BUT, HOW HOW ABOUT LUNCH?
NO, I GOT A FULL LOAD OF HOUSES TO DO TODAY.
OH, WELL. SEE YOU IN THE MORNING THEN?
OK.
FORGET SOMETHING?
WHAT HAPPENED TO MY TRUCK?
OH, SHIT! I TOTALLY FORGOT!
LAST NIGHT I WAS PRACTICING BACKING UP AND I KINDA BUMPED THE WALL, AND...
I WAS GONNA TELL YOU!
1

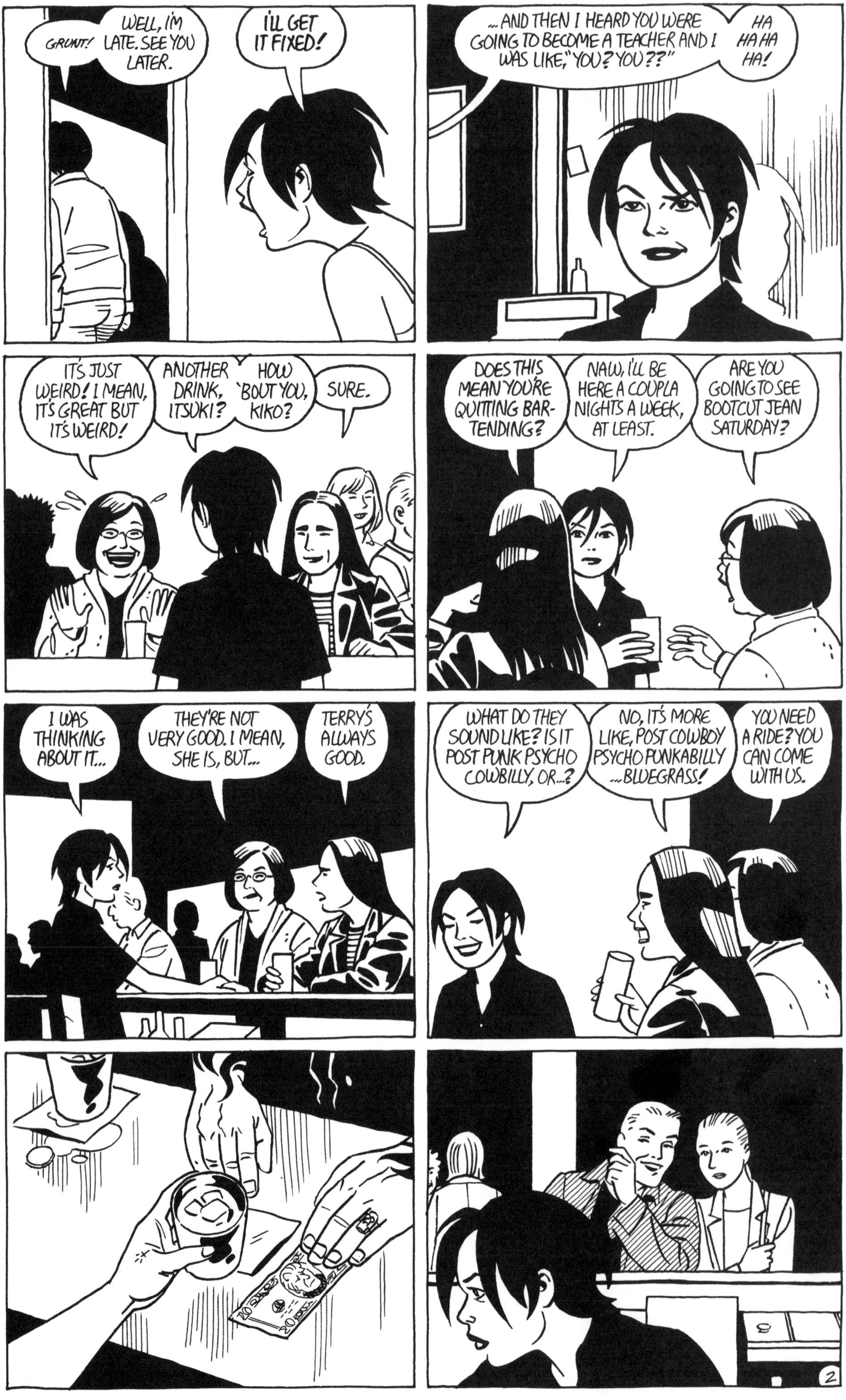
GRUNT!
WELL, I'M LATE. SEE YOU LATER.
I'LL GET IT FIXED!
...AND THEN I HEARD YOU WERE GOING TO BECOME A TEACHER AND I WAS LIKE, "YOU? YOU??"
HA HA HA HA!
IT'S JUST WEIRD! I MEAN, IT'S GREAT BUT IT'S WEIRD!
ANOTHER DRINK, ITSUKI?
HOW 'BOUT YOU, KIKO?
SURE.
DOES THIS MEAN YOU'RE QUITTING BAR-TENDING?
NAW, I'LL BE HERE A COUPLA NIGHTS A WEEK, AT LEAST.
ARE YOU GOING TO SEE BOOTCUT JEAN SATURDAY?
I WAS THINKING ABOUT IT...
THEY'RE NOT VERY GOOD. I MEAN, SHE IS, BUT...
TERRY'S ALWAYS GOOD.
WHAT DO THEY SOUND LIKE? IS IT POST PUNK PSYCHO COWBILLY, OR...?
NO, IT'S MORE LIKE, POST COWBOY PSYCHO PUNKABILLY ...BLUEGRASS!
YOU NEED A RIDE? YOU CAN COME WITH US.
2

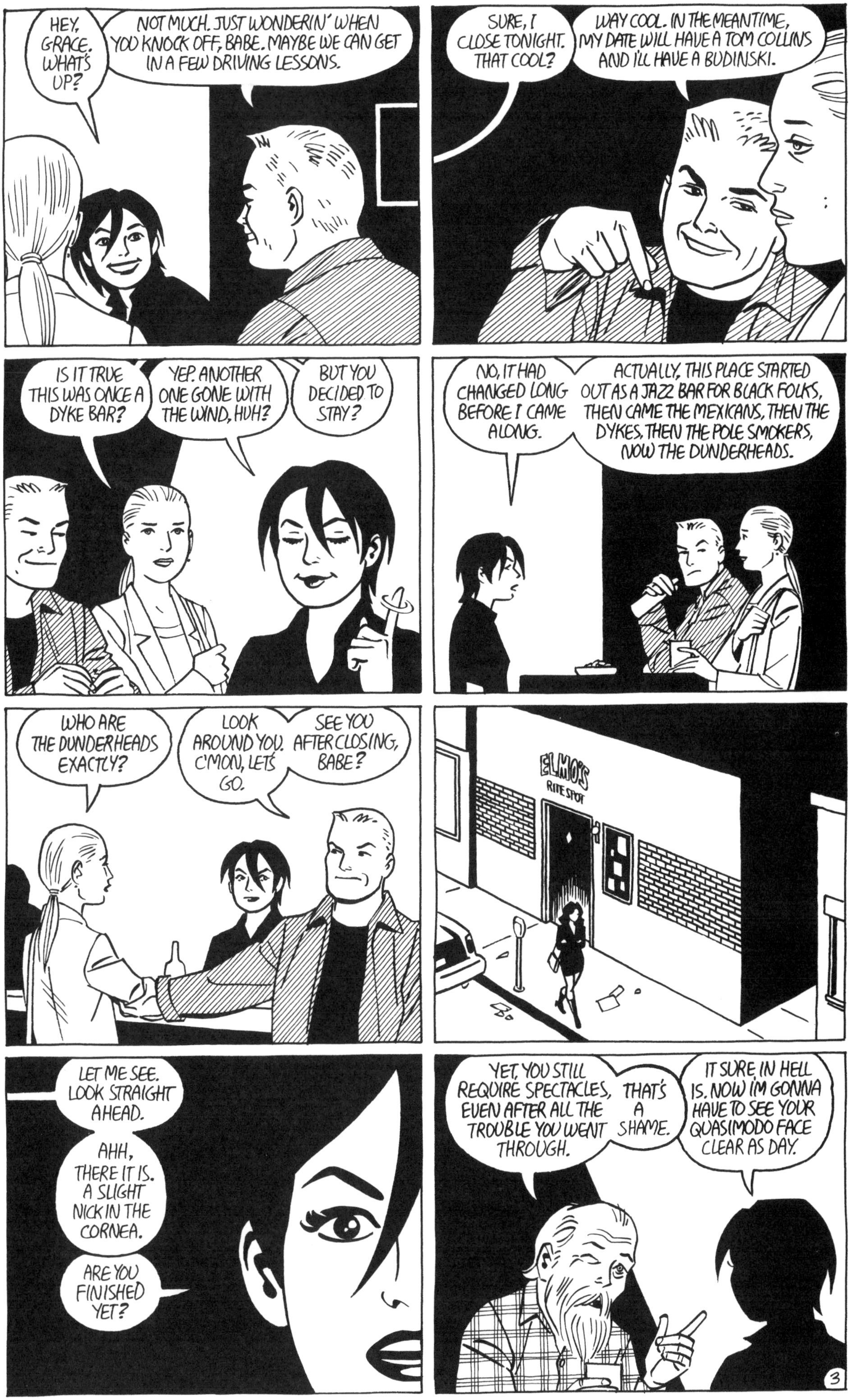
HEY, GRACE. WHAT'S UP?
NOT MUCH. JUST WONDERIN' WHEN YOU KNOCK OFF, BABE. MAYBE WE CAN GET IN A FEW DRIVING LESSONS.
SURE, I CLOSE TONIGHT. THAT COOL?
WAY COOL. IN THE MEANTIME, MY DATE WILL HAVE A TOM COLLINS AND I'LL HAVE A BUDINSKI.
IS IT TRUE THIS WAS ONCE A DYKE BAR?
YEP. ANOTHER ONE GONE WITH THE WIND, HUH?
BUT YOU DECIDED TO STAY?
NO, IT HAD CHANGED LONG BEFORE I CAME ALONG.
ACTUALLY, THIS PLACE STARTED OUT AS A JAZZ BAR FOR BLACK FOLKS, THEN CAME THE MEXICANS, THEN THE DYKES, THEN THE POLE SMOKERS, NOW THE DUNDERHEADS.
WHO ARE THE DUNDERHEADS EXACTLY?
LOOK AROUND YOU. C'MON, LET'S GO.
SEE YOU AFTER CLOSING, BABE?
ELMO'S
RITE SPOT
LET ME SEE. LOOK STRAIGHT AHEAD.
AHH, THERE IT IS. A SLIGHT NICK IN THE CORNEA.
ARE YOU FINISHED YET?
YET, YOU STILL REQUIRE SPECTACLES, EVEN AFTER ALL THE TROUBLE YOU WENT THROUGH.
THAT'S A SHAME.
IT SURE IN HELL IS. NOW I'M GONNA HAVE TO SEE YOUR QUASIMODO FACE CLEAR AS DAY.
3

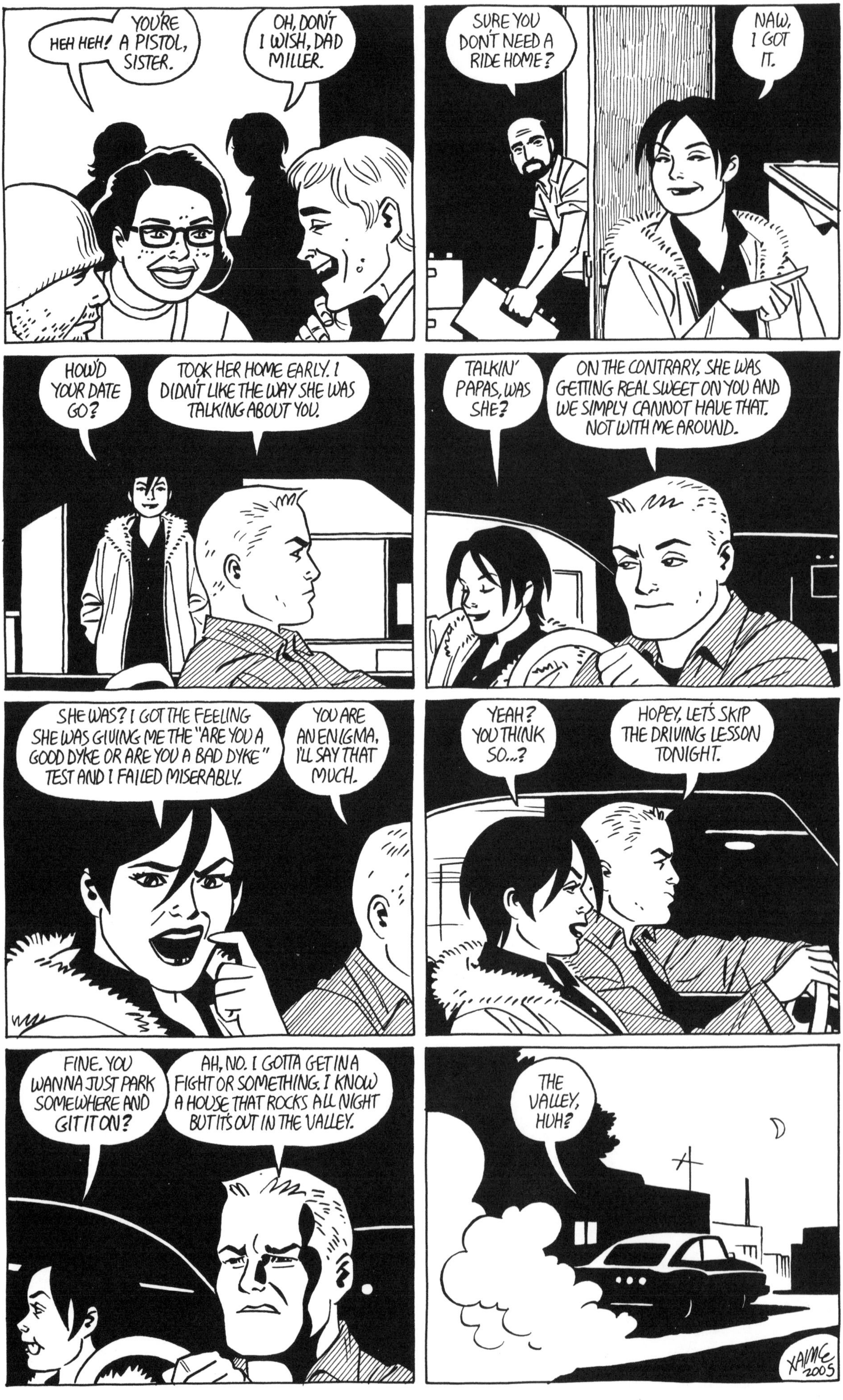
HEH HEH! YOU'RE A PISTOL, SISTER.
OH, DON'T I WISH, DAD MILLER.
SURE YOU DON'T NEED A RIDE HOME?
NAW, I GOT IT.
HOW'D YOUR DATE GO?
TOOK HER HOME EARLY. I DIDN'T LIKE THE WAY SHE WAS TALKING ABOUT YOU.
TALKIN' PAPAS, WAS SHE?
ON THE CONTRARY, SHE WAS GETTING REAL SWEET ON YOU AND WE SIMPLY CANNOT HAVE THAT. NOT WITH ME AROUND.
SHE WAS? I GOT THE FEELING SHE WAS GIVING ME THE "ARE YOU A GOOD DYKE OR ARE YOU A BAD DYKE" TEST AND I FAILED MISERABLY.
YOU ARE AN ENIGMA, I'LL SAY THAT MUCH.
YEAH? YOU THINK SO...?
HOPEY, LET'S SKIP THE DRIVING LESSON TONIGHT.
FINE. YOU WANNA JUST PARK SOMEWHERE AND GIT IT ON?
AH, NO. I GOTTA GET IN A FIGHT OR SOMETHING. I KNOW A HOUSE THAT ROCKS ALL NIGHT BUT IT'S OUT IN THE VALLEY.
THE VALLEY, HUH?
XAIME 2005

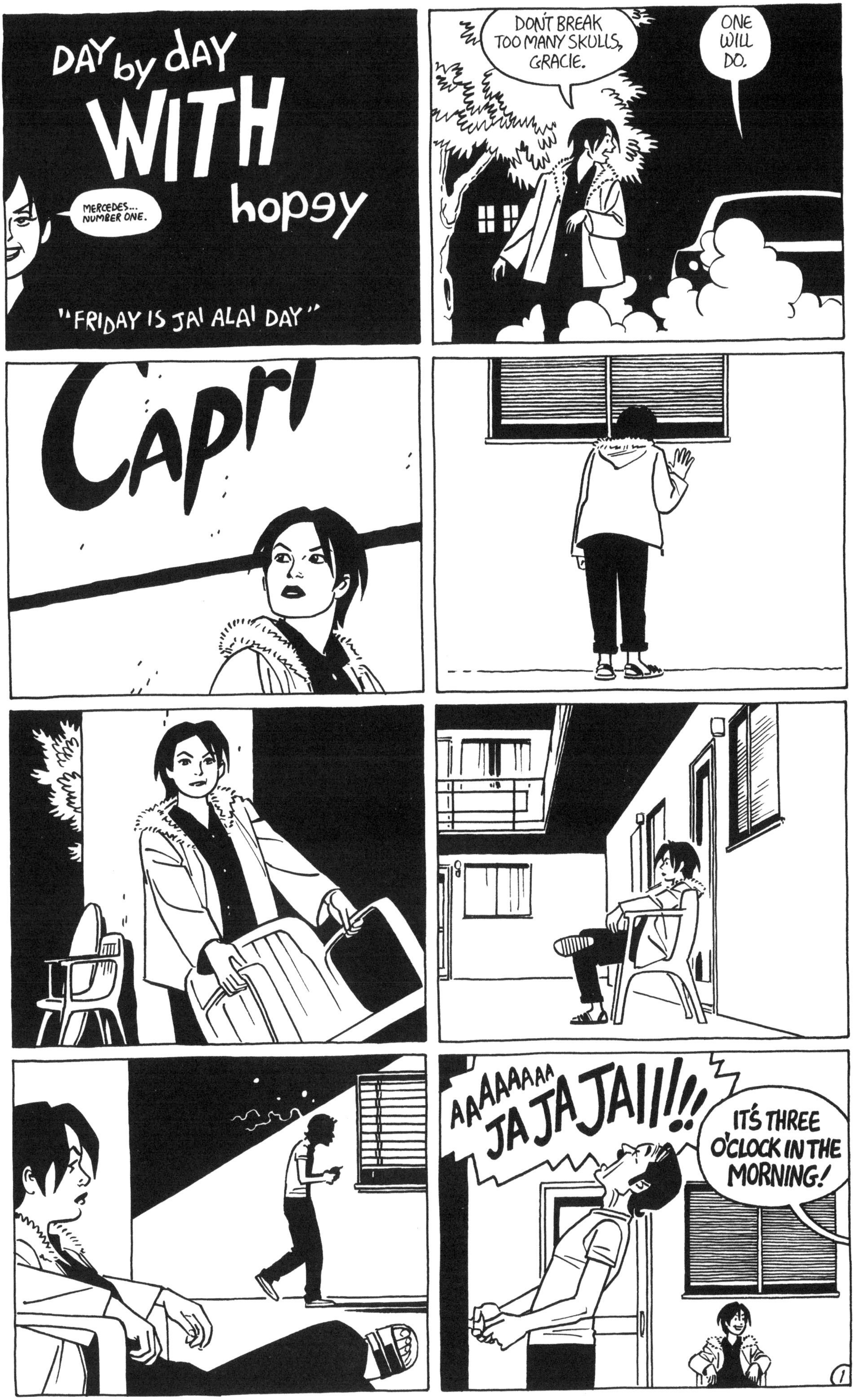
DAY by day WITH hopey
MERCEDES... NUMBER ONE.
"FRIDAY IS JAI ALAI DAY"
DON'T BREAK TOO MANY SKULLS, GRACIE.
ONE WILL DO.
Capri
AAAAAAAA JA JA JAIII!!!
IT'S THREE O'CLOCK IN THE MORNING!
1

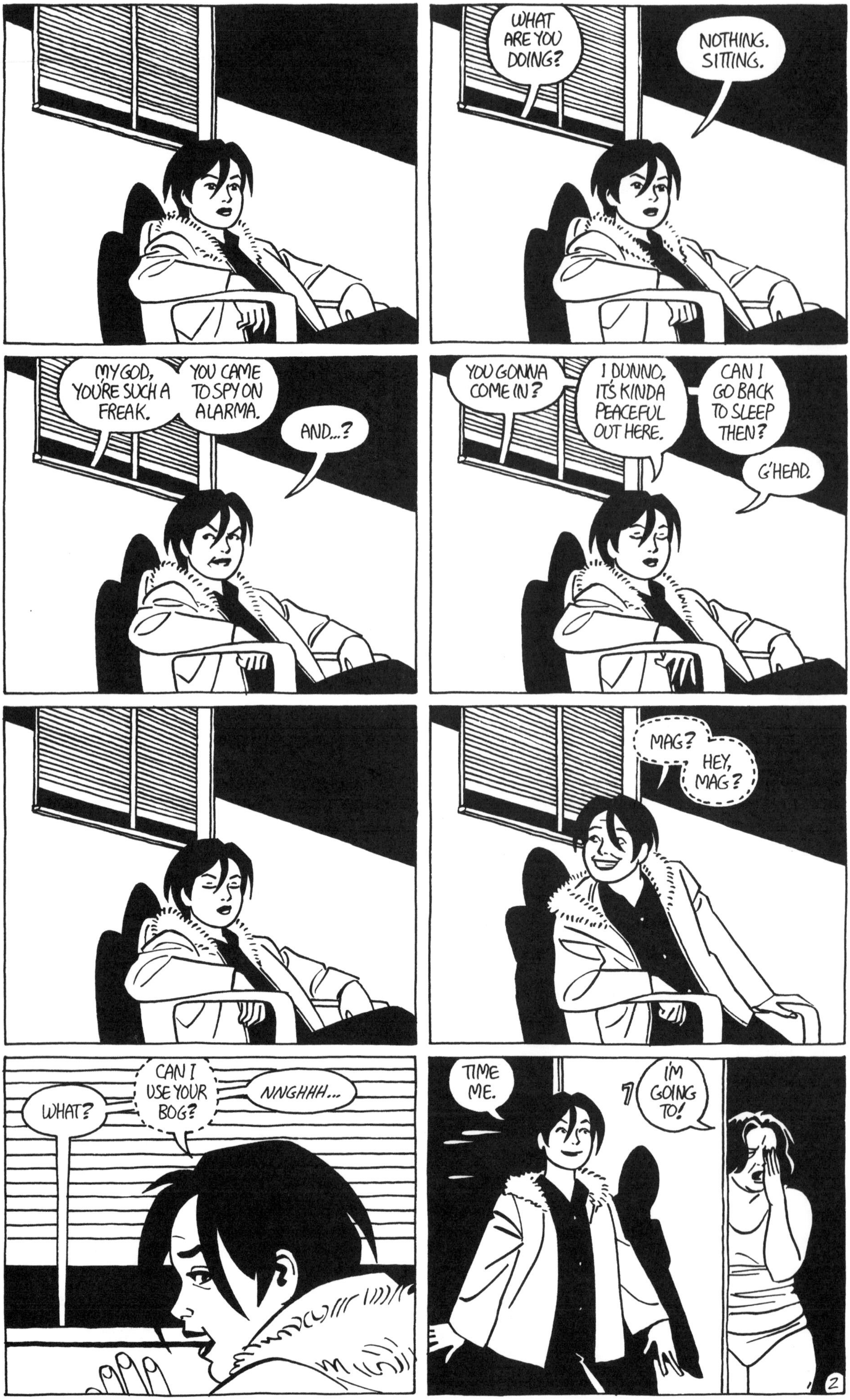
WHAT ARE YOU DOING?
NOTHING. SITTING.
MY GOD, YOU'RE SUCH A FREAK.
YOU CAME TO SPY ON ALARMA.
AND...?
YOU GONNA COME IN?
I DUNNO, IT'S KINDA PEACEFUL OUT HERE.
CAN I GO BACK TO SLEEP THEN?
G'HEAD.
MAG?
HEY, MAG?
WHAT?
CAN I USE YOUR BOG?
NNGHHH...
TIME ME.
I'M GOING TO!
2

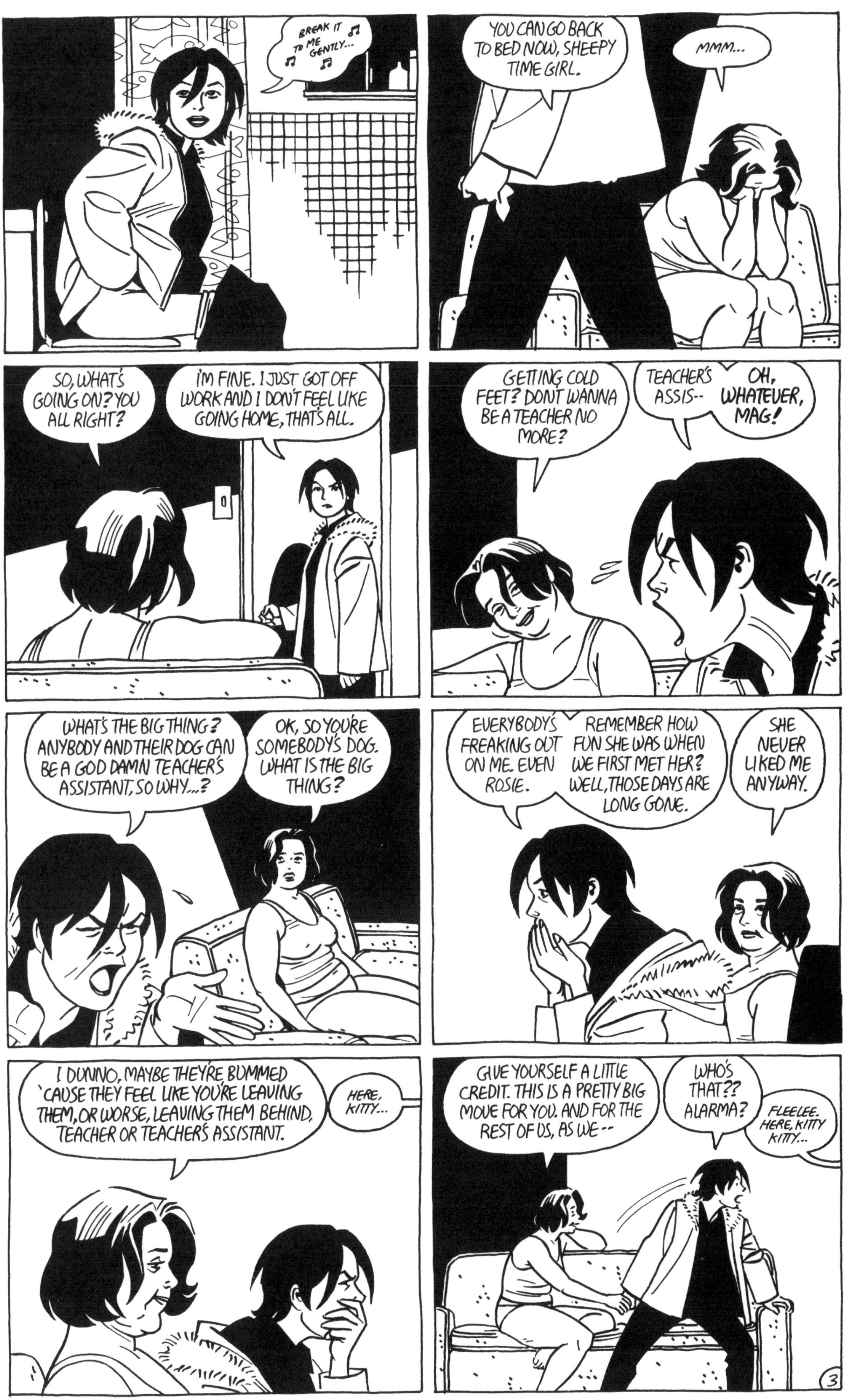
BREAK IT TO ME GENTLY...
YOU CAN GO BACK TO BED NOW, SHEEPY TIME GIRL.
MMM...
SO, WHAT'S GOING ON? YOU ALL RIGHT?
I'M FINE. I JUST GOT OFF WORK AND I DON'T FEEL LIKE GOING HOME, THAT'S ALL.
GETTING COLD FEET? DONT WANNA BE A TEACHER NO MORE?
TEACHER'S ASSIS--
OH, WHATEVER, MAG!
WHAT'S THE BIG THING? ANYBODY AND THEIR DOG CAN BE A GOD DAMN TEACHER'S ASSISTANT, SO WHY...?
OK, SO YOU'RE SOMEBODY'S DOG. WHAT IS THE BIG THING?
EVERYBODY'S FREAKING OUT ON ME. EVEN ROSIE.
REMEMBER HOW FUN SHE WAS WHEN WE FIRST MET HER? WELL, THOSE DAYS ARE LONG GONE.
SHE NEVER LIKED ME ANYWAY.
I DUNNO, MAYBE THEY'RE BUMMED 'CAUSE THEY FEEL LIKE YOU'RE LEAVING THEM, OR WORSE, LEAVING THEM BEHIND, TEACHER OR TEACHER'S ASSISTANT.
HERE, KITTY...
GIVE YOURSELF A LITTLE CREDIT. THIS IS A PRETTY BIG MOVE FOR YOU. AND FOR THE REST OF US, AS WE--
WHO'S THAT?? ALARMA?
FLEELEE. HERE, KITTY KITTY...
3

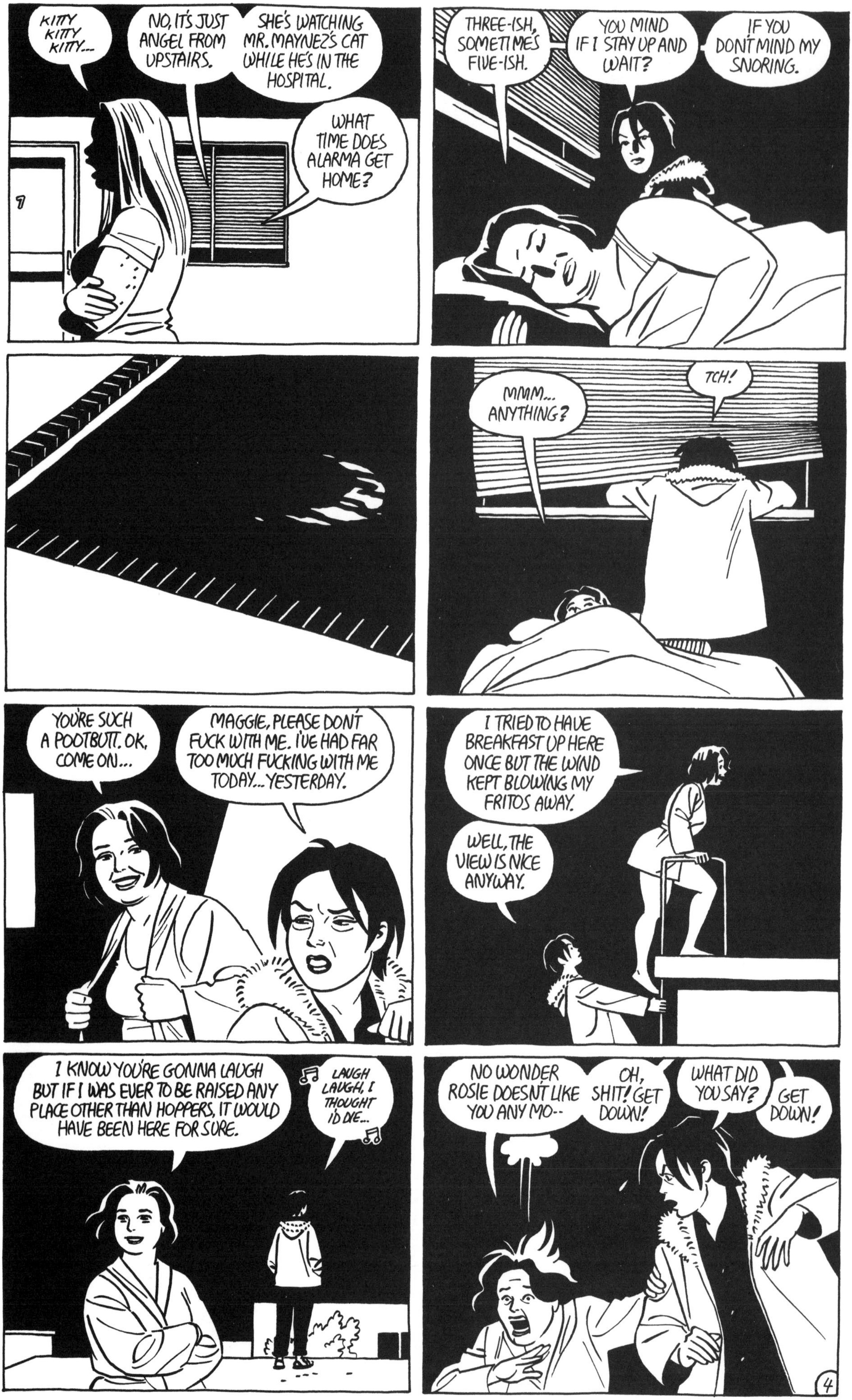
KITTY KITTY KITTY...
NO, IT'S JUST ANGEL FROM UPSTAIRS.
SHE'S WATCHING MR. MAYNEZ'S CAT WHILE HE'S IN THE HOSPITAL.
WHAT TIME DOES ALARMA GET HOME?
THREE-ISH, SOMETIMES FIVE-ISH.
YOU MIND IF I STAY UP AND WAIT?
IF YOU DON'T MIND MY SNORING.
MMM... ANYTHING?
TCH!
YOU'RE SUCH A POOTBUTT. OK, COME ON...
MAGGIE, PLEASE DON'T FUCK WITH ME. I'VE HAD FAR TOO MUCH FUCKING WITH ME TODAY... YESTERDAY.
I TRIED TO HAVE BREAKFAST UP HERE ONCE BUT THE WIND KEPT BLOWING MY FRITOS AWAY.
WELL, THE VIEW IS NICE ANYWAY.
I KNOW YOU'RE GONNA LAUGH BUT IF I WAS EVER TO BE RAISED ANY PLACE OTHER THAN HOPPERS, IT WOULD HAVE BEEN HERE FOR SURE.
LAUGH LAUGH, I THOUGHT I'D DIE...
NO WONDER ROSIE DOESN'T LIKE YOU ANY MO--
OH, SHIT! GET DOWN!
WHAT DID YOU SAY?
GET DOWN!
4

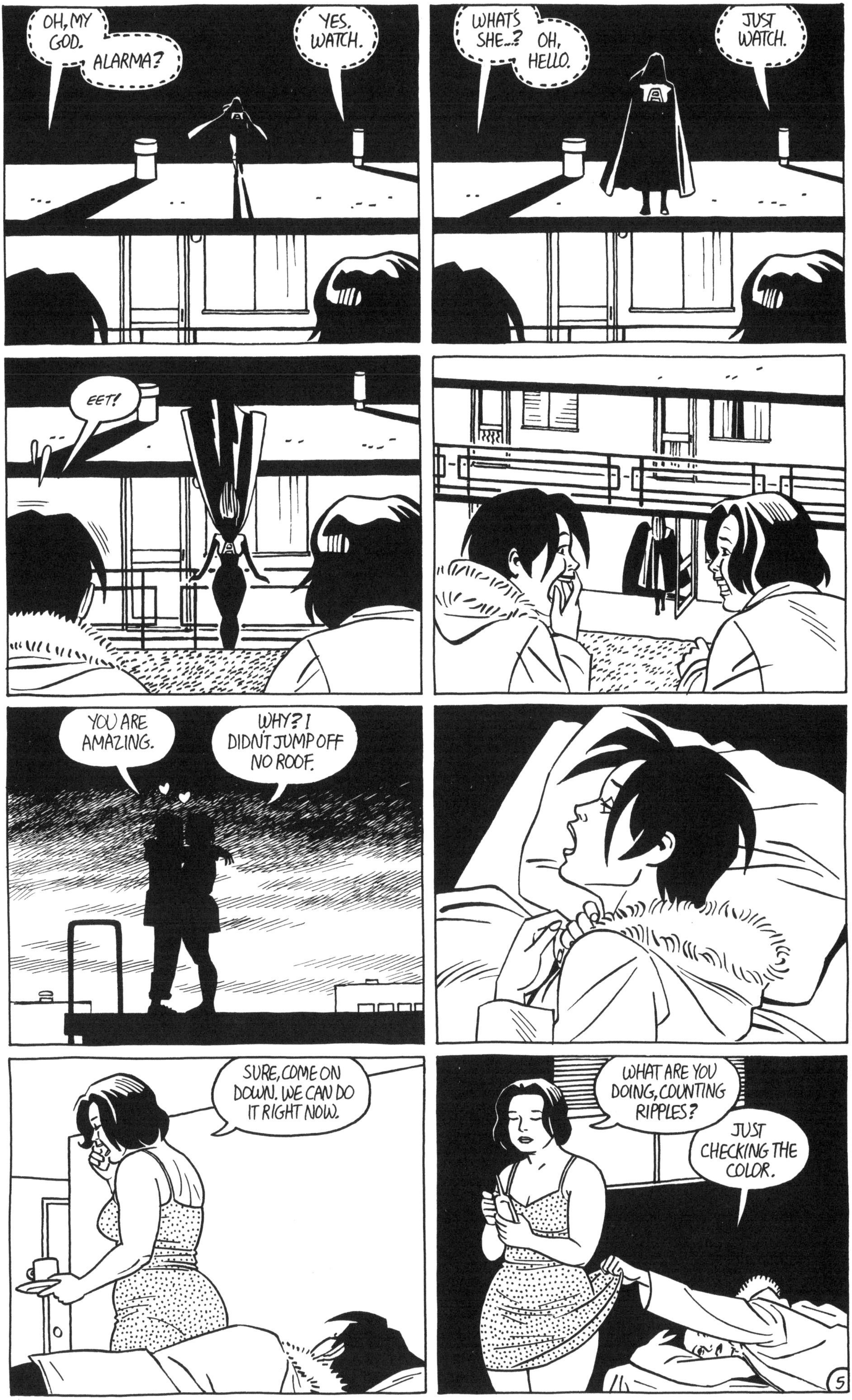
OH, MY GOD.
ALARMA?
YES. WATCH.
WHAT'S SHE..?
OH, HELLO.
JUST WATCH.
EET!
YOU ARE AMAZING.
WHY? I DIDN'T JUMP OFF NO ROOF.
SURE, COME ON DOWN. WE CAN DO IT RIGHT NOW.
WHAT ARE YOU DOING, COUNTING RIPPLES?
JUST CHECKING THE COLOR.
5

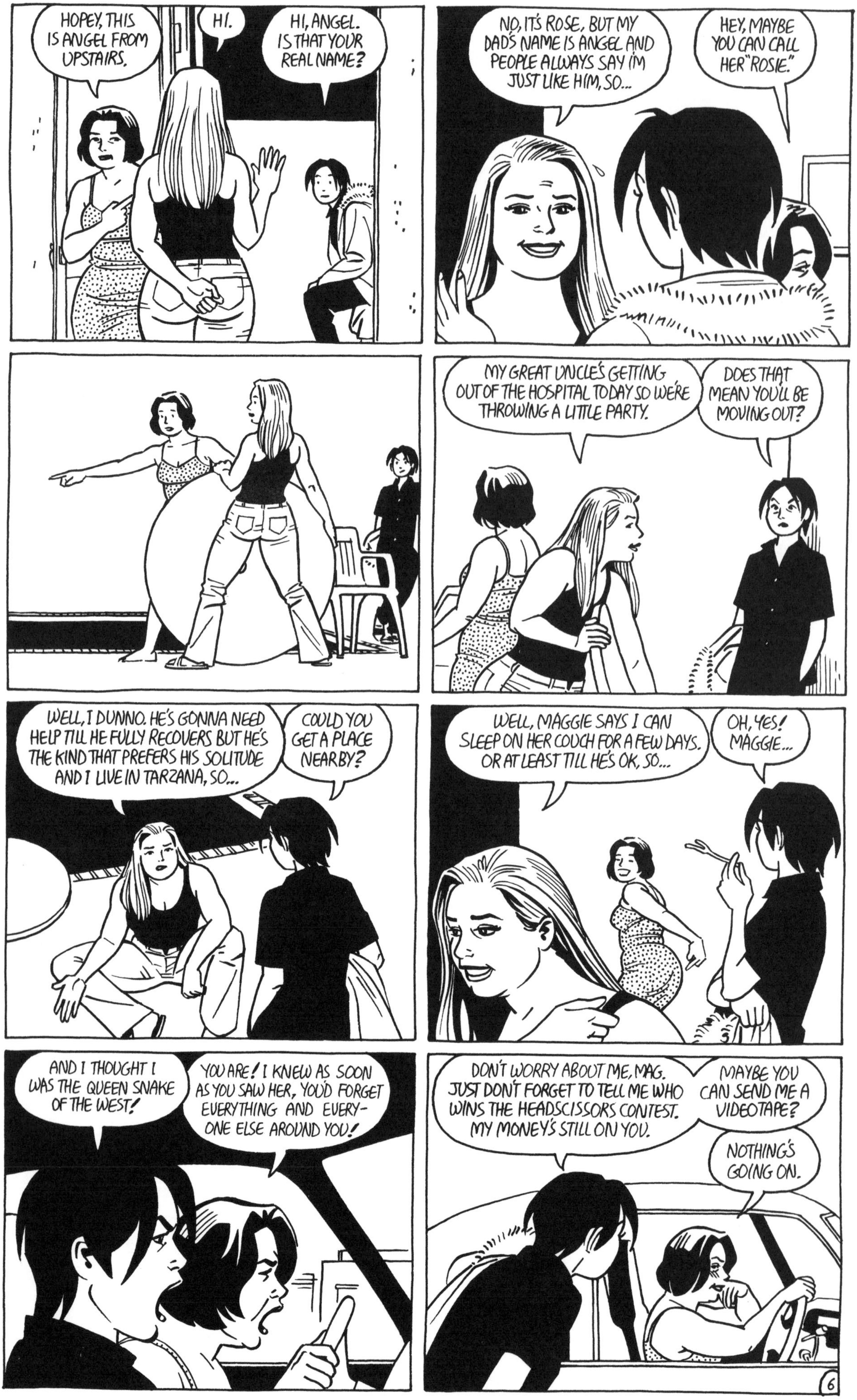
HOPEY, THIS IS ANGEL FROM UPSTAIRS.
HI.
HI, ANGEL. IS THAT YOUR REAL NAME?
NO, IT'S ROSE, BUT MY DAD'S NAME IS ANGEL AND PEOPLE ALWAYS SAY I'M JUST LIKE HIM, SO...
HEY, MAYBE YOU CAN CALL HER "ROSIE."
MY GREAT UNCLE'S GETTING OUT OF THE HOSPITAL TODAY SO WE'RE THROWING A LITTLE PARTY.
DOES THAT MEAN YOU'LL BE MOVING OUT?
WELL, I DUNNO. HE'S GONNA NEED HELP TILL HE FULLY RECOVERS BUT HE'S THE KIND THAT PREFERS HIS SOLITUDE AND I LIVE IN TARZANA, SO...
COULD YOU GET A PLACE NEARBY?
WELL, MAGGIE SAYS I CAN SLEEP ON HER COUCH FOR A FEW DAYS. OR AT LEAST TILL HE'S OK, SO...
OH, YES! MAGGIE...
AND I THOUGHT I WAS THE QUEEN SNAKE OF THE WEST!
YOU ARE! I KNEW AS SOON AS YOU SAW HER, YOU'D FORGET EVERYTHING AND EVERY-ONE ELSE AROUND YOU!
DON'T WORRY ABOUT ME, MAG. JUST DON'T FORGET TO TELL ME WHO WINS THE HEADSCISSORS CONTEST. MY MONEY'S STILL ON YOU.
MAYBE YOU CAN SEND ME A VIDEOTAPE?
NOTHING'S GOING ON.
6

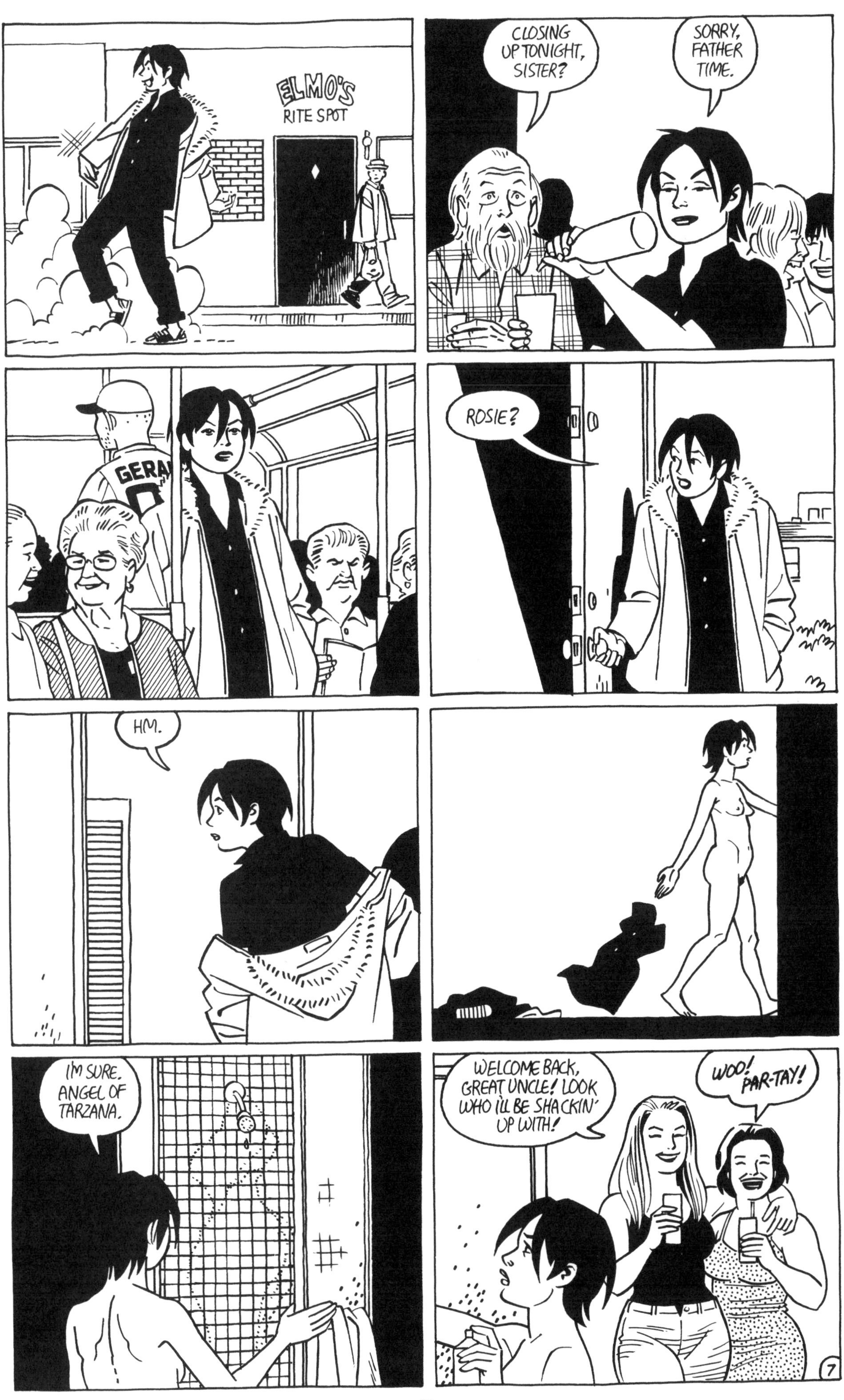
ELMO'S
RITE SPOT
CLOSING UP TONIGHT, SISTER?
SORRY, FATHER TIME.
GERA
ROSIE?
HM.
I'M SURE. ANGEL OF TARZANA.
WELCOME BACK, GREAT UNCLE! LOOK WHO I'LL BE SHACKIN' UP WITH!
WOO! PAR-TAY!
7

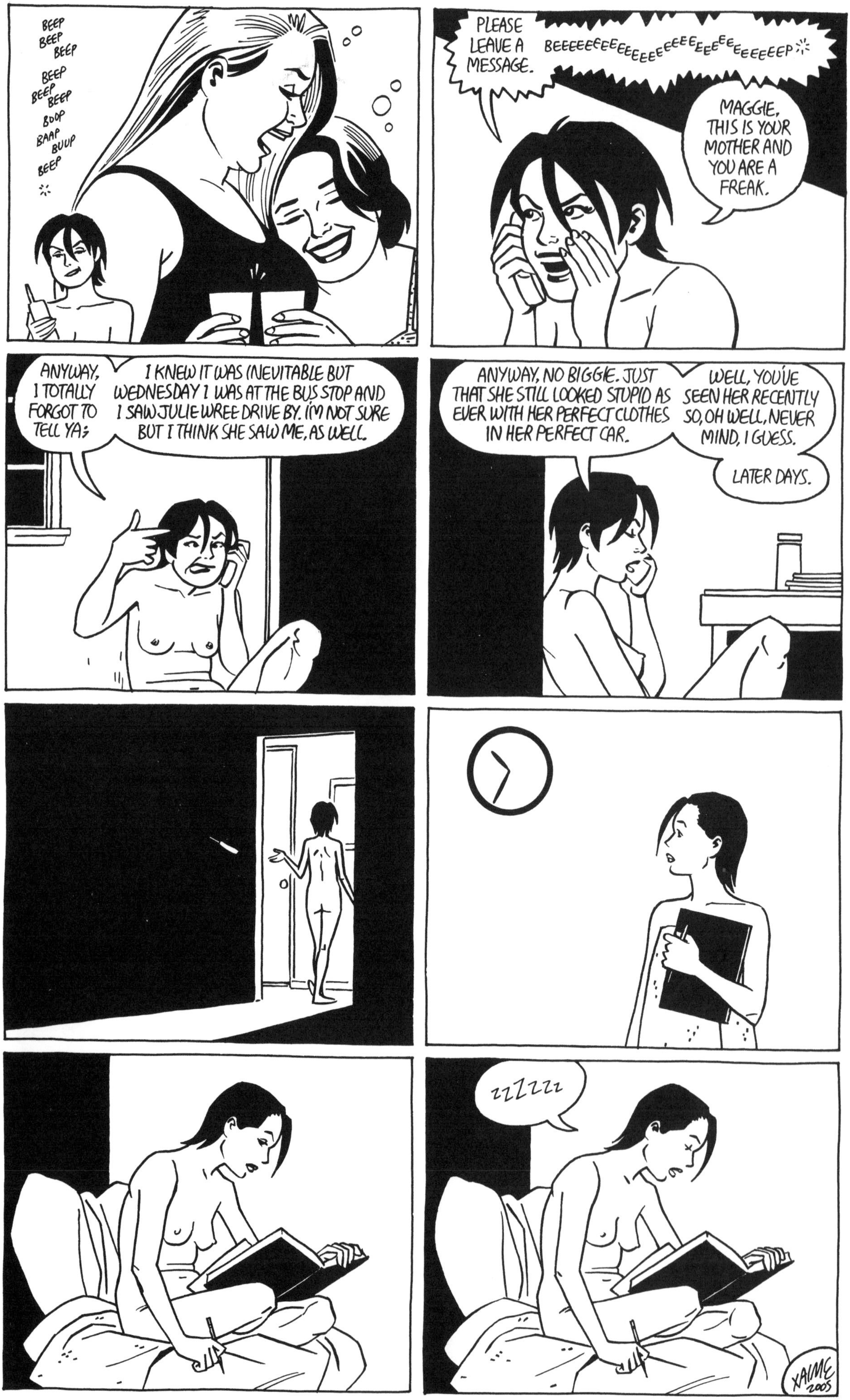
BEEP BEEP BEEP
BEEP BEEP BEEP
BOOP BAAP BUUP BEEP
PLEASE LEAVE A MESSAGE.
BEEEEEEEEEEEEEEEEEEEEEEEEEEEEEEEP
MAGGIE, THIS IS YOUR MOTHER AND YOU ARE A FREAK.
ANYWAY, I TOTALLY FORGOT TO TELL YA;
I KNEW IT WAS INEVITABLE BUT WEDNESDAY I WAS AT THE BUS STOP AND I SAW JULIE WREE DRIVE BY. I'M NOT SURE BUT I THINK SHE SAW ME, AS WELL.
ANYWAY, NO BIGGIE. JUST THAT SHE STILL LOOKED STUPID AS EVER WITH HER PERFECT CLOTHES IN HER PERFECT CAR.
WELL, YOU'VE SEEN HER RECENTLY SO, OH WELL, NEVER MIND, I GUESS.
LATER DAYS.
zzZZzz
XAIME 2005

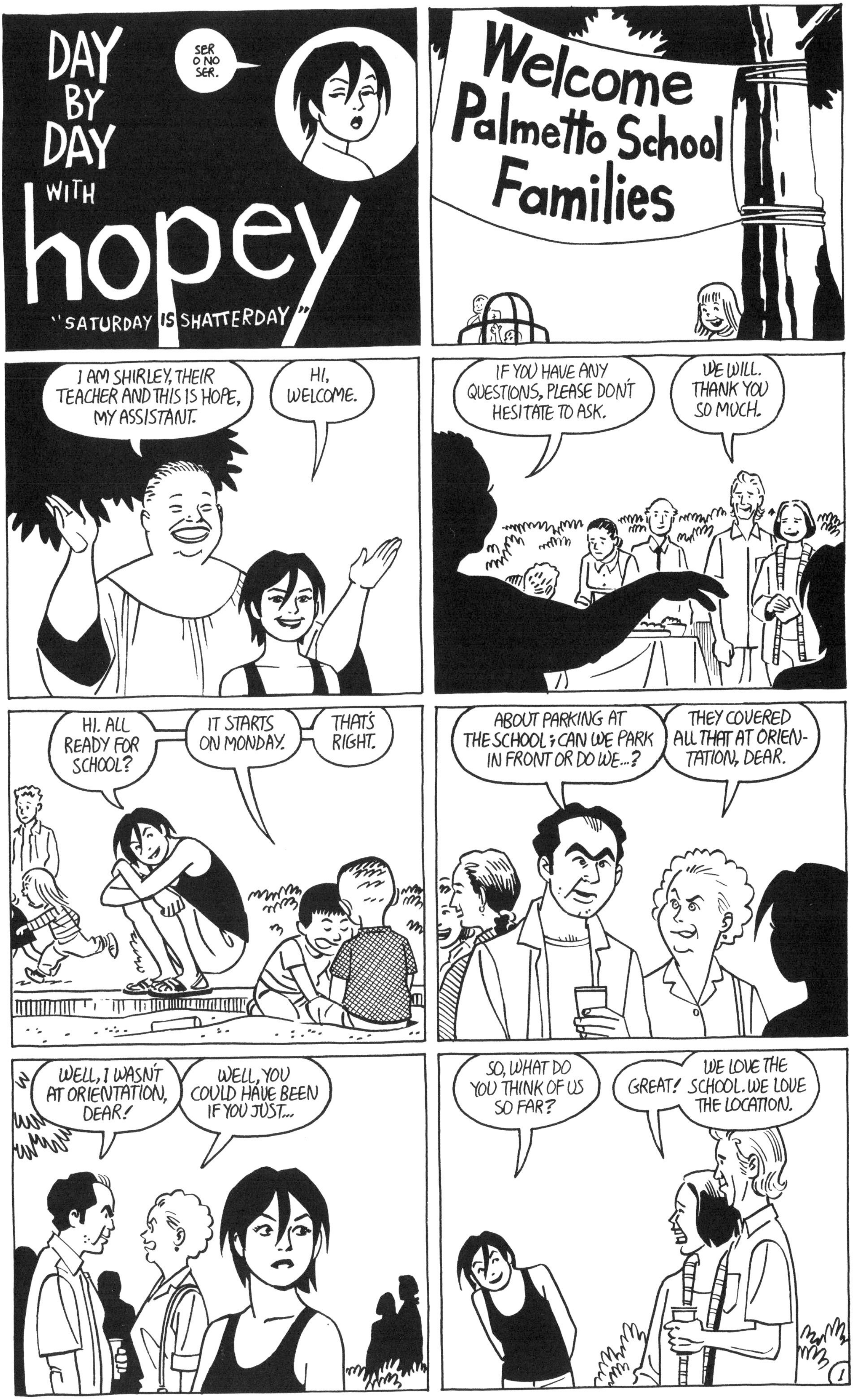
DAY BY DAY WITH hopey
"SATURDAY IS SHATTERDAY"
SER O NO SER.
Welcome Palmetto School Families
I AM SHIRLEY, THEIR TEACHER AND THIS IS HOPE, MY ASSISTANT.
HI, WELCOME.
IF YOU HAVE ANY QUESTIONS, PLEASE DON'T HESITATE TO ASK.
WE WILL. THANK YOU SO MUCH.
HI. ALL READY FOR SCHOOL?
IT STARTS ON MONDAY.
THAT'S RIGHT.
ABOUT PARKING AT THE SCHOOL; CAN WE PARK IN FRONT OR DO WE...?
THEY COVERED ALL THAT AT ORIENTATION, DEAR.
WELL, I WASN'T AT ORIENTATION, DEAR!
WELL, YOU COULD HAVE BEEN IF YOU JUST...
SO, WHAT DO YOU THINK OF US SO FAR?
GREAT!
WE LOVE THE SCHOOL. WE LOVE THE LOCATION.
1

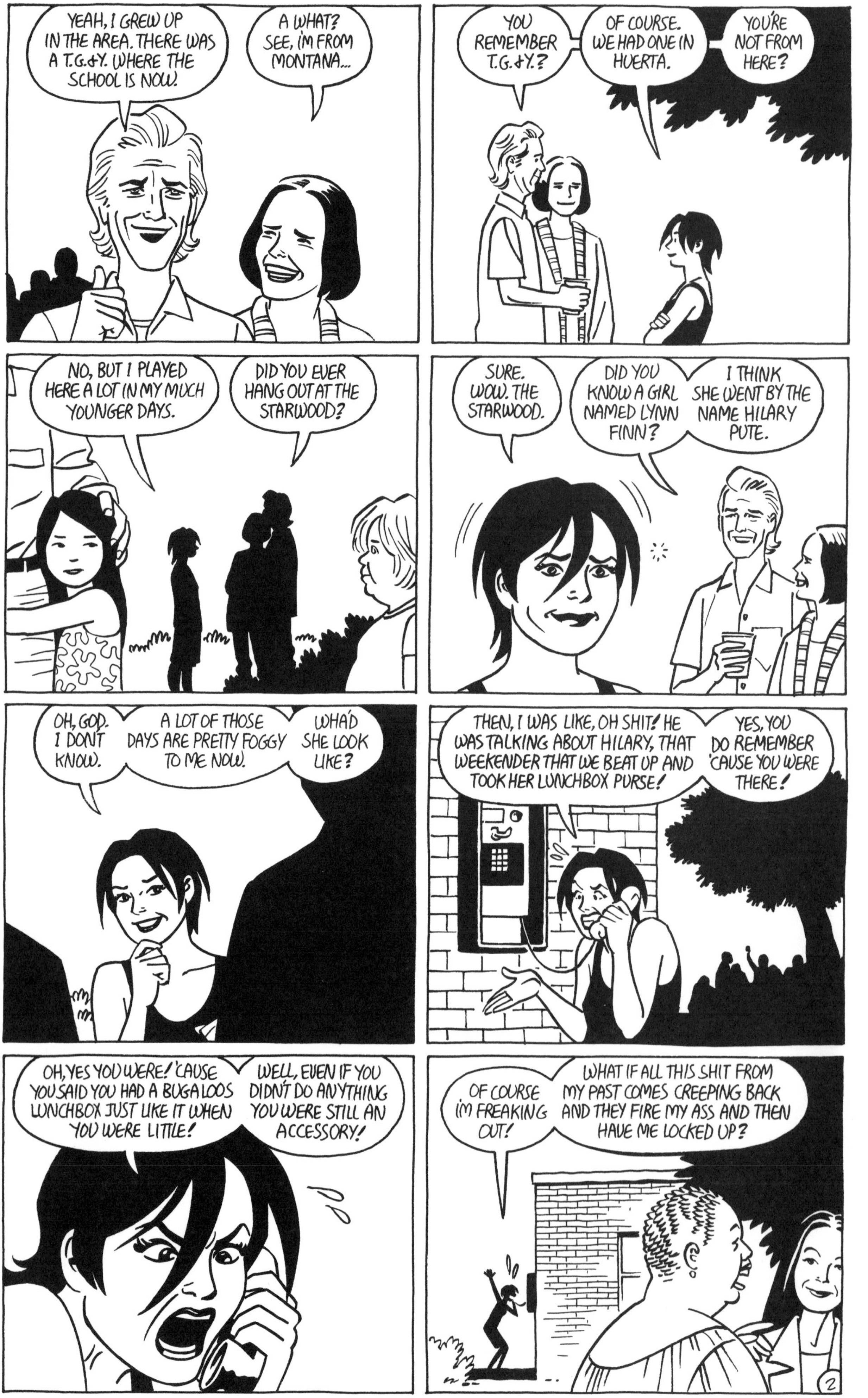
YEAH, I GREW UP IN THE AREA. THERE WAS A T.G.&Y. WHERE THE SCHOOL IS NOW.
A WHAT? SEE, I'M FROM MONTANA...
YOU REMEMBER T.G.&Y.?
OF COURSE. WE HAD ONE IN HUERTA.
YOU'RE NOT FROM HERE?
NO, BUT I PLAYED HERE A LOT IN MY MUCH YOUNGER DAYS.
DID YOU EVER HANG OUT AT THE STARWOOD?
SURE. WOW. THE STARWOOD.
DID YOU KNOW A GIRL NAMED LYNN FINN?
I THINK SHE WENT BY THE NAME HILARY PUTE.
OH, GOD. I DON'T KNOW.
A LOT OF THOSE DAYS ARE PRETTY FOGGY TO ME NOW.
WHA'D SHE LOOK LIKE?
THEN, I WAS LIKE, OH SHIT! HE WAS TALKING ABOUT HILARY, THAT WEEKENDER THAT WE BEAT UP AND TOOK HER LUNCHBOX PURSE!
YES, YOU DO REMEMBER 'CAUSE YOU WERE THERE!
OH, YES YOU WERE! 'CAUSE YOU SAID YOU HAD A BUGALOOS LUNCHBOX JUST LIKE IT WHEN YOU WERE LITTLE!
WELL, EVEN IF YOU DIDN'T DO ANYTHING YOU WERE STILL AN ACCESSORY!
OF COURSE I'M FREAKING OUT!
WHAT IF ALL THIS SHIT FROM MY PAST COMES CREEPING BACK AND THEY FIRE MY ASS AND THEN HAVE ME LOCKED UP?
2

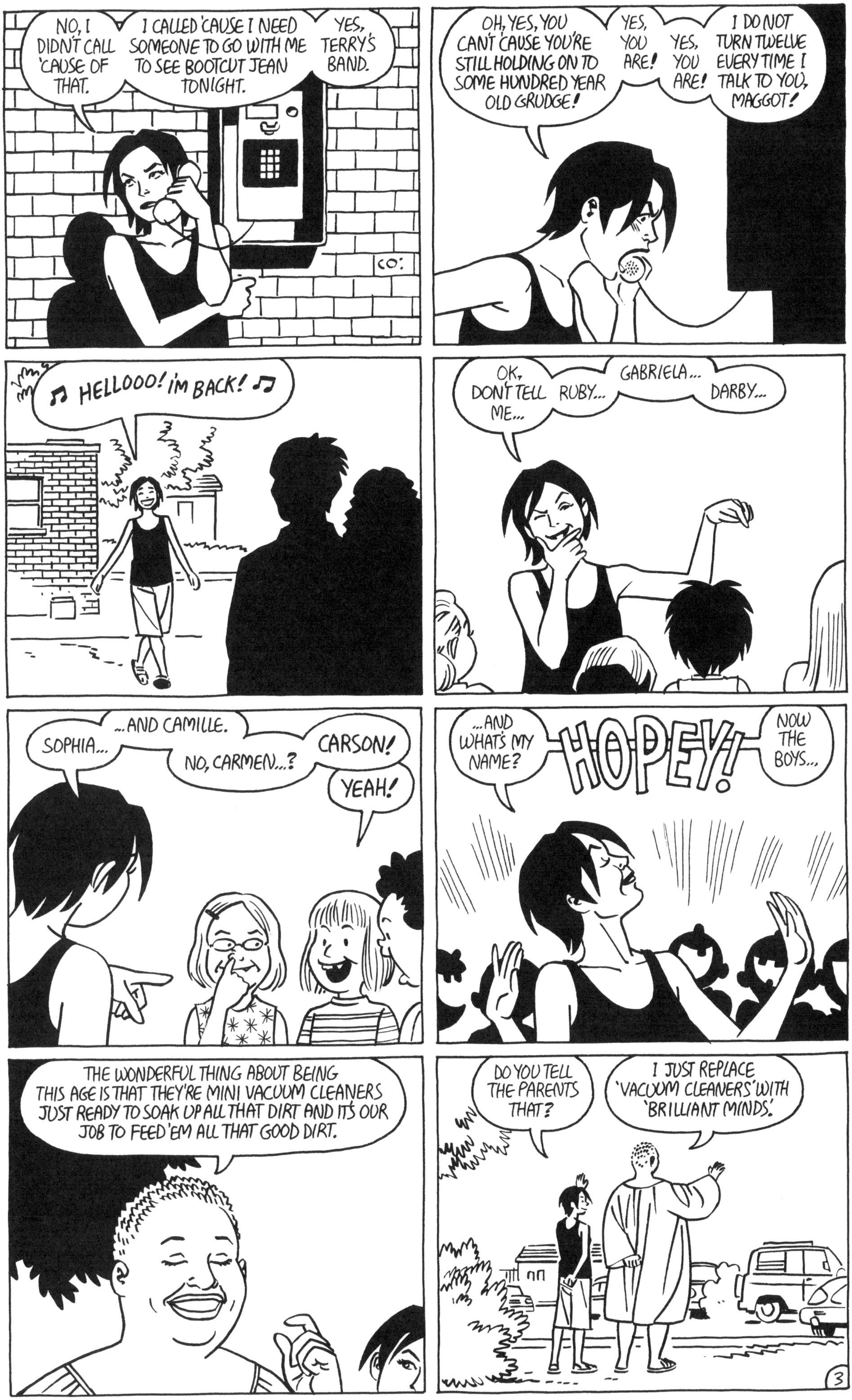
NO, I DIDN'T CALL 'CAUSE OF THAT.
I CALLED 'CAUSE I NEED SOMEONE TO GO WITH ME TO SEE BOOTCUT JEAN TONIGHT.
YES, TERRY'S BAND.
OH, YES, YOU CAN'T 'CAUSE YOU'RE STILL HOLDING ON TO SOME HUNDRED YEAR OLD GRUDGE!
YES, YOU ARE!
YES, YOU ARE!
I DO NOT TURN TWELVE EVERY TIME I TALK TO YOU, MAGGOT!
♫ HELLOOO! I'M BACK! ♫
OK, DON'T TELL ME...
RUBY...
GABRIELA...
DARBY...
SOPHIA...
...AND CAMILLE.
NO, CARMEN...?
CARSON!
YEAH!
...AND WHAT'S MY NAME?
HOPEY!
NOW THE BOYS...
THE WONDERFUL THING ABOUT BEING THIS AGE IS THAT THEY'RE MINI VACUUM CLEANERS JUST READY TO SOAK UP ALL THAT DIRT AND IT'S OUR JOB TO FEED 'EM ALL THAT GOOD DIRT.
DO YOU TELL THE PARENTS THAT?
I JUST REPLACE 'VACUUM CLEANERS' WITH 'BRILLIANT MINDS.'
3

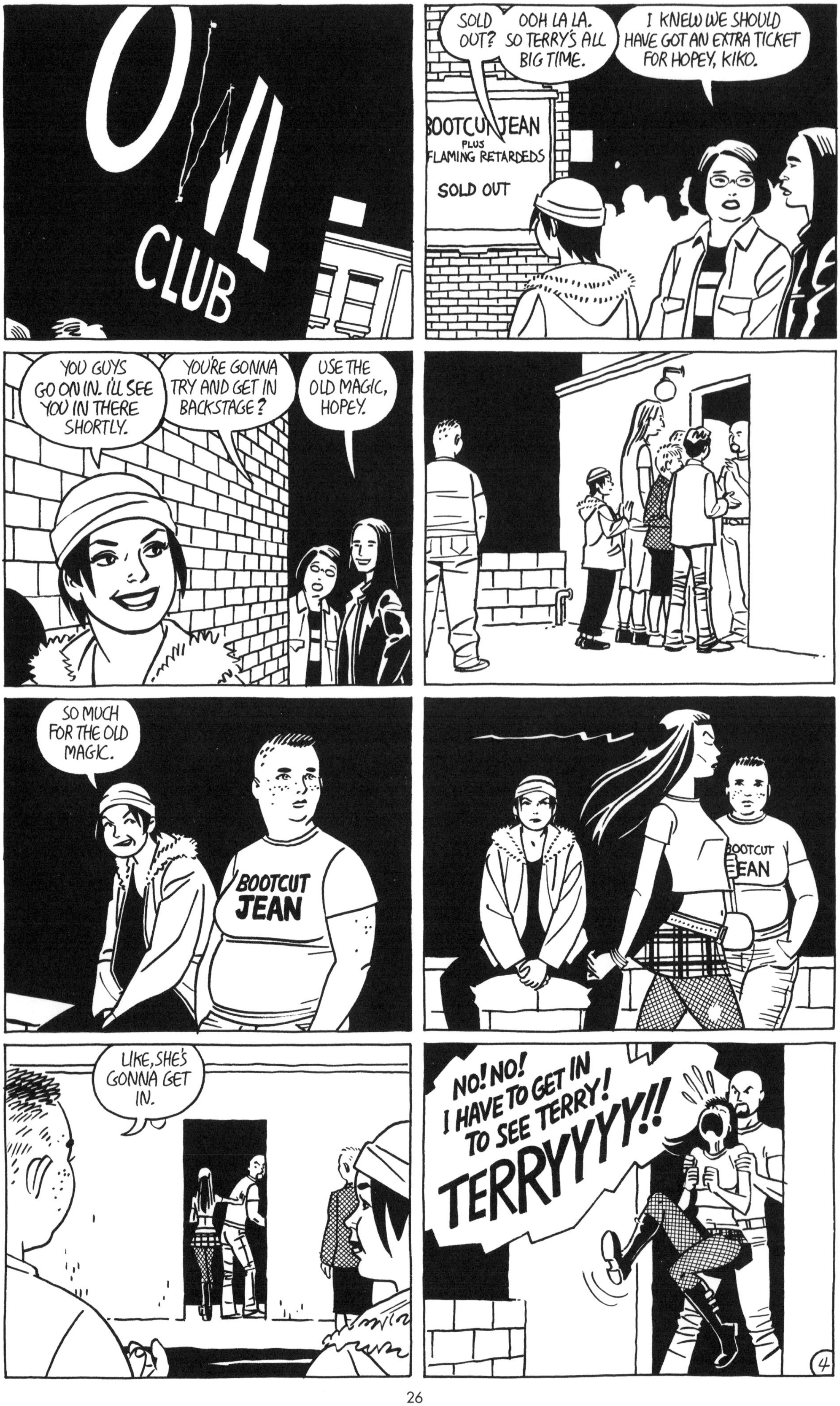
OWL
CLUB
SOLD OUT?
OOH LA LA. SO TERRY'S ALL BIG TIME.
I KNEW WE SHOULD HAVE GOT AN EXTRA TICKET FOR HOPEY, KIKO.
BOOTCUT JEAN PLUS FLAMING RETARDEDS
SOLD OUT
YOU GUYS GO ON IN. I'LL SEE YOU IN THERE SHORTLY.
YOU'RE GONNA TRY AND GET IN BACKSTAGE?
USE THE OLD MAGIC, HOPEY.
SO MUCH FOR THE OLD MAGIC.
BOOTCUT JEAN
LIKE, SHE'S GONNA GET IN.
NO! NO! I HAVE TO GET IN TO SEE TERRY!
TERRYYYY!!
4

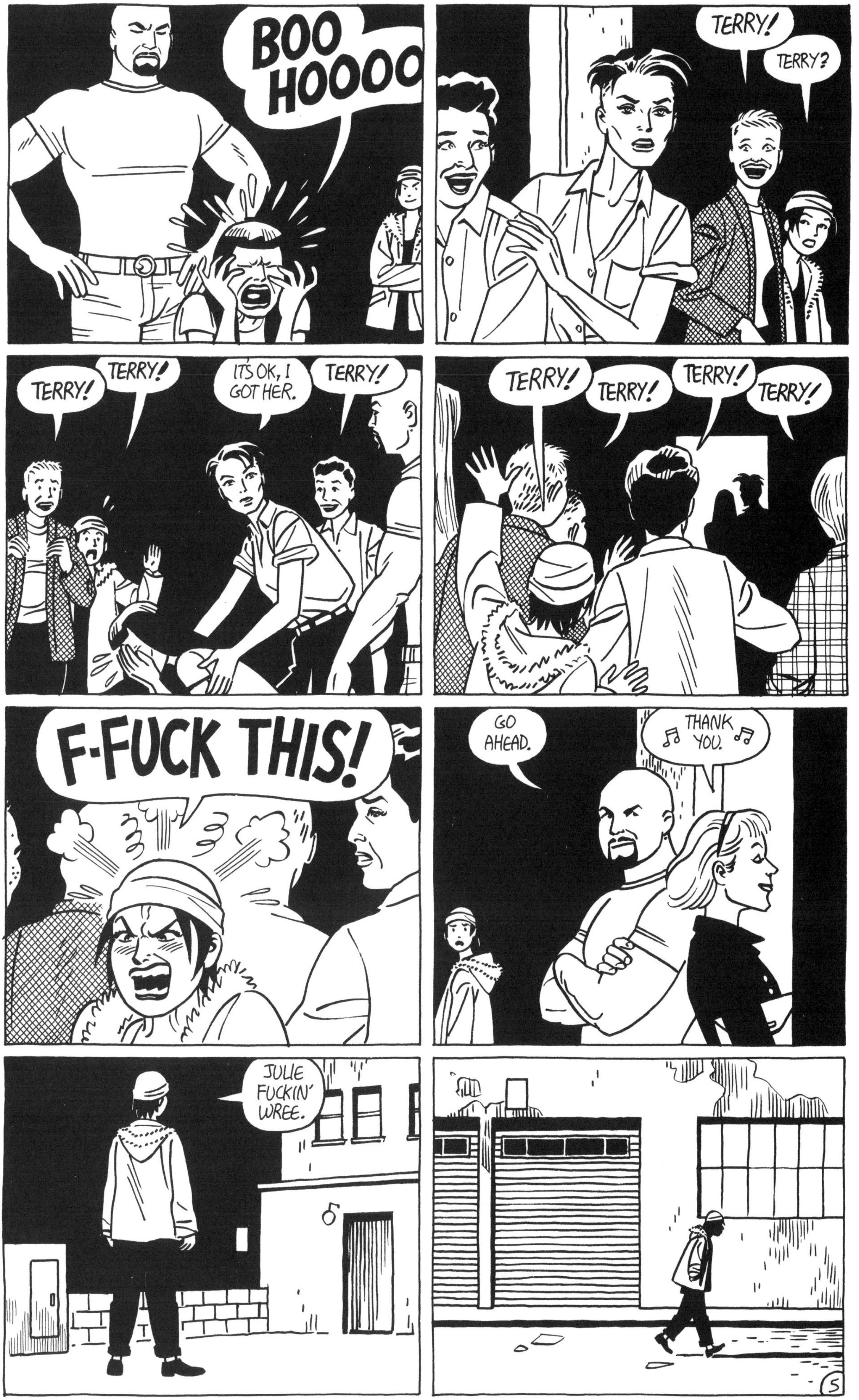
BOO HOOOO
TERRY!
TERRY?
TERRY!
TERRY!
IT'S OK, I GOT HER.
TERRY!
TERRY!
TERRY!
TERRY!
TERRY!
F-FUCK THIS!
GO AHEAD.
♫ THANK YOU. ♫
JULIE FUCKIN' WREE.
5

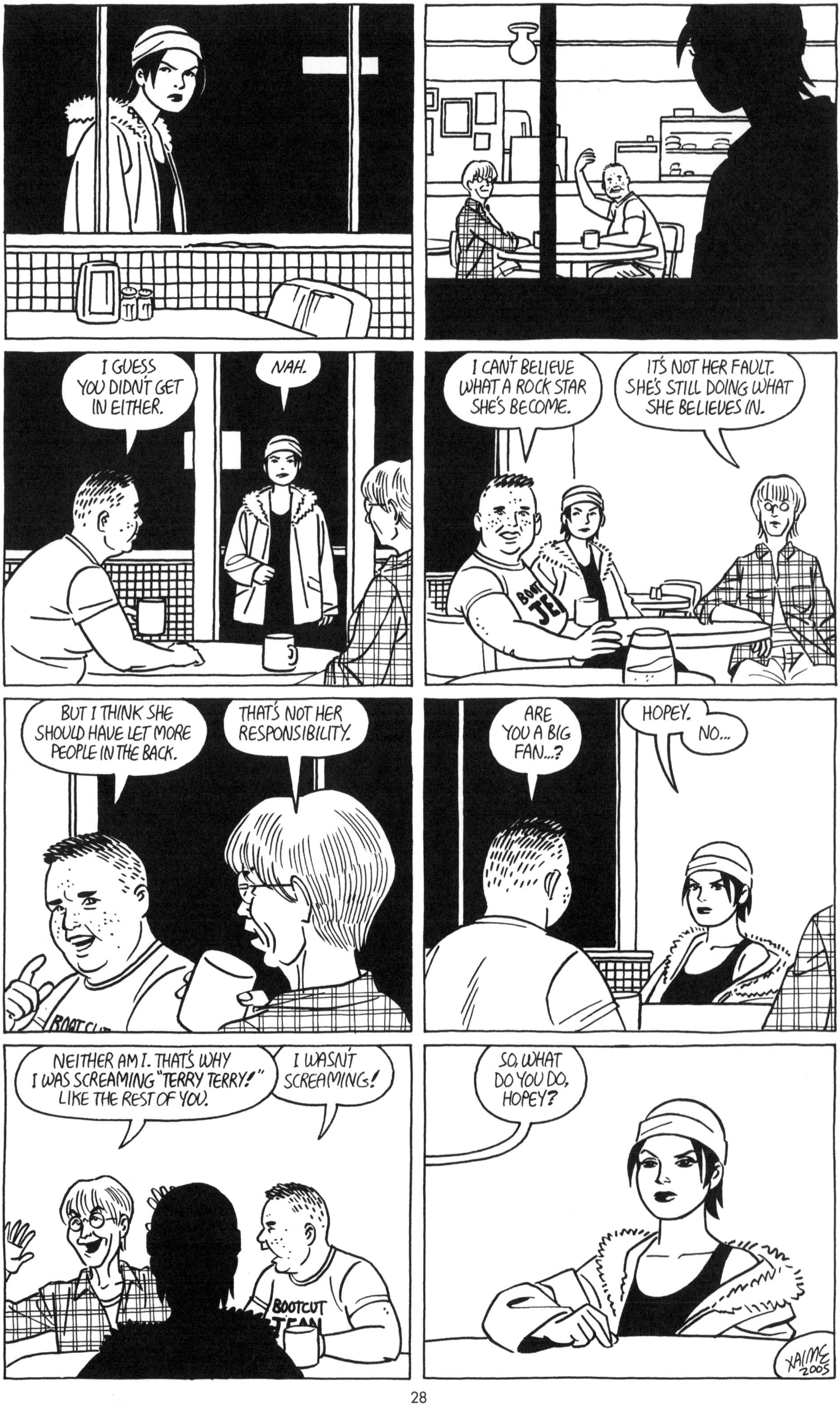
I GUESS YOU DIDN'T GET IN EITHER.
NAH.
I CAN'T BELIEVE WHAT A ROCK STAR SHE'S BECOME.
IT'S NOT HER FAULT. SHE'S STILL DOING WHAT SHE BELIEVES IN.
BUT I THINK SHE SHOULD HAVE LET MORE PEOPLE IN THE BACK.
THAT'S NOT HER RESPONSIBILITY.
ARE YOU A BIG FAN...?
HOPEY.
NO...
NEITHER AM I. THAT'S WHY I WAS SCREAMING "TERRY TERRY!" LIKE THE REST OF YOU.
I WASN'T SCREAMING!
BOOTCUT
SO, WHAT DO YOU DO, HOPEY?
XAIME 2005

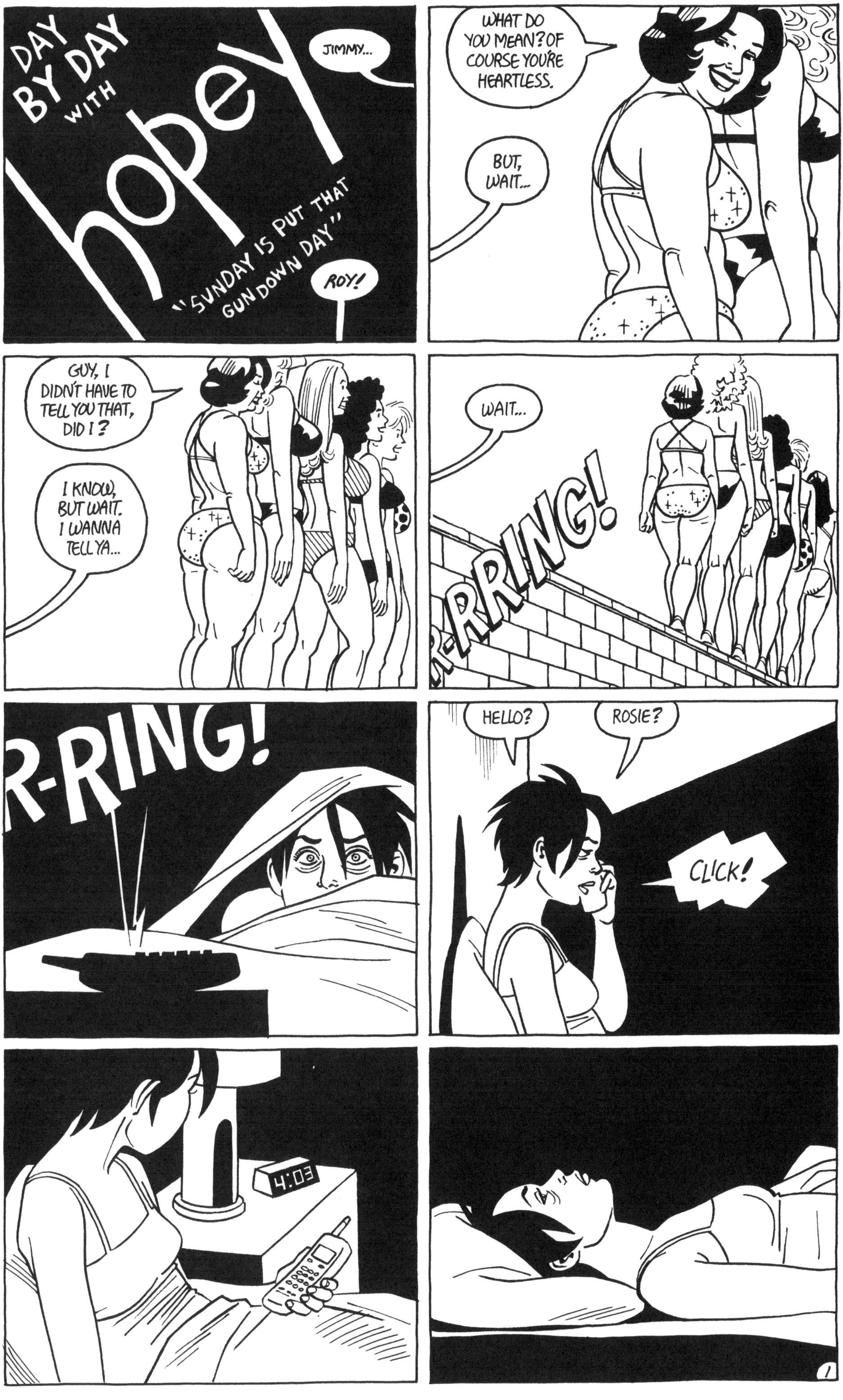
DAY BY DAY WITH
hopey
"SUNDAY IS PUT THAT GUN DOWN DAY"
JIMMY...
ROY!
WHAT DO YOU MEAN? OF COURSE YOU'RE HEARTLESS.
BUT, WAIT...
GUY, I DIDN'T HAVE TO TELL YOU THAT, DID I?
I KNOW, BUT WAIT. I WANNA TELL YA...
WAIT...
R-RRING!
R-RING!
HELLO?
ROSIE?
CLICK!
4:03
1

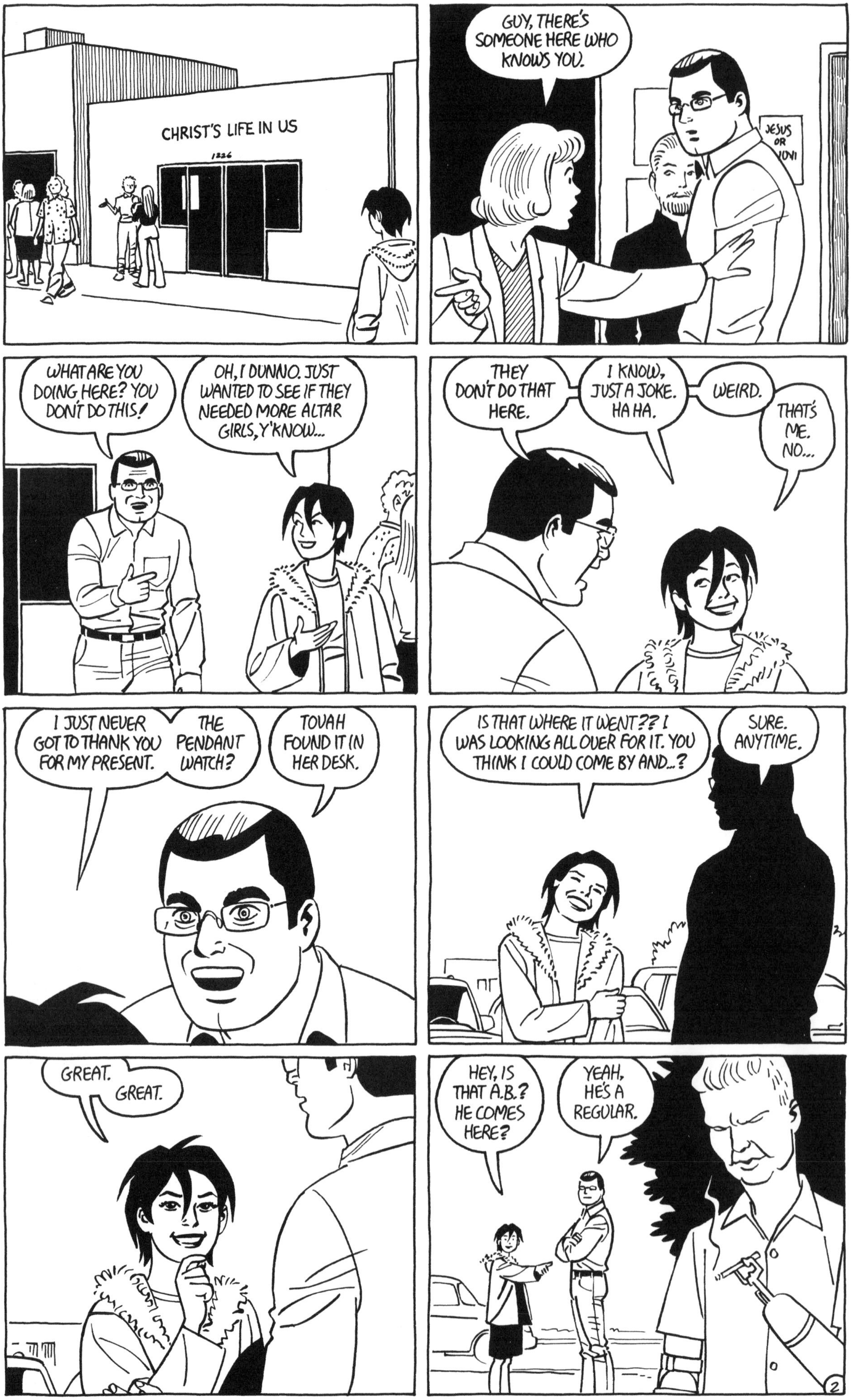
CHRIST'S LIFE IN US
1226
GUY, THERE'S SOMEONE HERE WHO KNOWS YOU.
JESUS OR
WHAT ARE YOU DOING HERE? YOU DON'T DO THIS!
OH, I DUNNO. JUST WANTED TO SEE IF THEY NEEDED MORE ALTAR GIRLS, Y'KNOW...
THEY DON'T DO THAT HERE.
I KNOW, JUST A JOKE. HA HA.
WEIRD.
THAT'S ME. NO...
I JUST NEVER GOT TO THANK YOU FOR MY PRESENT.
THE PENDANT WATCH?
TOVAH FOUND IT IN HER DESK.
IS THAT WHERE IT WENT?? I WAS LOOKING ALL OVER FOR IT. YOU THINK I COULD COME BY AND...?
SURE. ANYTIME.
GREAT. GREAT.
HEY, IS THAT A.B.? HE COMES HERE?
YEAH, HE'S A REGULAR.

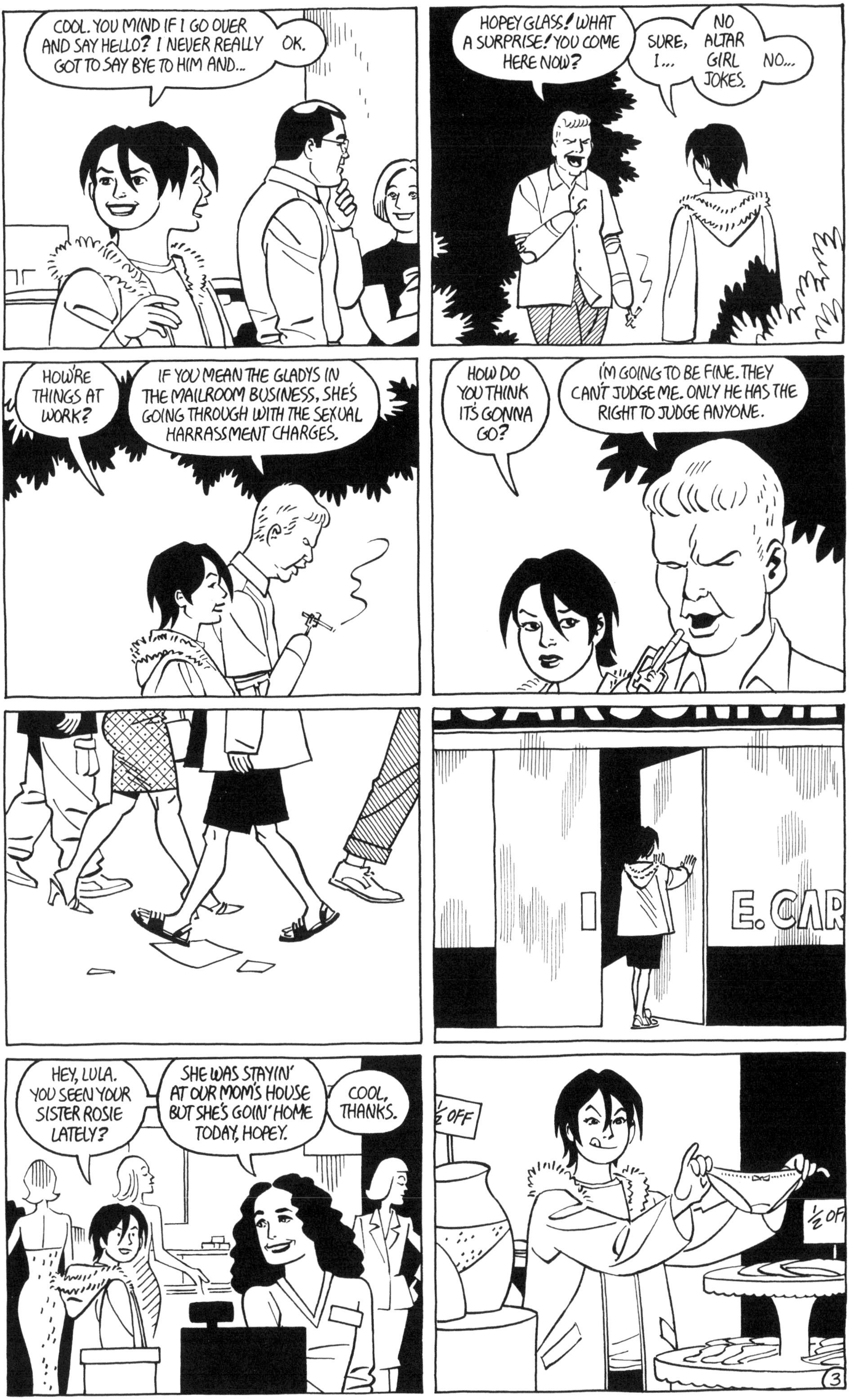
COOL. YOU MIND IF I GO OVER AND SAY HELLO? I NEVER REALLY GOT TO SAY BYE TO HIM AND...
OK.
HOPEY GLASS! WHAT A SURPRISE! YOU COME HERE NOW?
SURE, I...
NO ALTAR GIRL JOKES.
NO...
HOW'RE THINGS AT WORK?
IF YOU MEAN THE GLADYS IN THE MAILROOM BUSINESS, SHE'S GOING THROUGH WITH THE SEXUAL HARRASSMENT CHARGES.
HOW DO YOU THINK IT'S GONNA GO?
I'M GOING TO BE FINE. THEY CAN'T JUDGE ME. ONLY HE HAS THE RIGHT TO JUDGE ANYONE.
E. CAR
HEY, LULA. YOU SEEN YOUR SISTER ROSIE LATELY?
SHE WAS STAYIN' AT OUR MOM'S HOUSE BUT SHE'S GOIN' HOME TODAY, HOPEY.
COOL, THANKS.
½ OFF
½ OF
3

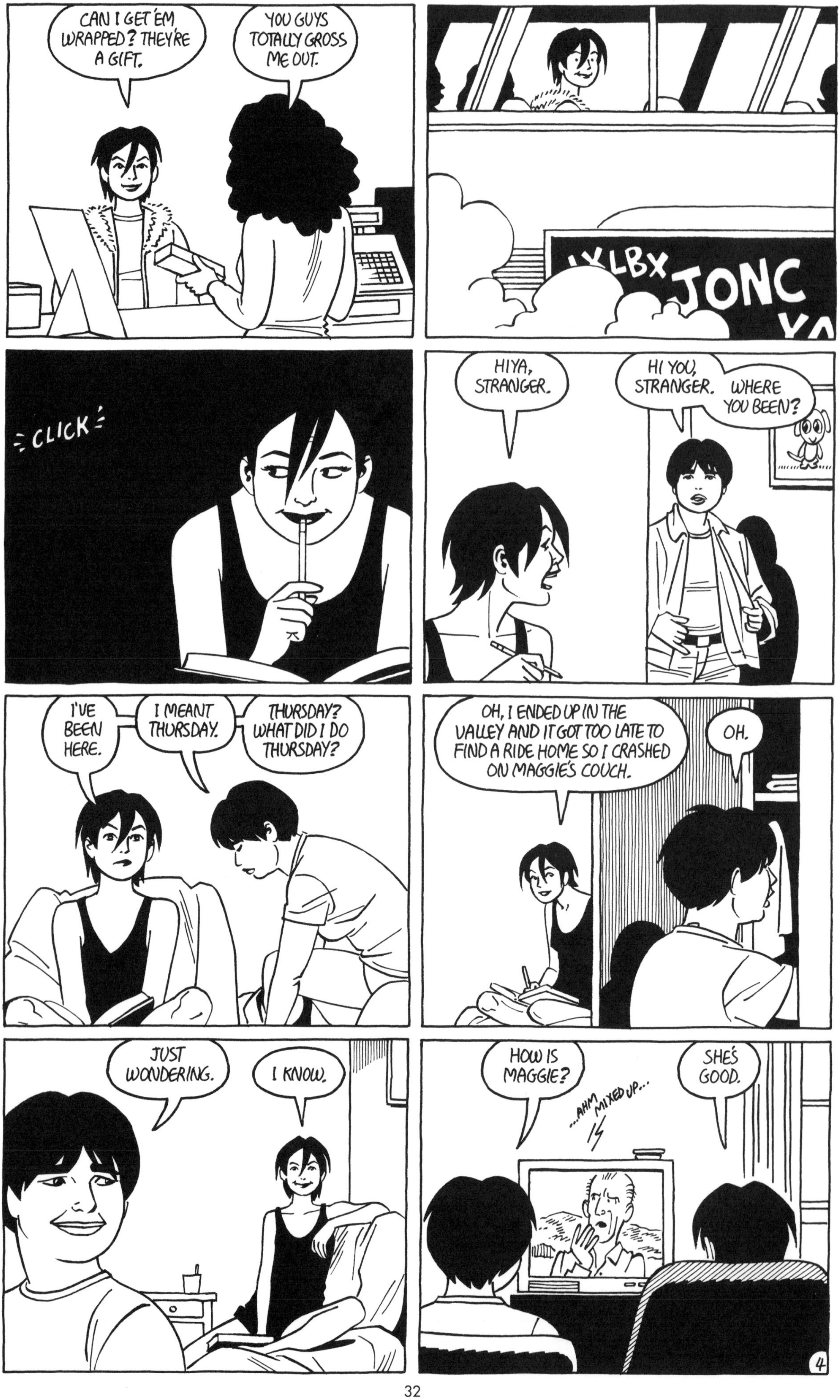
CAN I GET 'EM WRAPPED? THEY'RE A GIFT.
YOU GUYS TOTALLY GROSS ME OUT.
JONC
CLICK
HIYA, STRANGER.
HI YOU, STRANGER.
WHERE YOU BEEN?
I'VE BEEN HERE.
I MEANT THURSDAY.
THURSDAY? WHAT DID I DO THURSDAY?
OH, I ENDED UP IN THE VALLEY AND IT GOT TOO LATE TO FIND A RIDE HOME SO I CRASHED ON MAGGIE'S COUCH.
OH.
JUST WONDERING.
I KNOW.
HOW IS MAGGIE?
...AHM MIXED UP...
SHE'S GOOD.
4

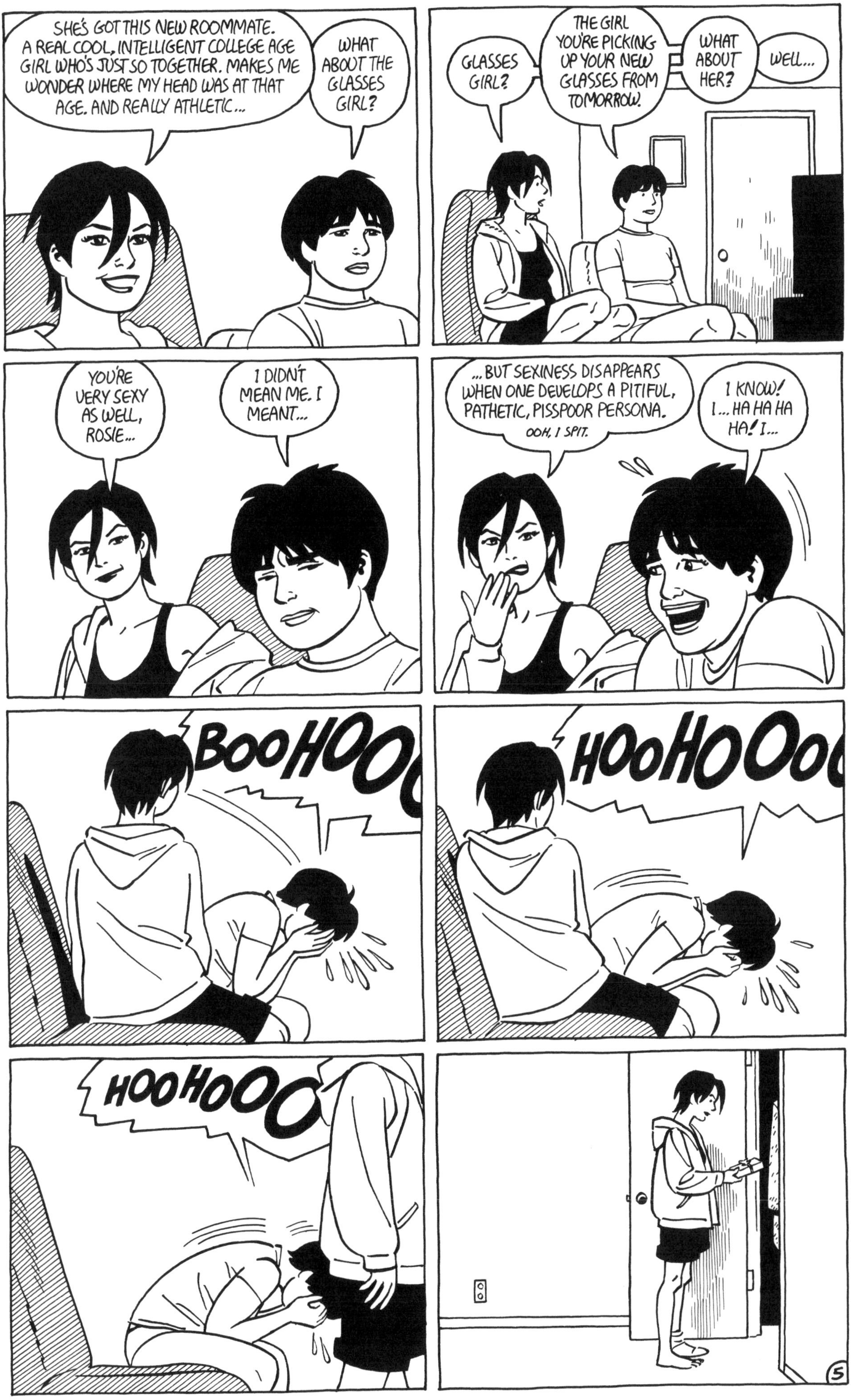
SHE'S GOT THIS NEW ROOMMATE. A REAL COOL, INTELLIGENT COLLEGE AGE GIRL WHO'S JUST SO TOGETHER. MAKES ME WONDER WHERE MY HEAD WAS AT THAT AGE. AND REALLY ATHLETIC...
WHAT ABOUT THE GLASSES GIRL?
GLASSES GIRL?
THE GIRL YOU'RE PICKING UP YOUR NEW GLASSES FROM TOMORROW.
WHAT ABOUT HER?
WELL...
YOU'RE VERY SEXY AS WELL, ROSIE...
I DIDN'T MEAN ME. I MEANT...
...BUT SEXINESS DISAPPEARS WHEN ONE DEVELOPS A PITIFUL, PATHETIC, PISSPOOR PERSONA.
OOH, I SPIT.
I KNOW! I... HA HA HA HA! I...
BOOHOOO
HOOHOOOO
HOOHOOO
5

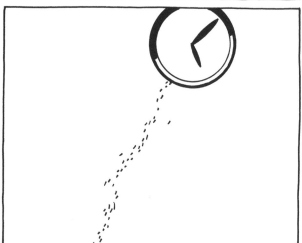

♪ ...RIDIN' 'ROUND TOWN WITH ALL THE WINDOWS DOWN...♪

ELMO'S NITE SPOT

CLOSING UP TONIGHT, SISTER?

NO, I GOTTA GET UP EARLY.

WHAT? NO NICKNAME TONIGHT? HOW ABOUT KRIS KRINGLE? I USED TO GET RICHARD CHAMBERLAIN BACK IN THE DAY.

WHAT IS YOUR NAME ANYWAY? YOU'RE HERE EVERY NIGHT ON THAT SAME STOOL...

HONEST JOE, AT YOUR SERVICE.

I'VE BEEN COMING HERE OFF AND ON SINCE FIFTY-TWO. A LOTTA GREAT MUSIC CAME OUT OF THESE WALLS. THURSTY NEWELL, ARNIE RODRIGUEZ, JOE BANKS, LESTER TALLEY. I WAS HERE THE NIGHT MINGUS SAT IN.

6

I THOUGHT I HEARD IT ALL TILL THAT ONE NIGHT.

I REMEMBER THEM PLAYING AND I JUST SAT THERE ALL FROZE UP. I DIDN'T DARE MOVE. I DIDN'T WANNA SPOIL THE MOST PERFECT NIGHT OF MY LIFE.

YOU COULD HAVE KILLED ME THE NEXT DAY AND I WOULDA BEEN JUST FINE.

BUT YOU, IT LOOKS LIKE TOMORROW STARTS A WHOLE NEW LIFE FOR YOU, SISTER.

YEH...

WHEN I STARTED GOING TO THESE CLASSES AND WE GOT OUR FIRST ASSIGNMENT, I TOOK MY WORK HOME AND I READ THE FIRST PAGE AND...

AND THEN...

AND THEN I READ THE FIRST PAGE AGAIN...

...AND AGAIN...

AND I DIDN'T KNOW WHAT THE HELL IT WAS SAYING. BUT, HERE I AM. HOW I GOT HERE IS A TOTAL MYSTERY, BUT...

AMAZING, ISN'T IT?

NOW, THIS PAST WEEK I'VE BEEN GOING OVER ALL THE STUFF I'M SUPPOSED TO KNOW FOR THE CLASS AND I'VE BEEN READING THAT FIRST PAGE OVER AN' OVER AND I DON'T KNOW WHAT THE HELL IT'S SAYING.

WHAT TIME ARE YOU SUPPOSED TO BE AT THE SCHOOL?

SEVEN FORTY-FIVE.

THAT'S ALL YOU NEED TO KNOW, SISTER.

CHEERS.

THANKS, POOPDECK PAPPY.

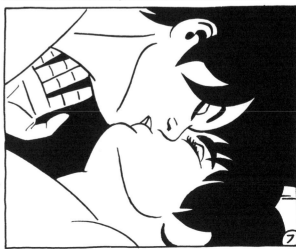

7

35

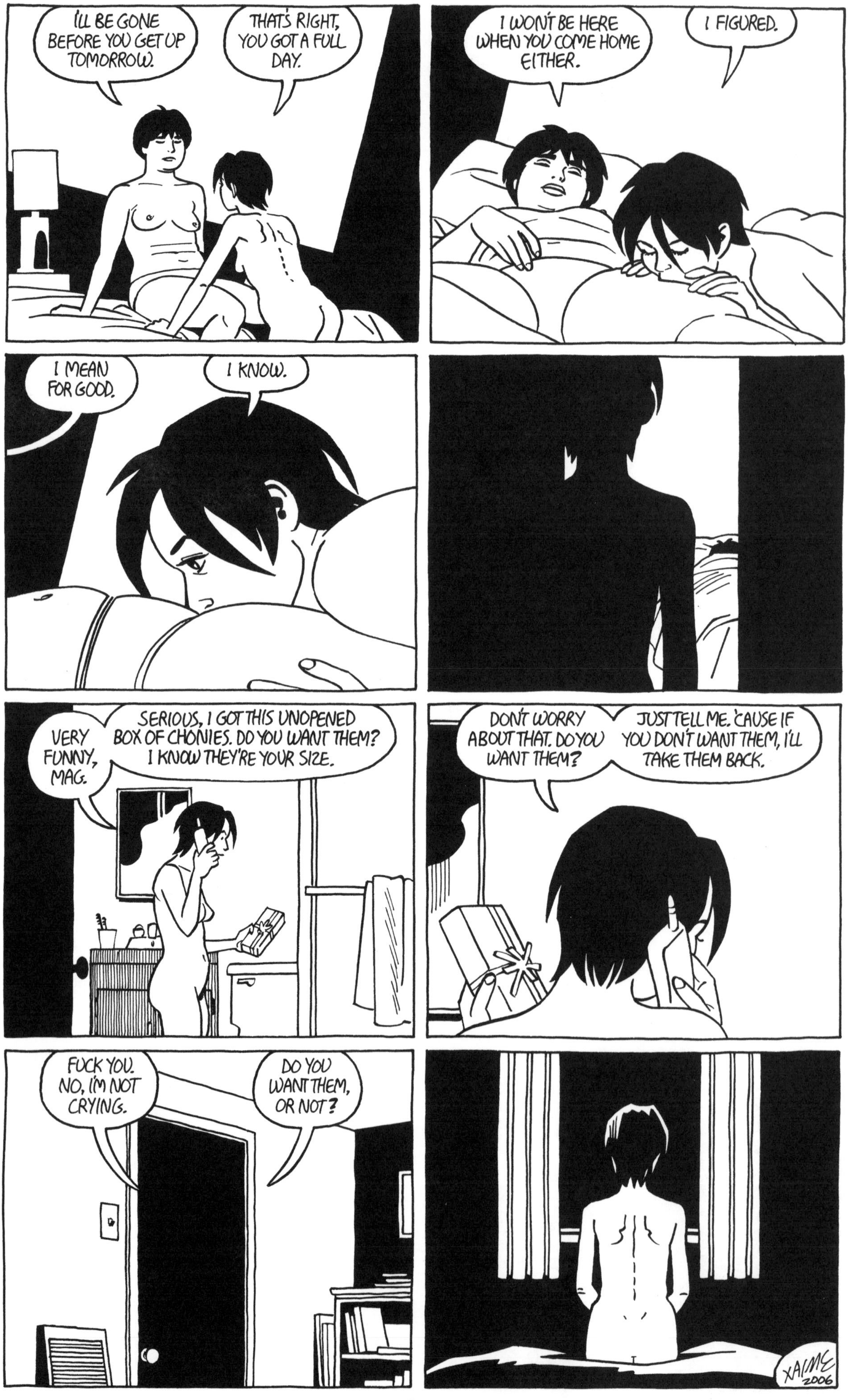
I'LL BE GONE BEFORE YOU GET UP TOMORROW.
THAT'S RIGHT, YOU GOT A FULL DAY.
I WON'T BE HERE WHEN YOU COME HOME EITHER.
I FIGURED.
I MEAN FOR GOOD.
I KNOW.
VERY FUNNY, MAG.
SERIOUS, I GOT THIS UNOPENED BOX OF CHONIES. DO YOU WANT THEM? I KNOW THEY'RE YOUR SIZE.
DON'T WORRY ABOUT THAT. DO YOU WANT THEM?
JUST TELL ME. 'CAUSE IF YOU DON'T WANT THEM, I'LL TAKE THEM BACK.
FUCK YOU. NO, I'M NOT CRYING.
DO YOU WANT THEM, OR NOT?
XAIME 2006

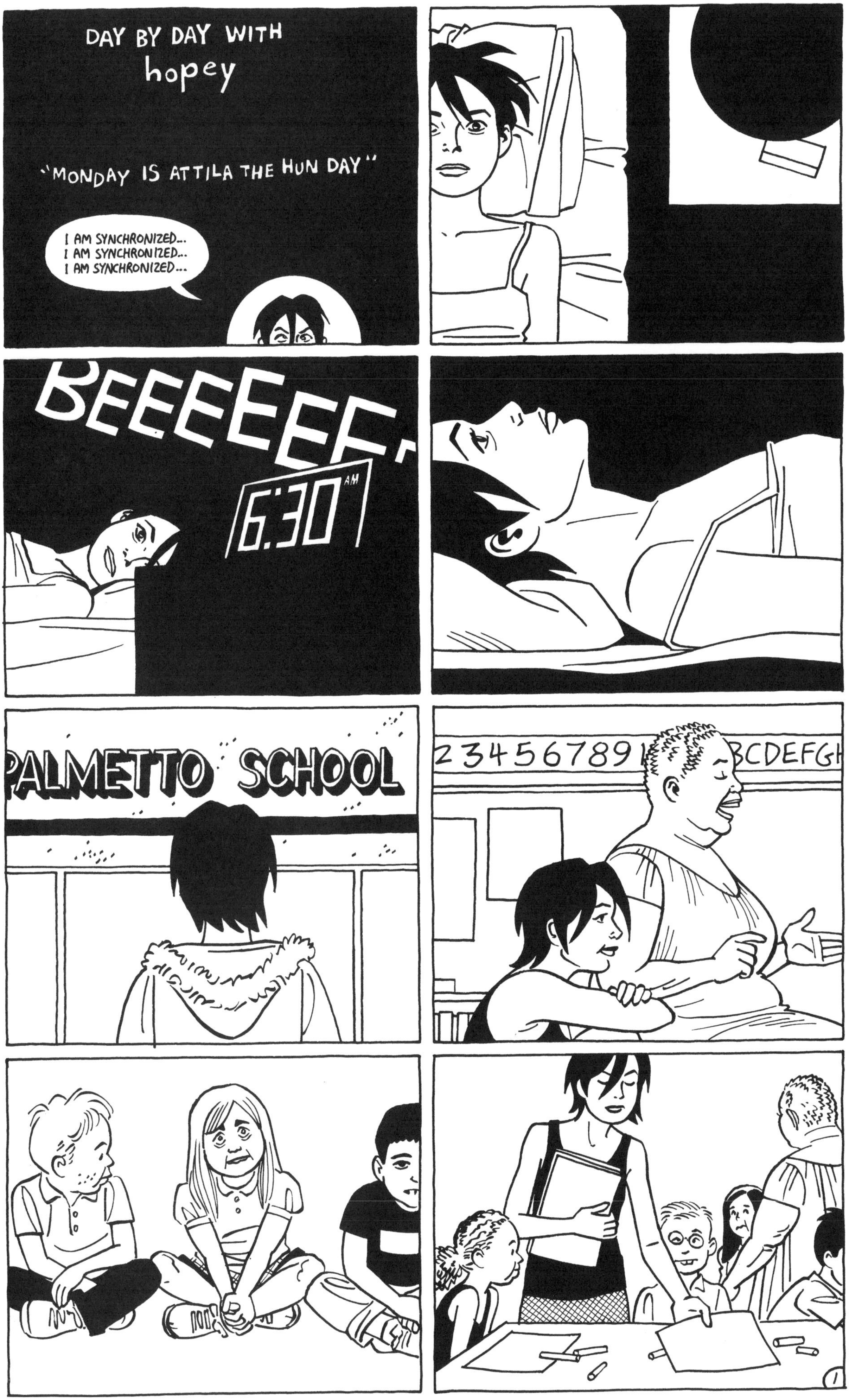
DAY BY DAY WITH
hopey
"MONDAY IS ATTILA THE HUN DAY"
I AM SYNCHRONIZED... I AM SYNCHRONIZED... I AM SYNCHRONIZED...
BEEEEEE
6:30 AM
PALMETTO SCHOOL
23456789
BCDEFG

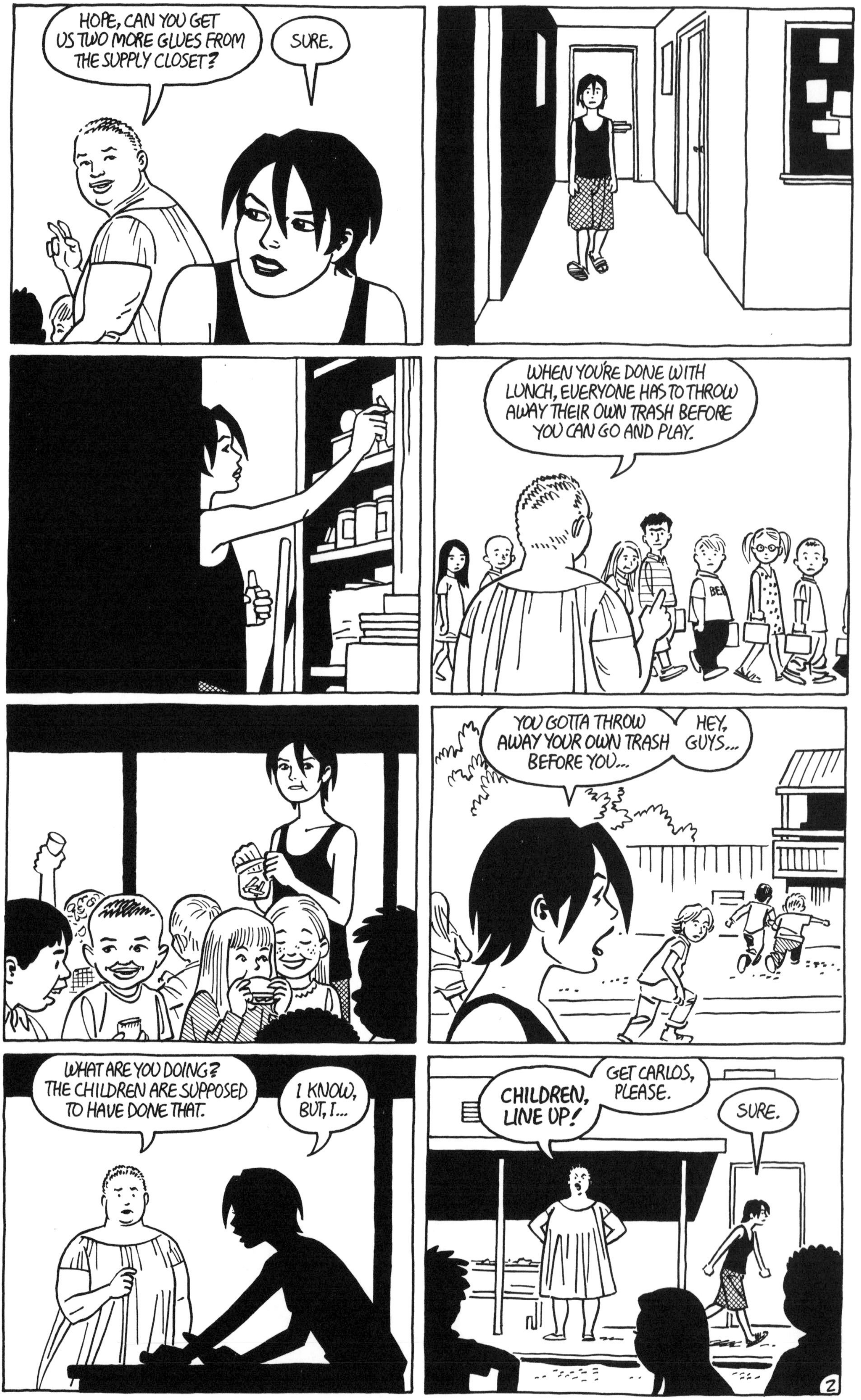
HOPE, CAN YOU GET US TWO MORE GLUES FROM THE SUPPLY CLOSET?
SURE.
WHEN YOU'RE DONE WITH LUNCH, EVERYONE HAS TO THROW AWAY THEIR OWN TRASH BEFORE YOU CAN GO AND PLAY.
YOU GOTTA THROW AWAY YOUR OWN TRASH BEFORE YOU...
HEY, GUYS...
WHAT ARE YOU DOING? THE CHILDREN ARE SUPPOSED TO HAVE DONE THAT.
I KNOW, BUT, I...
CHILDREN, LINE UP!
GET CARLOS, PLEASE.
SURE.
2

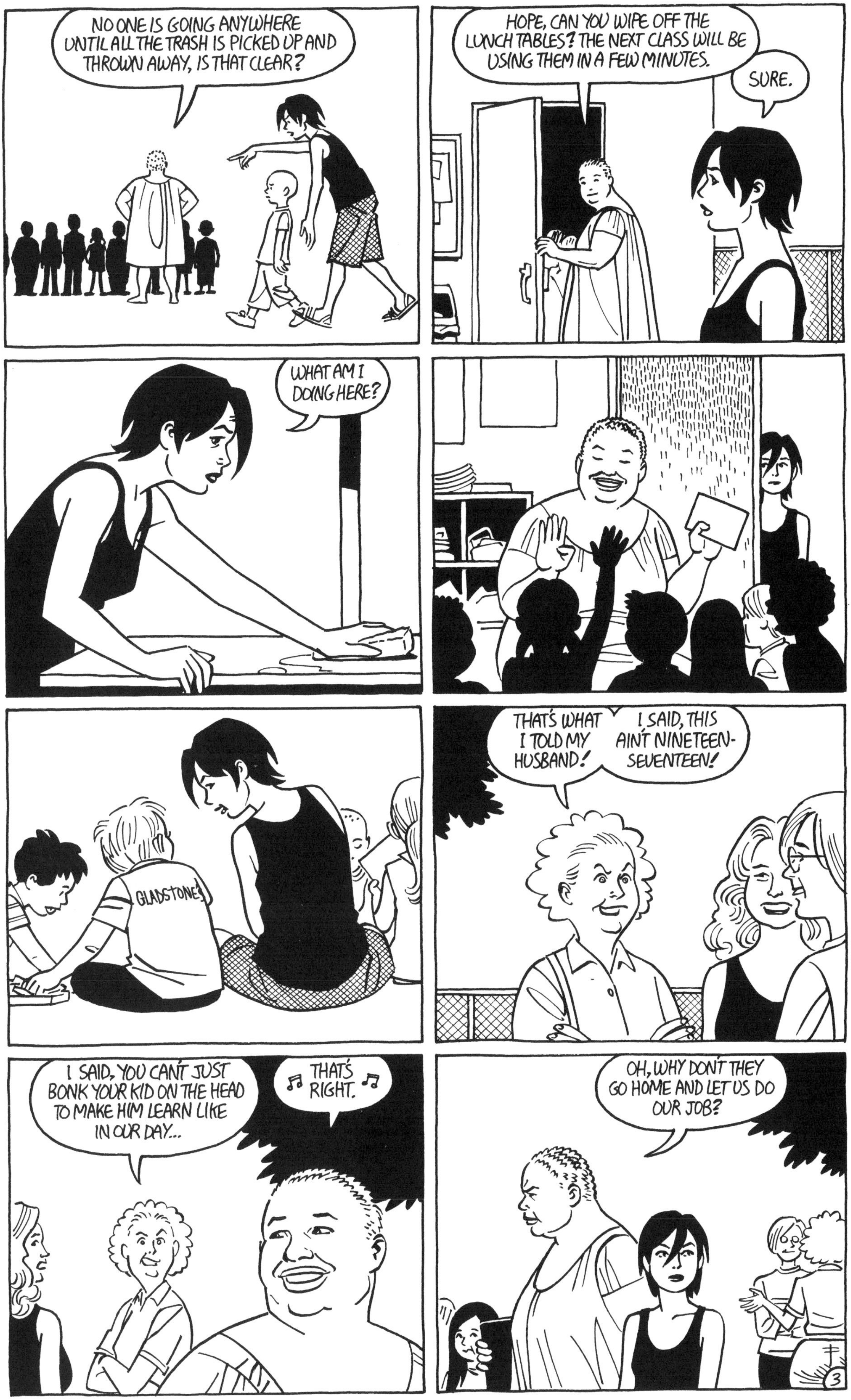
NO ONE IS GOING ANYWHERE UNTIL ALL THE TRASH IS PICKED UP AND THROWN AWAY, IS THAT CLEAR?
HOPE, CAN YOU WIPE OFF THE LUNCH TABLES? THE NEXT CLASS WILL BE USING THEM IN A FEW MINUTES.
SURE.
WHAT AM I DOING HERE?
GLADSTONES
THAT'S WHAT I TOLD MY HUSBAND!
I SAID, THIS AIN'T NINETEEN-SEVENTEEN!
I SAID, YOU CAN'T JUST BONK YOUR KID ON THE HEAD TO MAKE HIM LEARN LIKE IN OUR DAY...
♫ THAT'S RIGHT. ♫
OH, WHY DON'T THEY GO HOME AND LET US DO OUR JOB?
3

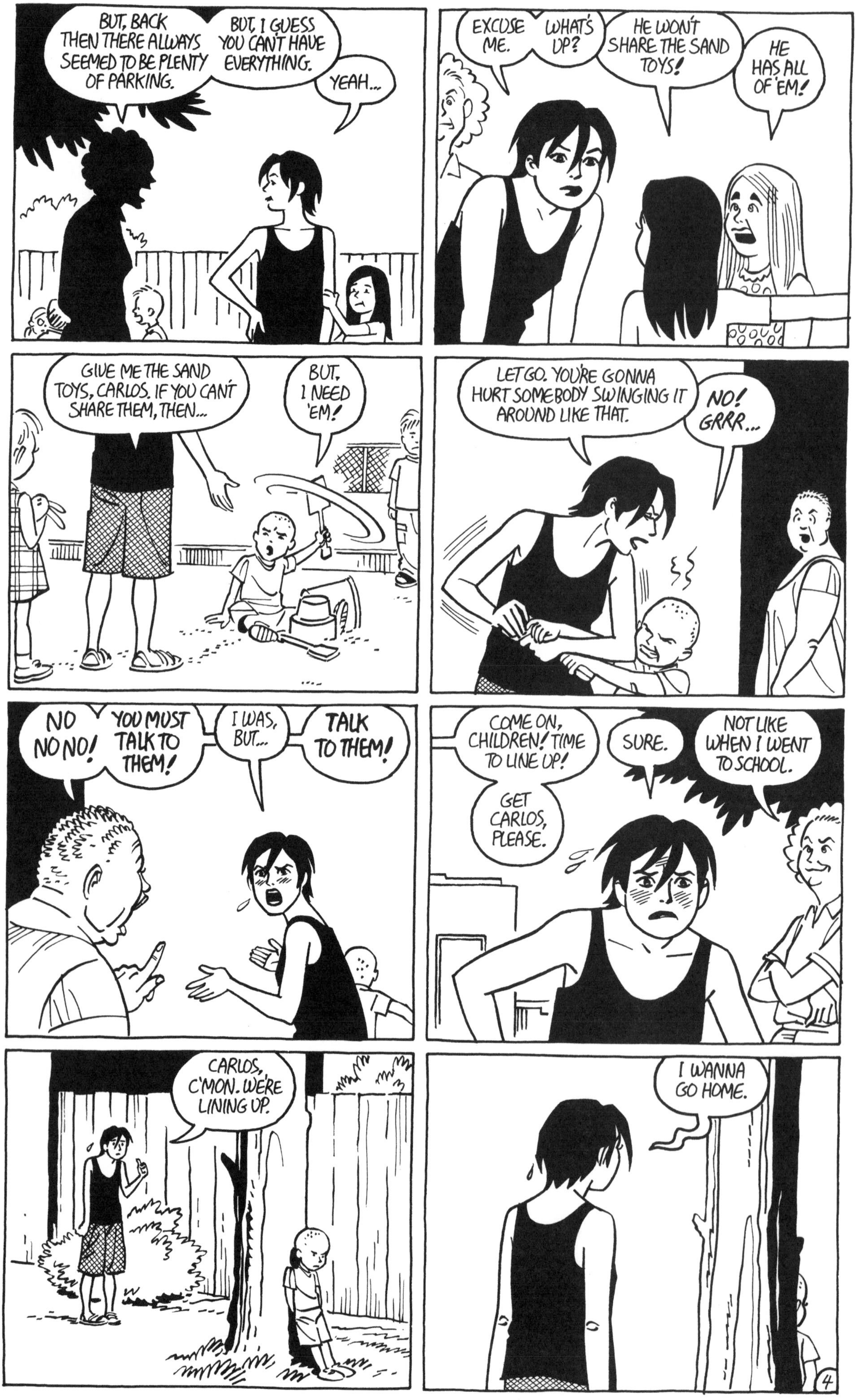
BUT, BACK THEN THERE ALWAYS SEEMED TO BE PLENTY OF PARKING.
BUT, I GUESS YOU CAN'T HAVE EVERYTHING.
YEAH...
EXCUSE ME.
WHAT'S UP?
HE WON'T SHARE THE SAND TOYS!
HE HAS ALL OF 'EM!
GIVE ME THE SAND TOYS, CARLOS. IF YOU CAN'T SHARE THEM, THEN...
BUT, I NEED 'EM!
LET GO. YOU'RE GONNA HURT SOMEBODY SWINGING IT AROUND LIKE THAT.
NO! GRRR...
NO NO NO!
YOU MUST TALK TO THEM!
I WAS, BUT...
TALK TO THEM!
COME ON, CHILDREN! TIME TO LINE UP!
GET CARLOS, PLEASE.
SURE.
NOT LIKE WHEN I WENT TO SCHOOL.
CARLOS, C'MON. WE'RE LINING UP.
I WANNA GO HOME.
4

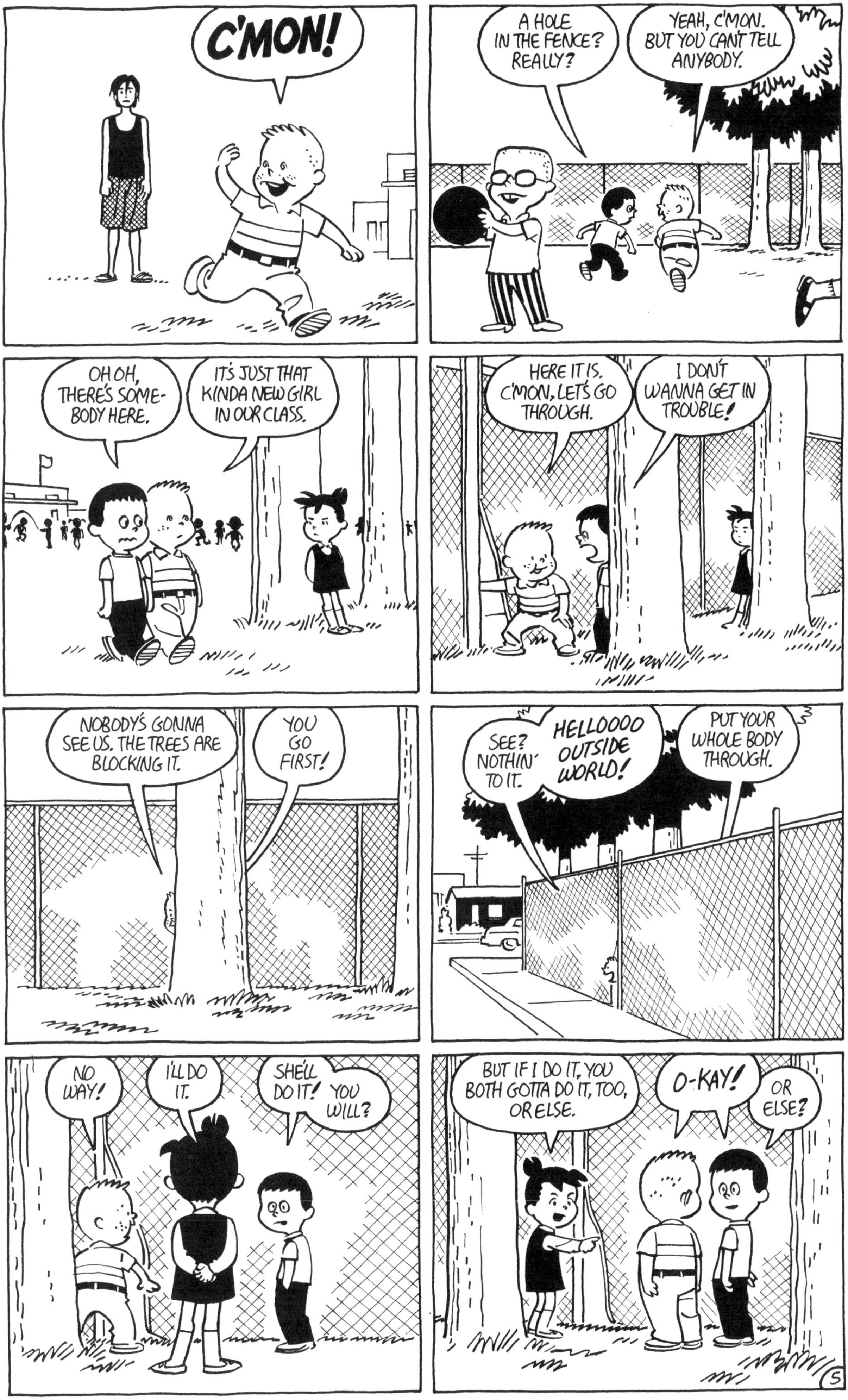
C'MON!
A HOLE IN THE FENCE? REALLY?
YEAH, C'MON. BUT YOU CAN'T TELL ANYBODY.
OH OH, THERE'S SOME-BODY HERE.
IT'S JUST THAT KINDA NEW GIRL IN OUR CLASS.
HERE IT IS. C'MON, LET'S GO THROUGH.
I DON'T WANNA GET IN TROUBLE!
NOBODY'S GONNA SEE US. THE TREES ARE BLOCKING IT.
YOU GO FIRST!
SEE? NOTHIN' TO IT.
HELLOOOO OUTSIDE WORLD!
PUT YOUR WHOLE BODY THROUGH.
NO WAY!
I'LL DO IT.
SHE'LL DO IT!
YOU WILL?
BUT IF I DO IT, YOU BOTH GOTTA DO IT, TOO, OR ELSE.
O-KAY!
OR ELSE?
5

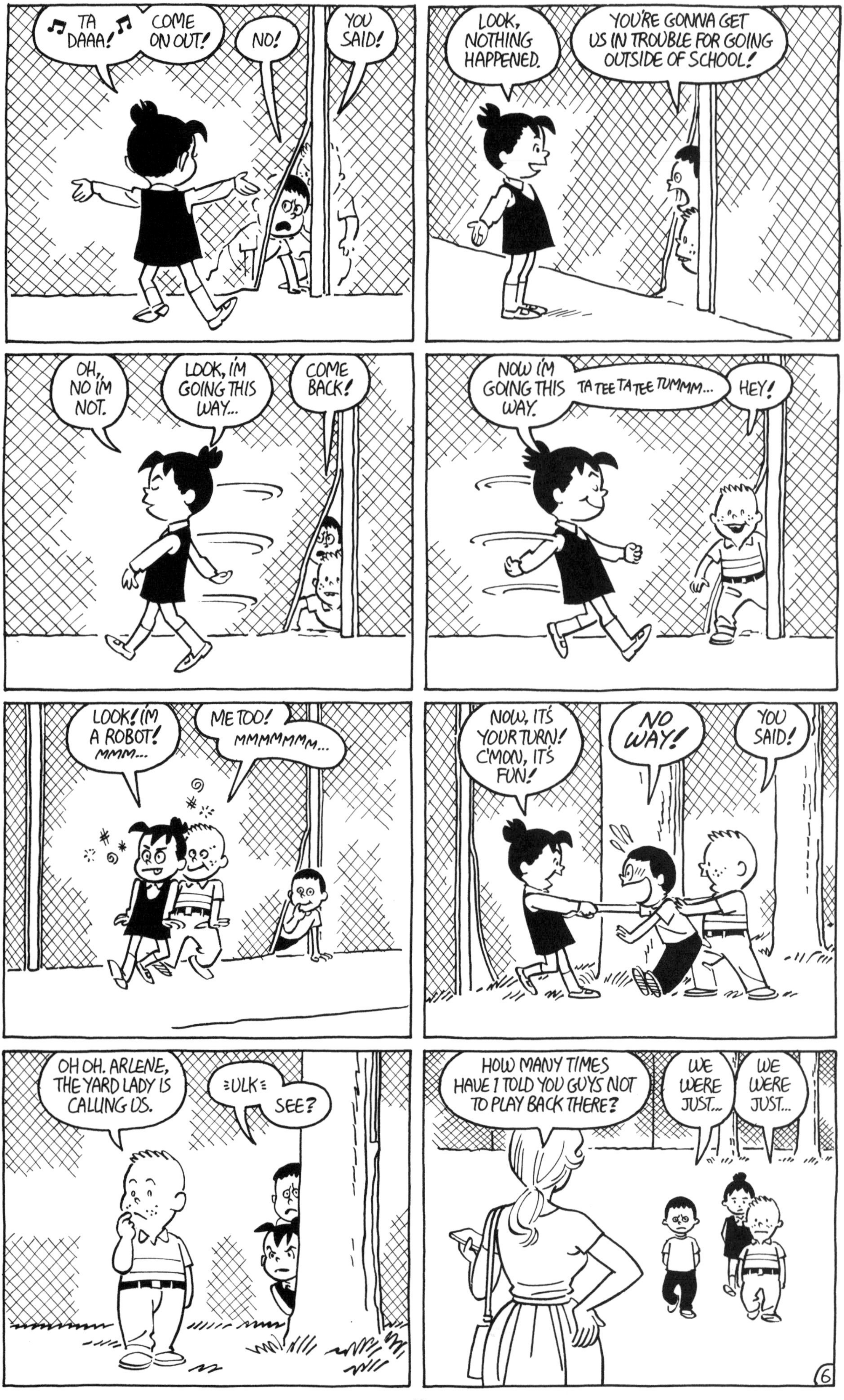
TA DAAA!
COME ON OUT!
NO!
YOU SAID!
LOOK, NOTHING HAPPENED.
YOU'RE GONNA GET US IN TROUBLE FOR GOING OUTSIDE OF SCHOOL!
OH, NO I'M NOT.
LOOK, I'M GOING THIS WAY...
COME BACK!
NOW I'M GOING THIS WAY.
TA TEE TA TEE TUMMM...
HEY!
LOOK! I'M A ROBOT! MMM...
ME TOO! MMMMMMM...
NOW, IT'S YOUR TURN! C'MON, IT'S FUN!
NO WAY!
YOU SAID!
OH OH. ARLENE, THE YARD LADY IS CALLING US.
ULK
SEE?
HOW MANY TIMES HAVE I TOLD YOU GUYS NOT TO PLAY BACK THERE?
WE WERE JUST...
WE WERE JUST...
6

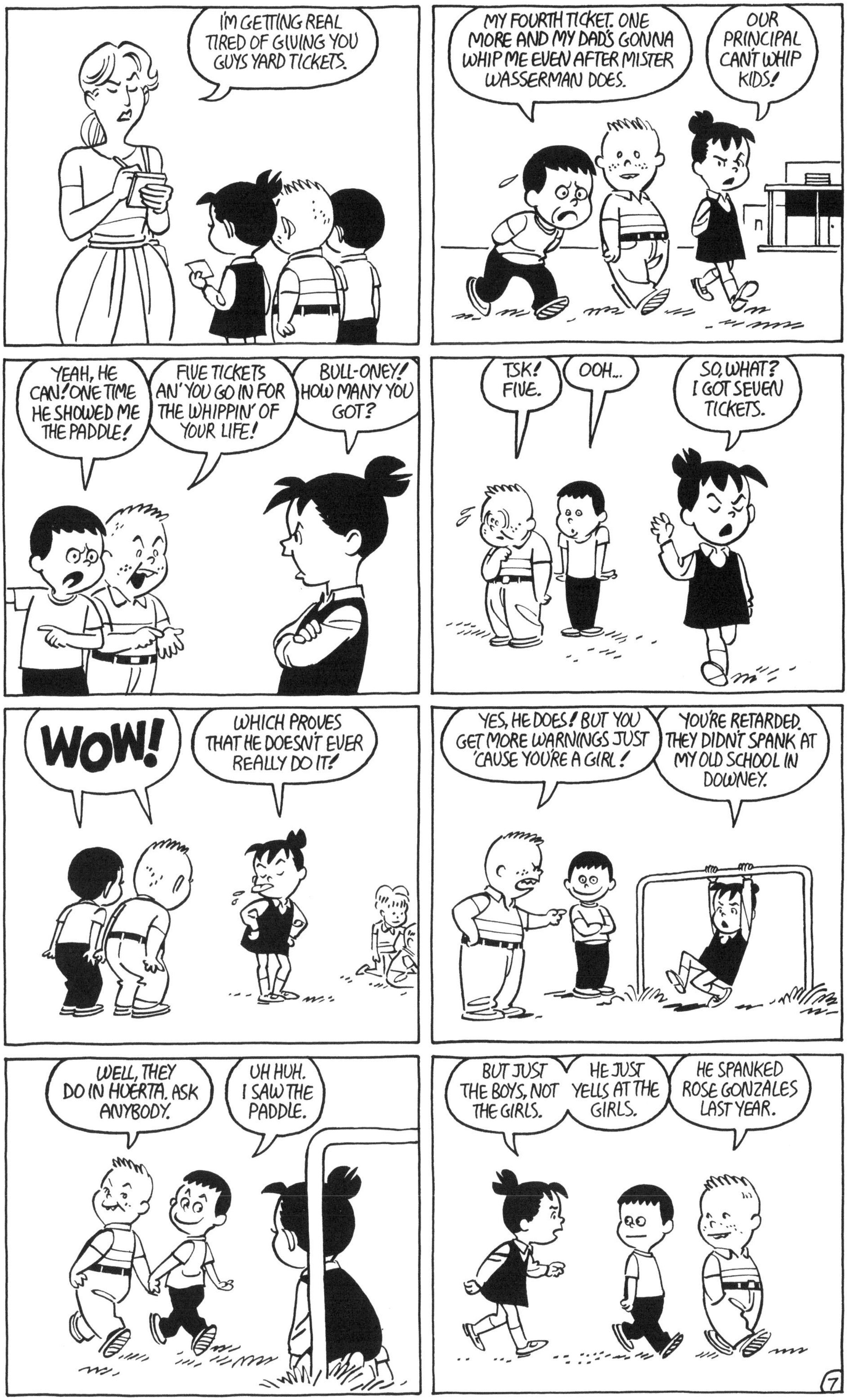
I'M GETTING REAL TIRED OF GIVING YOU GUYS YARD TICKETS.
MY FOURTH TICKET. ONE MORE AND MY DAD'S GONNA WHIP ME EVEN AFTER MISTER WASSERMAN DOES.
OUR PRINCIPAL CAN'T WHIP KIDS!
YEAH, HE CAN! ONE TIME HE SHOWED ME THE PADDLE!
FIVE TICKETS AN' YOU GO IN FOR THE WHIPPIN' OF YOUR LIFE!
BULL-ONEY! HOW MANY YOU GOT?
TSK! FIVE.
OOH...
SO, WHAT? I GOT SEVEN TICKETS.
WOW!
WHICH PROVES THAT HE DOESN'T EVER REALLY DO IT!
YES, HE DOES! BUT YOU GET MORE WARNINGS JUST 'CAUSE YOU'RE A GIRL!
YOU'RE RETARDED. THEY DIDN'T SPANK AT MY OLD SCHOOL IN DOWNEY.
WELL, THEY DO IN HUERTA. ASK ANYBODY.
UH HUH. I SAW THE PADDLE.
BUT JUST THE BOYS, NOT THE GIRLS.
HE JUST YELLS AT THE GIRLS.
HE SPANKED ROSE GONZALES LAST YEAR.
7

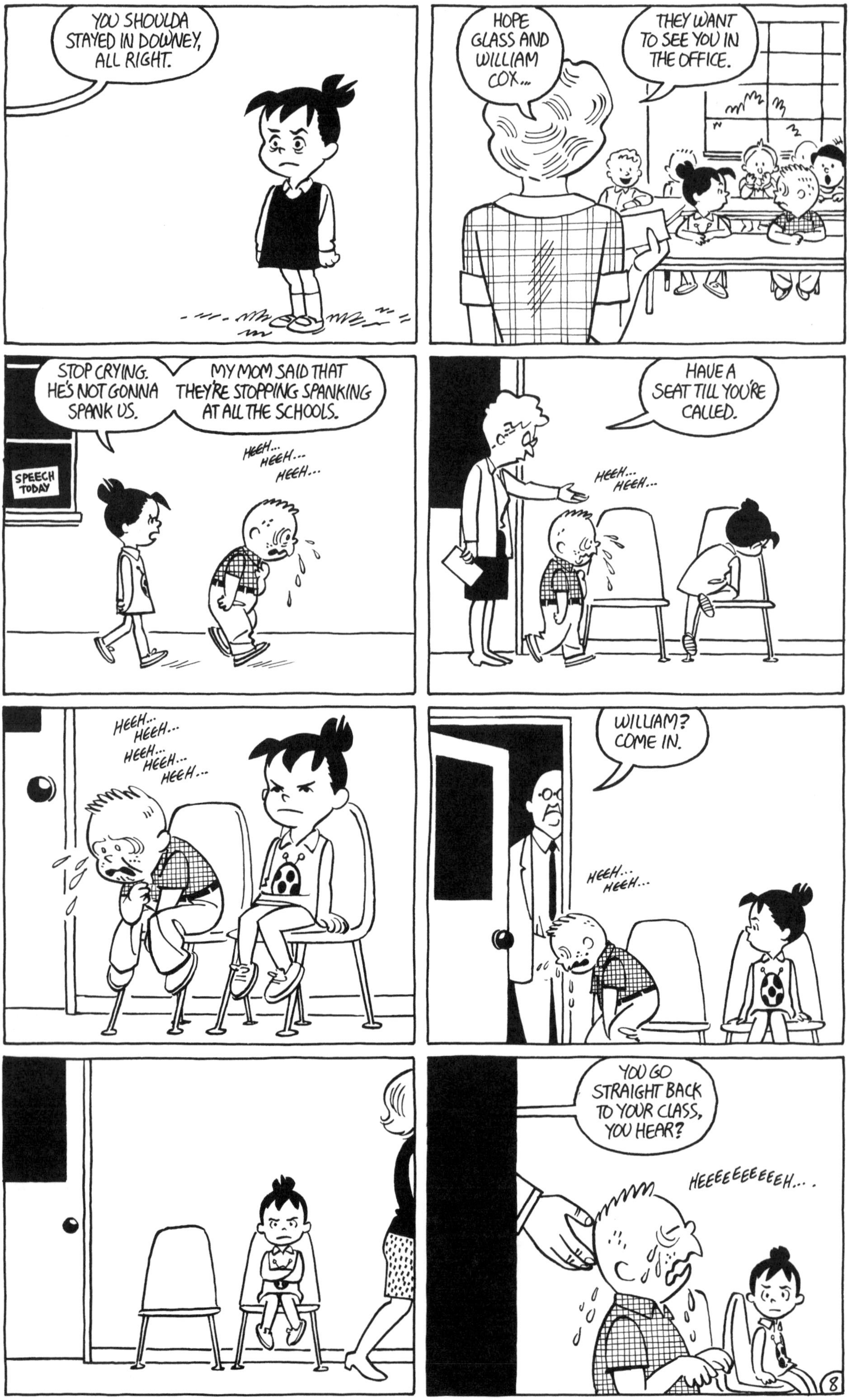
YOU SHOULDA STAYED IN DOWNEY, ALL RIGHT.
HOPE GLASS AND WILLIAM COX...
THEY WANT TO SEE YOU IN THE OFFICE.
STOP CRYING. HE'S NOT GONNA SPANK US.
MY MOM SAID THAT THEY'RE STOPPING SPANKING AT ALL THE SCHOOLS.
SPEECH TODAY
HEEH... HEEH... HEEH...
HAVE A SEAT TILL YOU'RE CALLED.
HEEH... HEEH...
HEEH... HEEH... HEEH... HEEH... HEEH...
WILLIAM? COME IN.
HEEH... HEEH...
YOU GO STRAIGHT BACK TO YOUR CLASS, YOU HEAR?
HEEEEEEEEEEH....
8

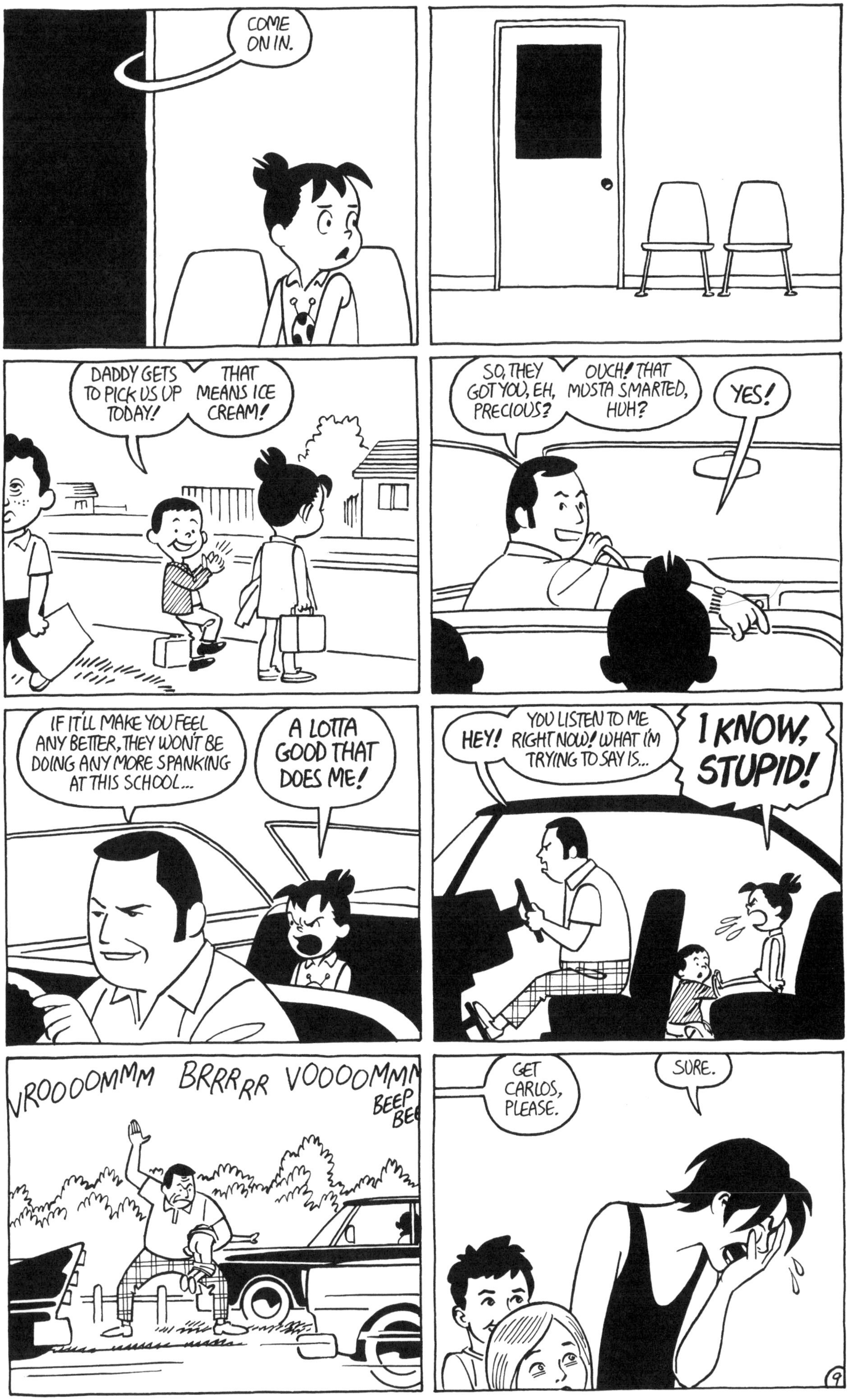
COME ON IN.
DADDY GETS TO PICK US UP TODAY!
THAT MEANS ICE CREAM!
SO, THEY GOT YOU, EH, PRECIOUS?
OUCH! THAT MUSTA SMARTED, HUH?
YES!
IF IT'LL MAKE YOU FEEL ANY BETTER, THEY WON'T BE DOING ANY MORE SPANKING AT THIS SCHOOL...
A LOTTA GOOD THAT DOES ME!
HEY!
YOU LISTEN TO ME RIGHT NOW! WHAT I'M TRYING TO SAY IS...
I KNOW, STUPID!
VROOOOMMM BRRRRR VOOOOMMM
BEEP
GET CARLOS, PLEASE.
SURE.
9

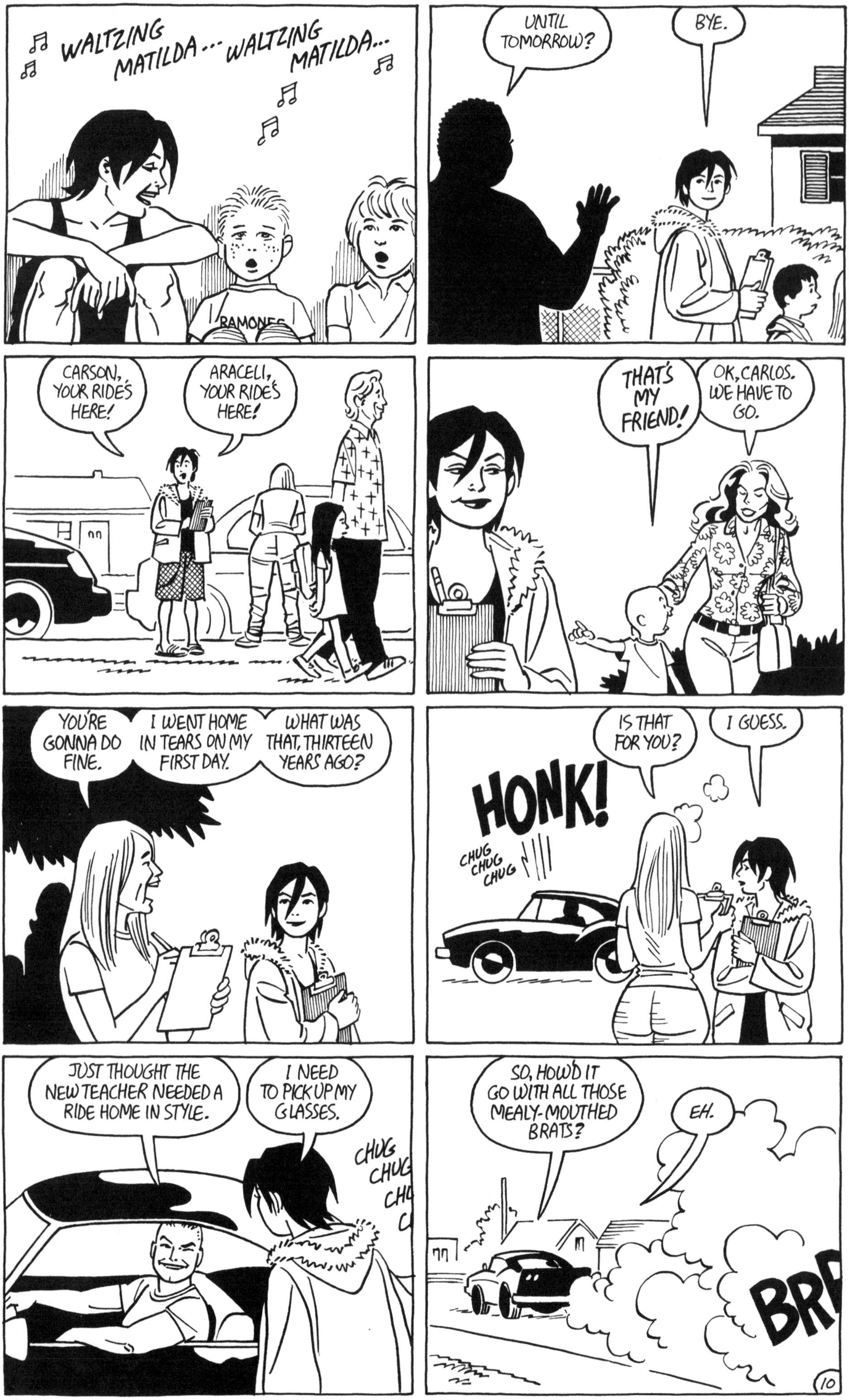
WALTZING MATILDA... WALTZING MATILDA...
RAMONES
UNTIL TOMORROW?
BYE.
CARSON, YOUR RIDE'S HERE!
ARACELI, YOUR RIDE'S HERE!
THAT'S MY FRIEND!
OK, CARLOS. WE HAVE TO GO.
YOU'RE GONNA DO FINE.
I WENT HOME IN TEARS ON MY FIRST DAY.
WHAT WAS THAT, THIRTEEN YEARS AGO?
HONK!
CHUG CHUG CHUG
IS THAT FOR YOU?
I GUESS.
JUST THOUGHT THE NEW TEACHER NEEDED A RIDE HOME IN STYLE.
I NEED TO PICK UP MY GLASSES.
SO, HOW'D IT GO WITH ALL THOSE MEALY-MOUTHED BRATS?
EH.
10

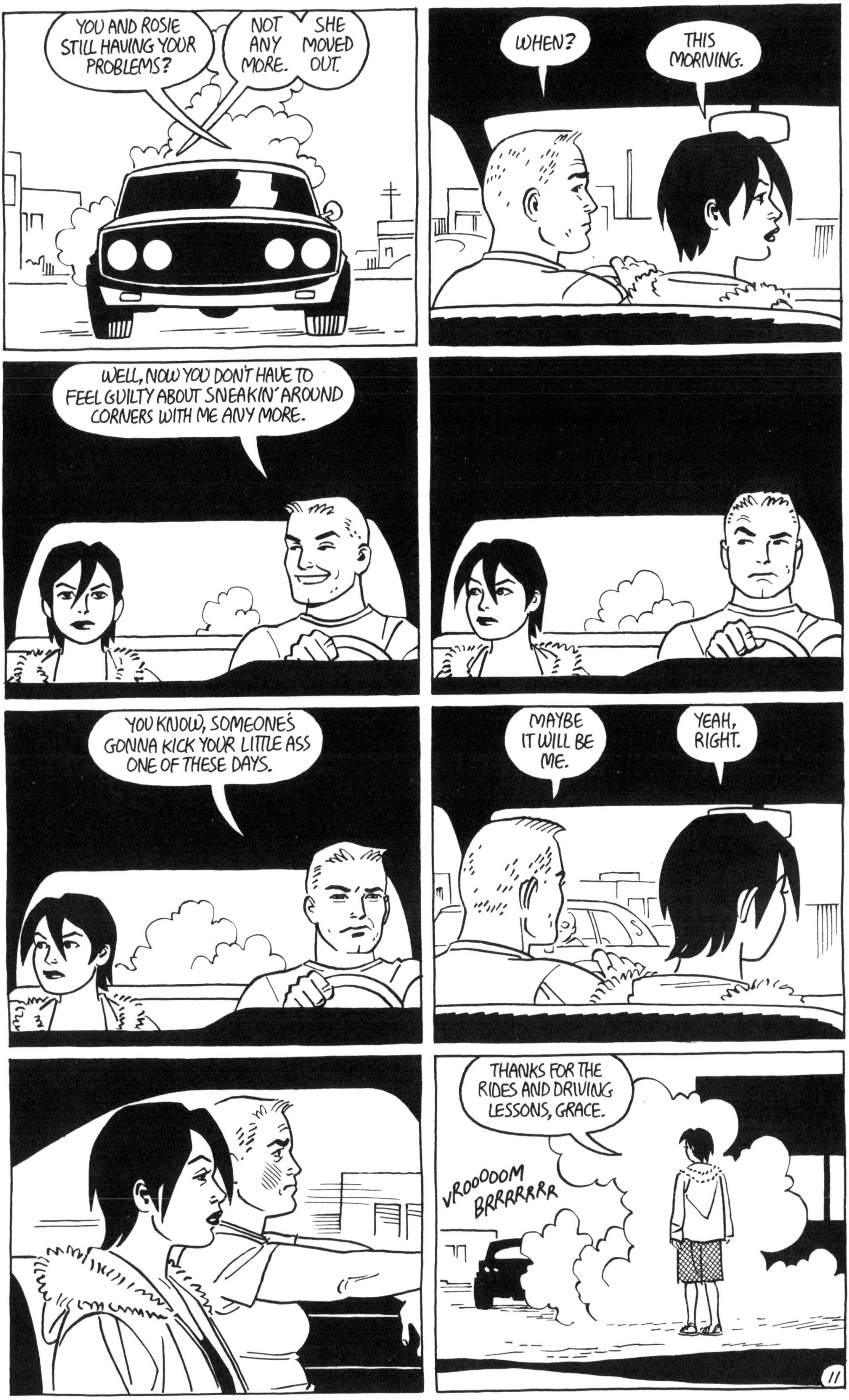
YOU AND ROSIE STILL HAVING YOUR PROBLEMS?
NOT ANY MORE.
SHE MOVED OUT.
WHEN?
THIS MORNING.
WELL, NOW YOU DON'T HAVE TO FEEL GUILTY ABOUT SNEAKIN' AROUND CORNERS WITH ME ANY MORE.
YOU KNOW, SOMEONE'S GONNA KICK YOUR LITTLE ASS ONE OF THESE DAYS.
MAYBE IT WILL BE ME.
YEAH, RIGHT.
THANKS FOR THE RIDES AND DRIVING LESSONS, GRACE.
VROOOOOOM
BRRRRRRR
11

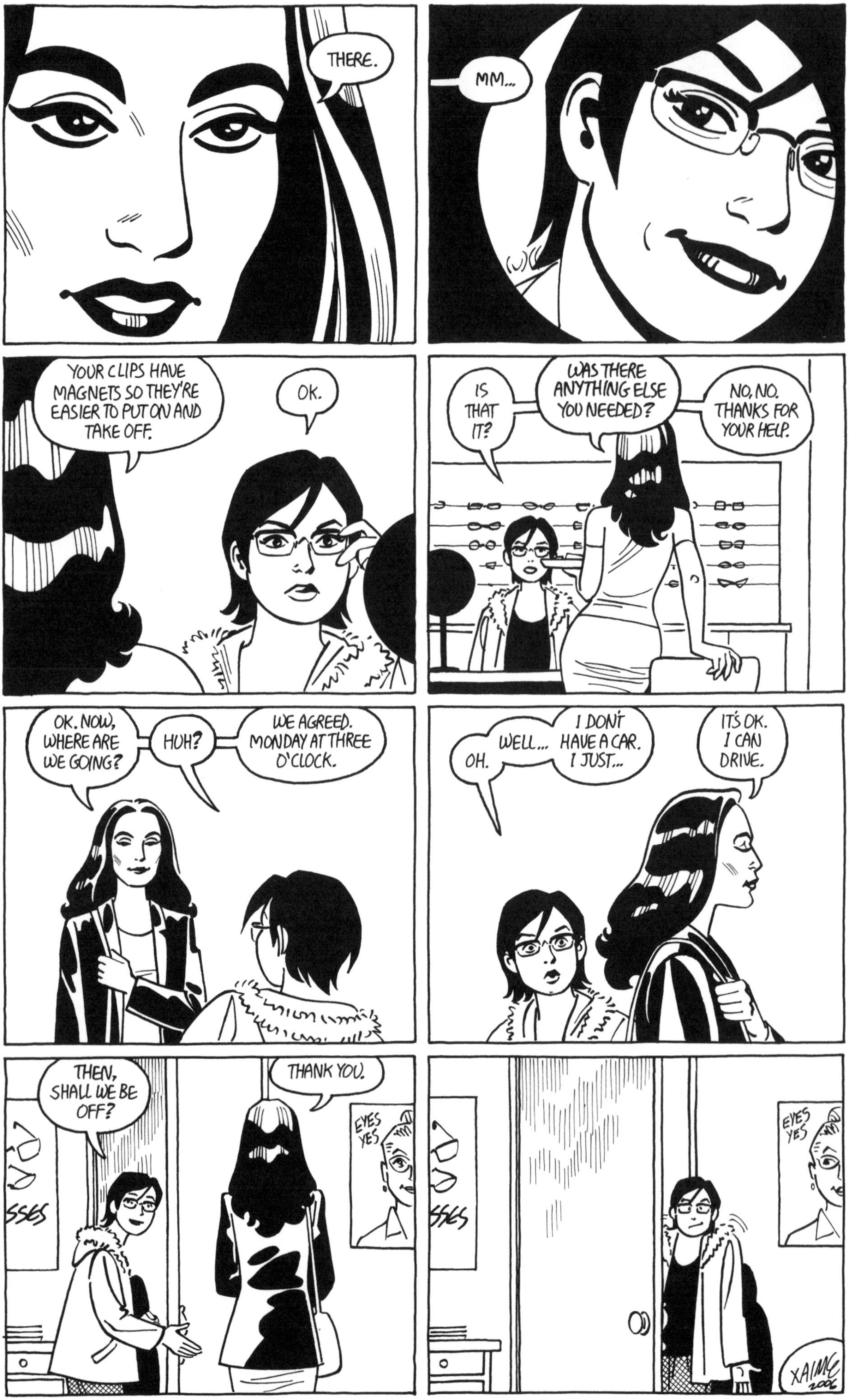
THERE.
MM...
YOUR CLIPS HAVE MAGNETS SO THEY'RE EASIER TO PUT ON AND TAKE OFF.
OK.
IS THAT IT?
WAS THERE ANYTHING ELSE YOU NEEDED?
NO, NO. THANKS FOR YOUR HELP.
OK. NOW, WHERE ARE WE GOING?
HUH?
WE AGREED. MONDAY AT THREE O'CLOCK.
OH.
WELL...
I DON'T HAVE A CAR. I JUST...
IT'S OK. I CAN DRIVE.
THEN, SHALL WE BE OFF?
THANK YOU.
EYES YES
SSES
EYES YES
SSES
XAIME 2006

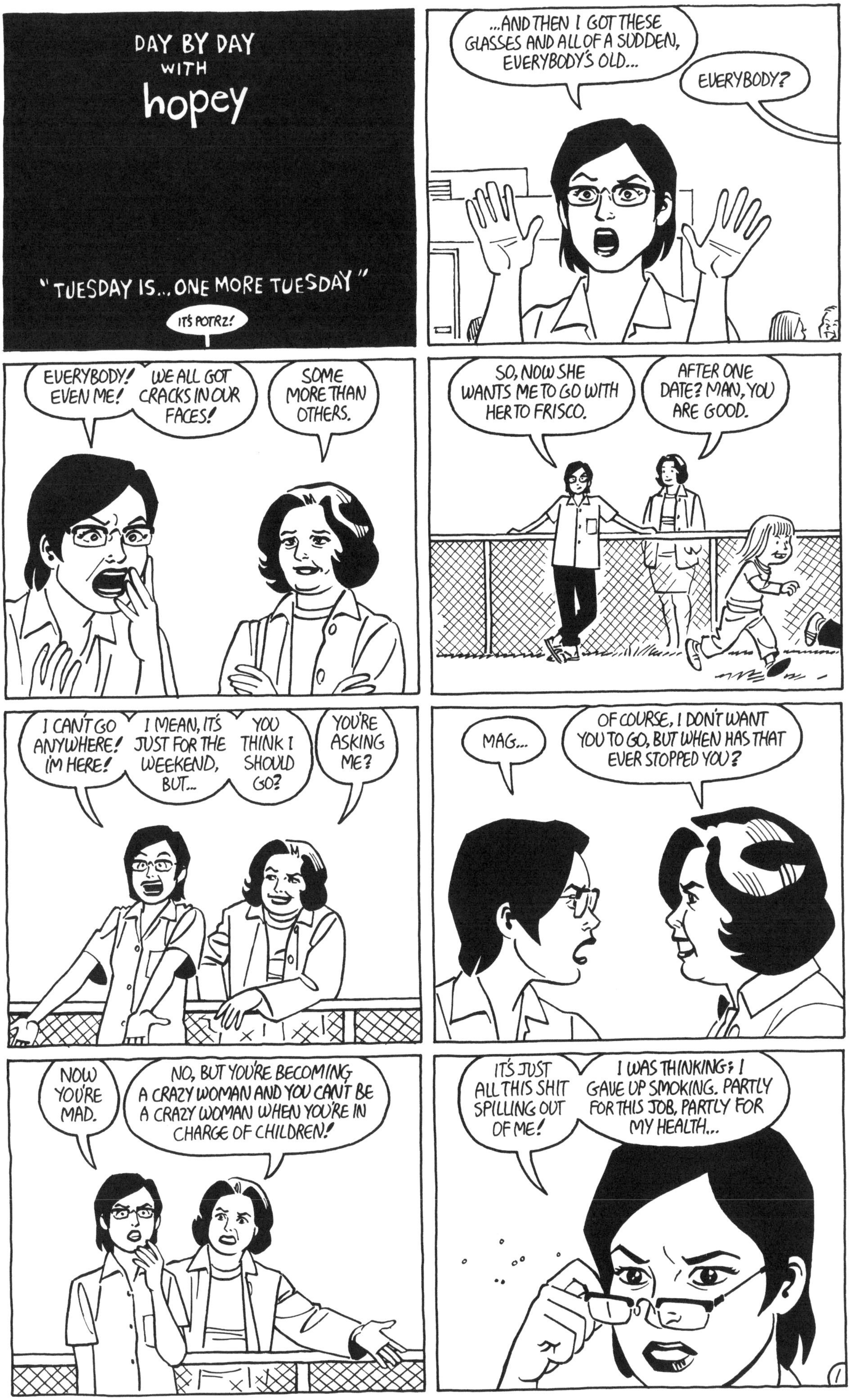

DAY BY DAY WITH hopey
"TUESDAY IS... ONE MORE TUESDAY"
IT'S POTRZ!
...AND THEN I GOT THESE GLASSES AND ALL OF A SUDDEN, EVERYBODY'S OLD...
EVERYBODY?
EVERYBODY! EVEN ME!
WE ALL GOT CRACKS IN OUR FACES!
SOME MORE THAN OTHERS.
SO, NOW SHE WANTS ME TO GO WITH HER TO FRISCO.
AFTER ONE DATE? MAN, YOU ARE GOOD.
I CAN'T GO ANYWHERE! I'M HERE!
I MEAN, IT'S JUST FOR THE WEEKEND, BUT...
YOU THINK I SHOULD GO?
YOU'RE ASKING ME?
MAG...
OF COURSE, I DON'T WANT YOU TO GO, BUT WHEN HAS THAT EVER STOPPED YOU?
NOW YOU'RE MAD.
NO, BUT YOU'RE BECOMING A CRAZY WOMAN AND YOU CAN'T BE A CRAZY WOMAN WHEN YOU'RE IN CHARGE OF CHILDREN!
IT'S JUST ALL THIS SHIT SPILLING OUT OF ME!
I WAS THINKING; I GAVE UP SMOKING. PARTLY FOR THIS JOB, PARTLY FOR MY HEALTH...

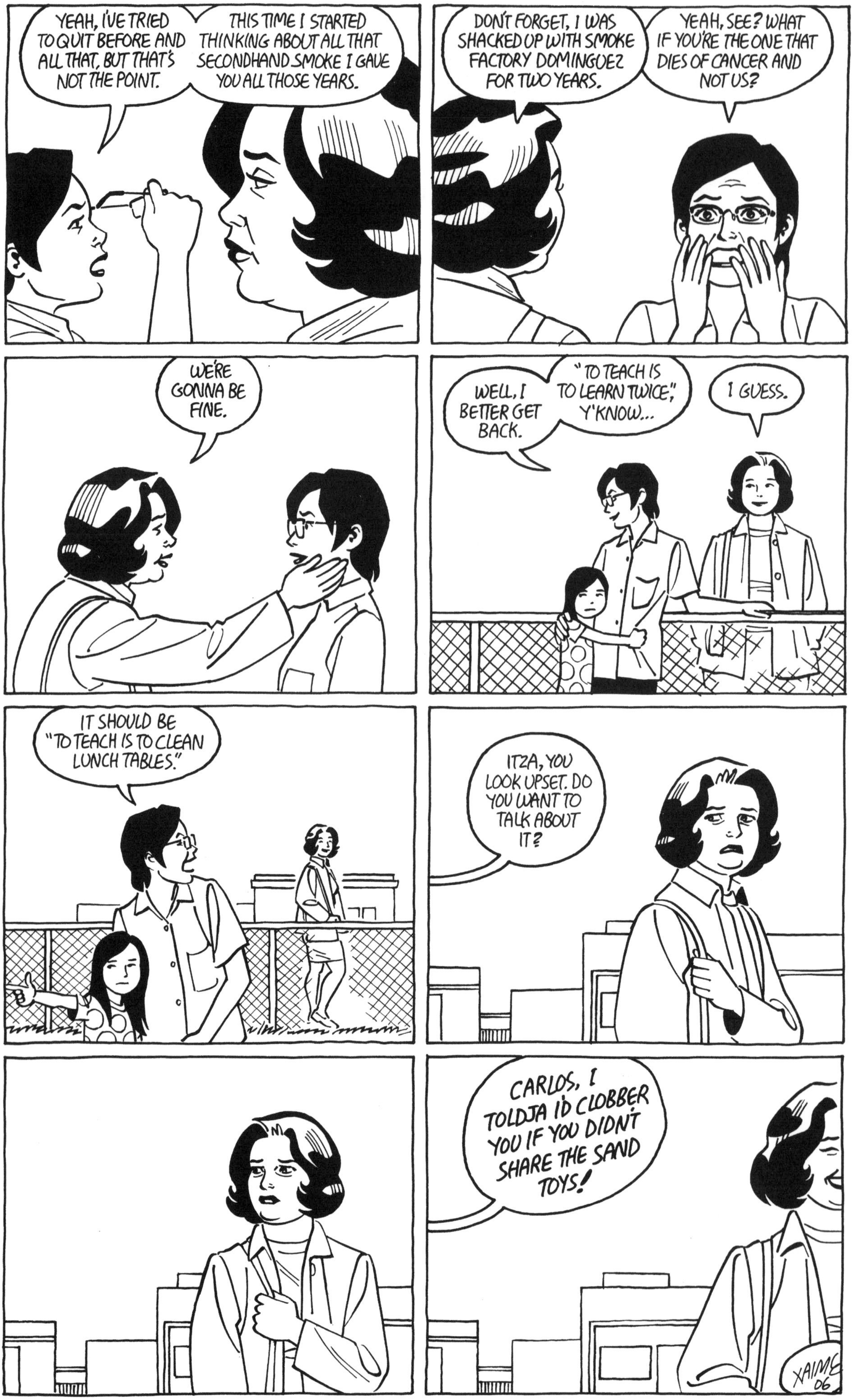
YEAH, I'VE TRIED TO QUIT BEFORE AND ALL THAT, BUT THAT'S NOT THE POINT.
THIS TIME I STARTED THINKING ABOUT ALL THAT SECONDHAND SMOKE I GAVE YOU ALL THOSE YEARS.
DON'T FORGET, I WAS SHACKED UP WITH SMOKE FACTORY DOMINGUEZ FOR TWO YEARS.
YEAH, SEE? WHAT IF YOU'RE THE ONE THAT DIES OF CANCER AND NOT US?
WE'RE GONNA BE FINE.
WELL, I BETTER GET BACK.
"TO TEACH IS TO LEARN TWICE," Y'KNOW...
I GUESS.
IT SHOULD BE "TO TEACH IS TO CLEAN LUNCH TABLES."
ITZA, YOU LOOK UPSET. DO YOU WANT TO TALK ABOUT IT?
CARLOS, I TOLDJA I'D CLOBBER YOU IF YOU DIDN'T SHARE THE SAND TOYS!
XAIME 06

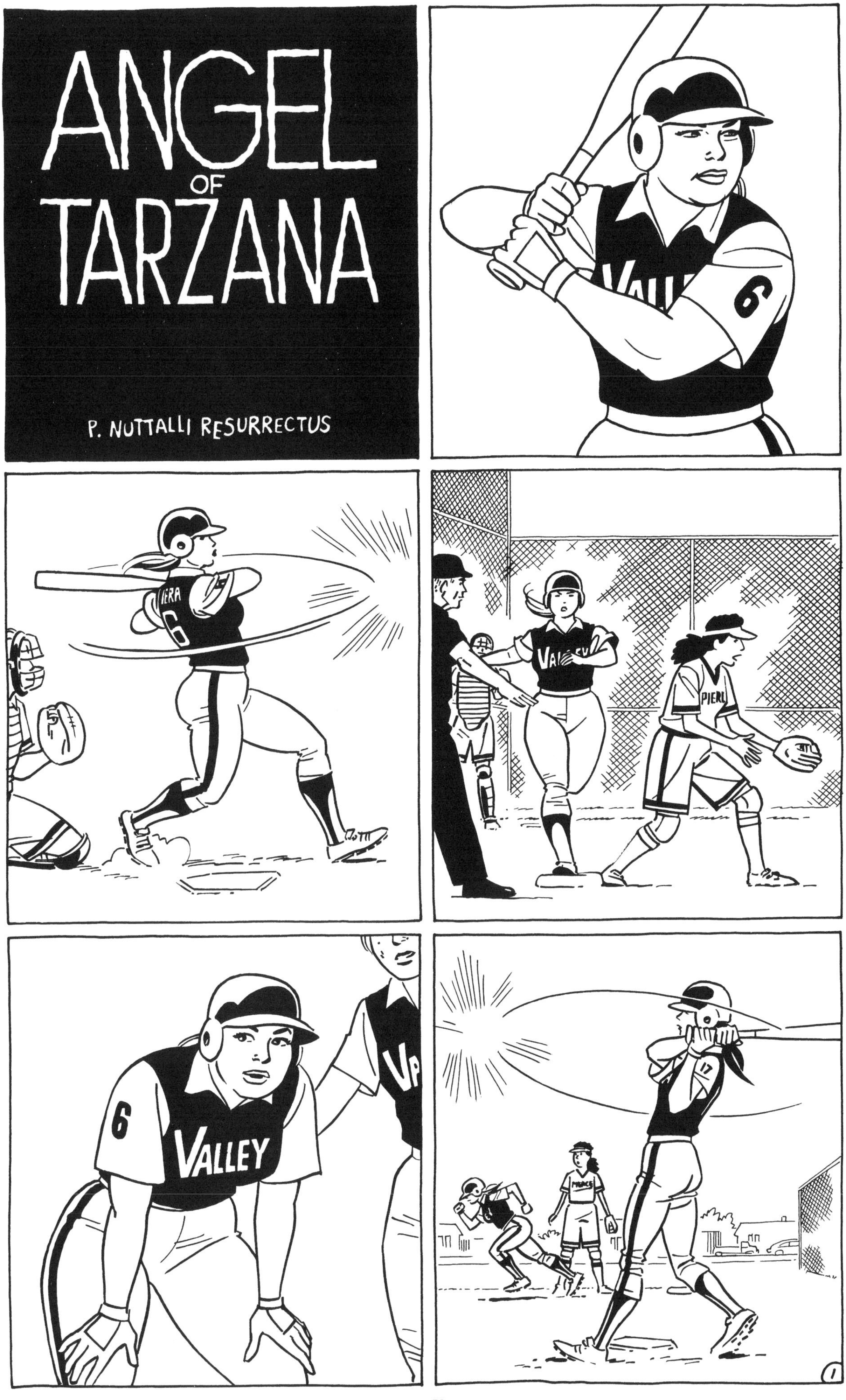
ANGEL OF TARZANA
P. NUTTALLI RESURRECTUS
6
PIERA
VALLEY
6
VALLEY
17
1

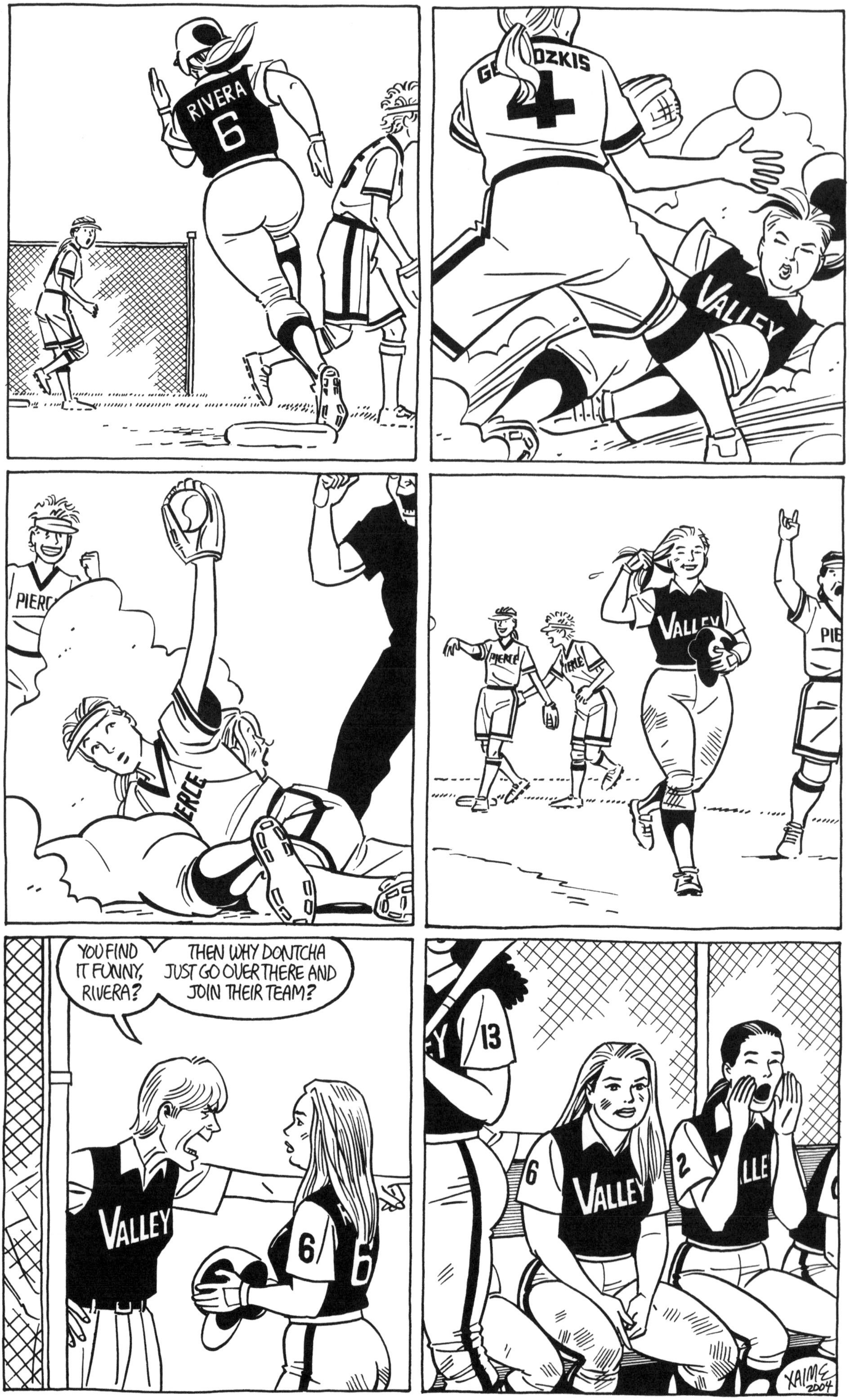
RIVERA
6
GE ODZKIS
4
VALLEY
PIERCE
YOU FIND IT FUNNY, RIVERA?
THEN WHY DONTCHA JUST GO OVER THERE AND JOIN THEIR TEAM?
13
VALLEY
XAIME 2004

ANGEL OF

TARZANA

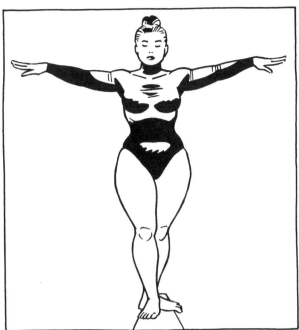

YAYY!

WOOo!

9.25?!

NO WAY! YOU WERE BETTER THAN KATY ANN KLUNK!

OH, WELL. GOODBYE, STATE CHAMPIONSHIPS. SIGH...

VALLEY

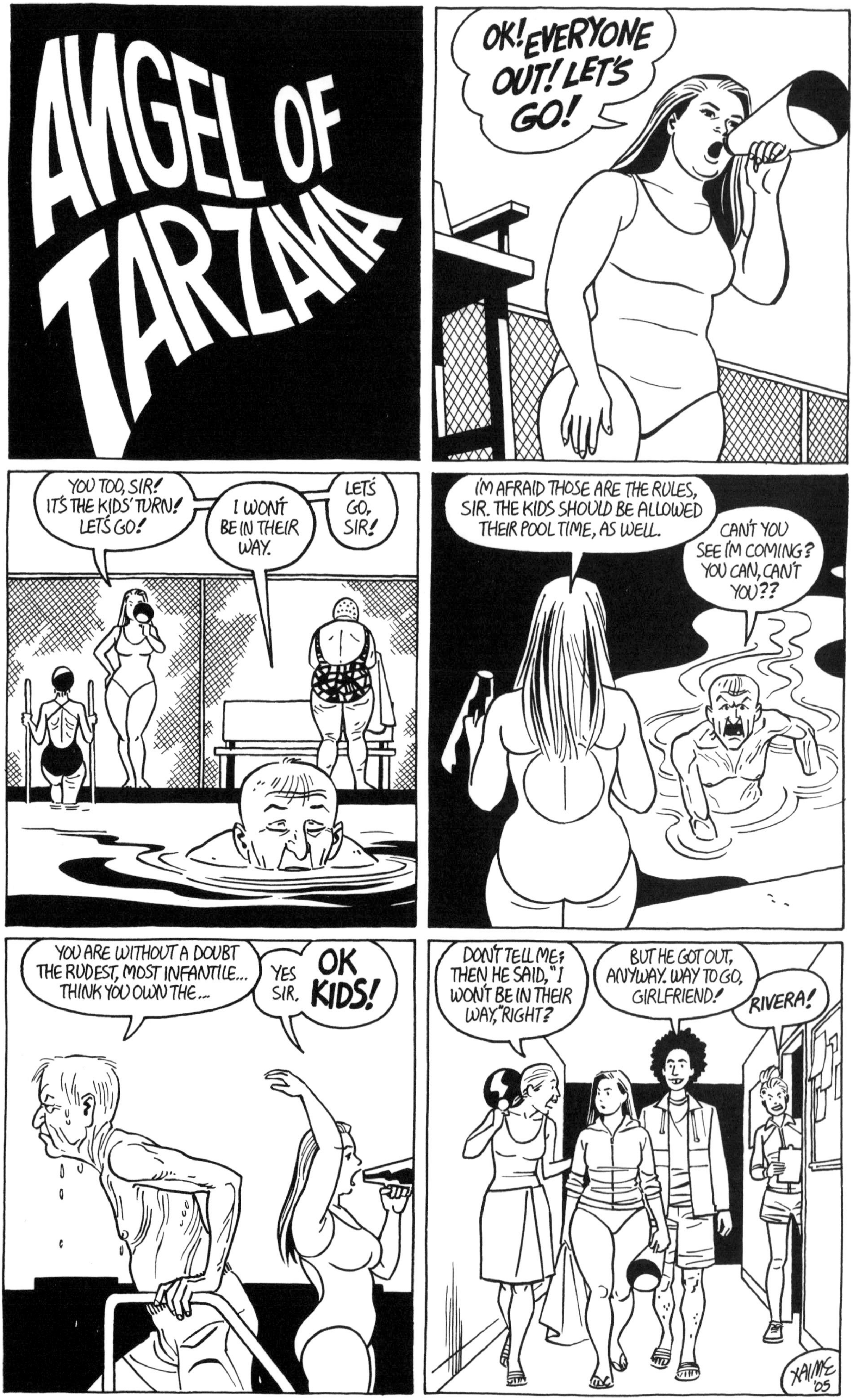
ANGEL OF TARZANA
OK! EVERYONE OUT! LET'S GO!
YOU TOO, SIR! IT'S THE KIDS' TURN! LET'S GO!
I WON'T BE IN THEIR WAY.
LET'S GO, SIR!
I'M AFRAID THOSE ARE THE RULES, SIR. THE KIDS SHOULD BE ALLOWED THEIR POOL TIME, AS WELL.
CAN'T YOU SEE I'M COMING? YOU CAN, CAN'T YOU??
YOU ARE WITHOUT A DOUBT THE RUDEST, MOST INFANTILE... THINK YOU OWN THE...
YES SIR.
OK KIDS!
DON'T TELL ME; THEN HE SAID, "I WON'T BE IN THEIR WAY," RIGHT?
BUT HE GOT OUT, ANYWAY. WAY TO GO, GIRLFRIEND!
RIVERA!
XAIME '05

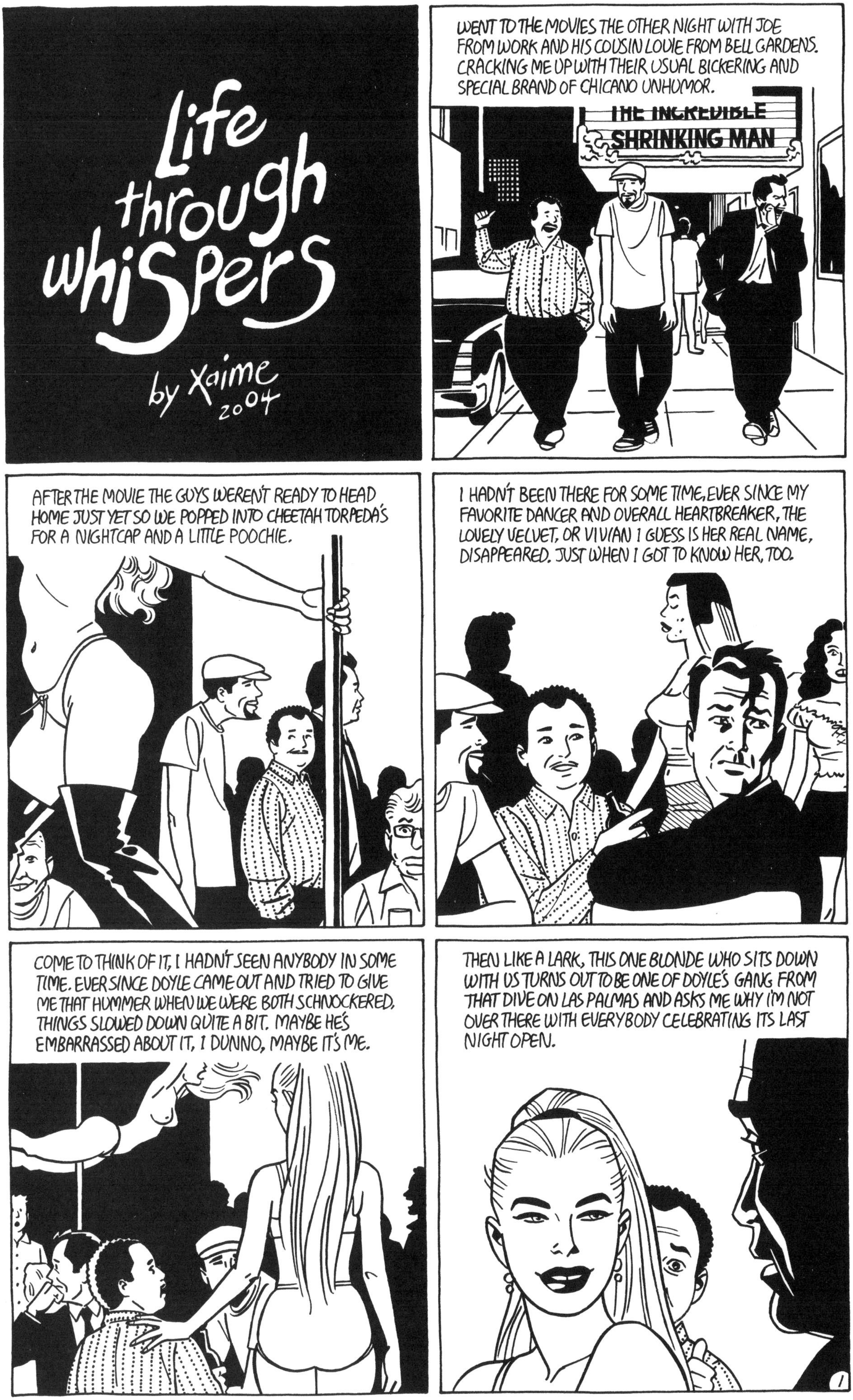
Life through whispers
by Xaime 2004
WENT TO THE MOVIES THE OTHER NIGHT WITH JOE FROM WORK AND HIS COUSIN LOUIE FROM BELL GARDENS. CRACKING ME UP WITH THEIR USUAL BICKERING AND SPECIAL BRAND OF CHICANO UNHUMOR.
THE INCREDIBLE SHRINKING MAN
AFTER THE MOVIE THE GUYS WEREN'T READY TO HEAD HOME JUST YET SO WE POPPED INTO CHEETAH TORPEDA'S FOR A NIGHTCAP AND A LITTLE POOCHIE.
I HADN'T BEEN THERE FOR SOME TIME, EVER SINCE MY FAVORITE DANCER AND OVERALL HEARTBREAKER, THE LOVELY VELVET, OR VIVIAN I GUESS IS HER REAL NAME, DISAPPEARED. JUST WHEN I GOT TO KNOW HER, TOO.
COME TO THINK OF IT, I HADN'T SEEN ANYBODY IN SOME TIME. EVER SINCE DOYLE CAME OUT AND TRIED TO GIVE ME THAT HUMMER WHEN WE WERE BOTH SCHNOCKERED, THINGS SLOWED DOWN QUITE A BIT. MAYBE HE'S EMBARRASSED ABOUT IT, I DUNNO, MAYBE IT'S ME.
THEN LIKE A LARK, THIS ONE BLONDE WHO SITS DOWN WITH US TURNS OUT TO BE ONE OF DOYLE'S GANG FROM THAT DIVE ON LAS PALMAS AND ASKS ME WHY I'M NOT OVER THERE WITH EVERYBODY CELEBRATING ITS LAST NIGHT OPEN.
1

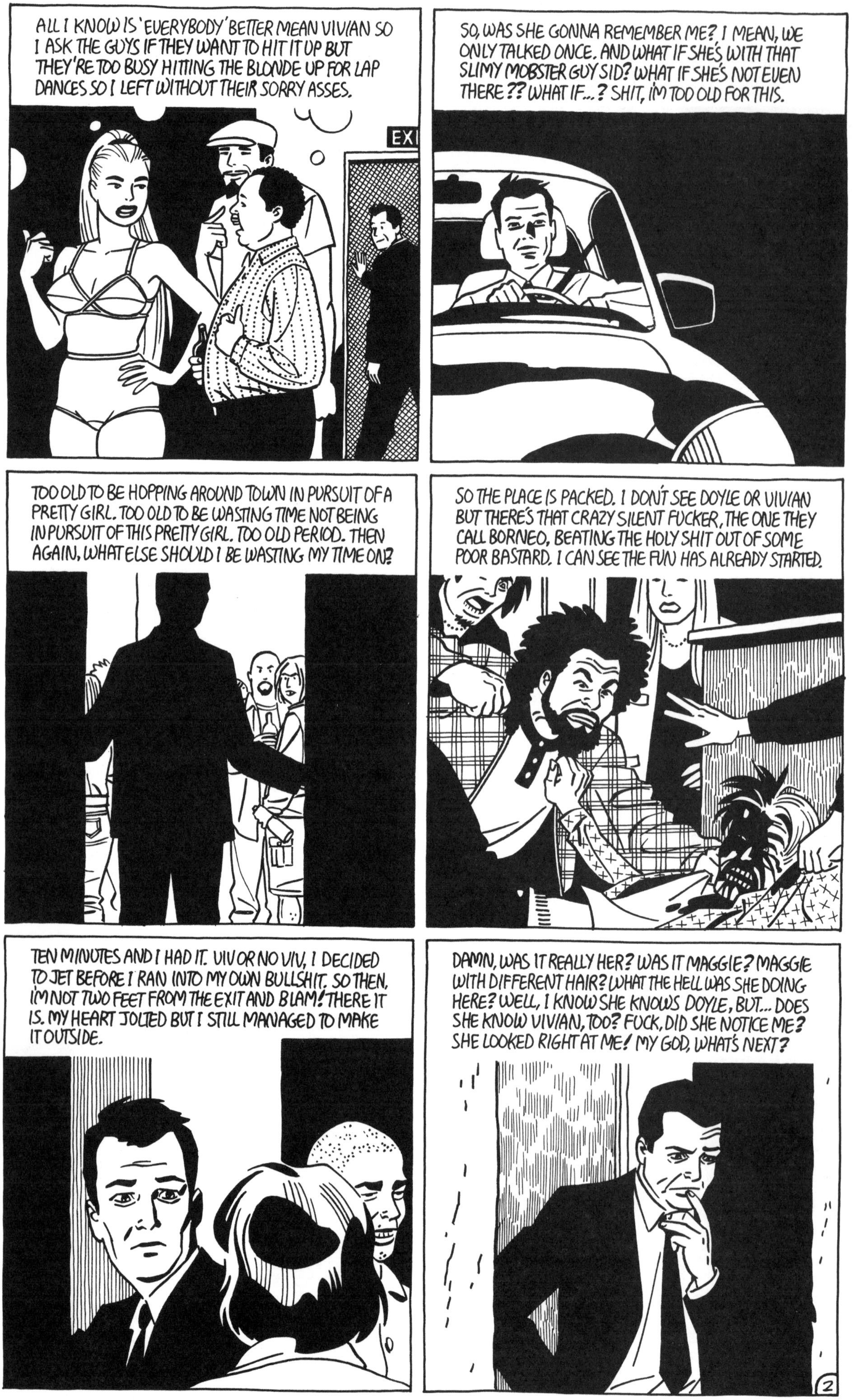
ALL I KNOW IS 'EVERYBODY' BETTER MEAN VIVIAN SO I ASK THE GUYS IF THEY WANT TO HIT IT UP BUT THEY'RE TOO BUSY HITTING THE BLONDE UP FOR LAP DANCES SO I LEFT WITHOUT THEIR SORRY ASSES.
EXI
SO, WAS SHE GONNA REMEMBER ME? I MEAN, WE ONLY TALKED ONCE. AND WHAT IF SHE'S WITH THAT SLIMY MOBSTER GUY SID? WHAT IF SHE'S NOT EVEN THERE?? WHAT IF...? SHIT, I'M TOO OLD FOR THIS.
TOO OLD TO BE HOPPING AROUND TOWN IN PURSUIT OF A PRETTY GIRL. TOO OLD TO BE WASTING TIME NOT BEING IN PURSUIT OF THIS PRETTY GIRL. TOO OLD PERIOD. THEN AGAIN, WHAT ELSE SHOULD I BE WASTING MY TIME ON?
SO THE PLACE IS PACKED. I DON'T SEE DOYLE OR VIVIAN BUT THERE'S THAT CRAZY SILENT FUCKER, THE ONE THEY CALL BORNEO, BEATING THE HOLY SHIT OUT OF SOME POOR BASTARD. I CAN SEE THE FUN HAS ALREADY STARTED.
TEN MINUTES AND I HAD IT. VIV OR NO VIV, I DECIDED TO JET BEFORE I RAN INTO MY OWN BULLSHIT. SO THEN, I'M NOT TWO FEET FROM THE EXIT AND BLAM! THERE IT IS. MY HEART JOLTED BUT I STILL MANAGED TO MAKE IT OUTSIDE.
DAMN, WAS IT REALLY HER? WAS IT MAGGIE? MAGGIE WITH DIFFERENT HAIR? WHAT THE HELL WAS SHE DOING HERE? WELL, I KNOW SHE KNOWS DOYLE, BUT... DOES SHE KNOW VIVIAN, TOO? FUCK, DID SHE NOTICE ME? SHE LOOKED RIGHT AT ME! MY GOD, WHAT'S NEXT?
2

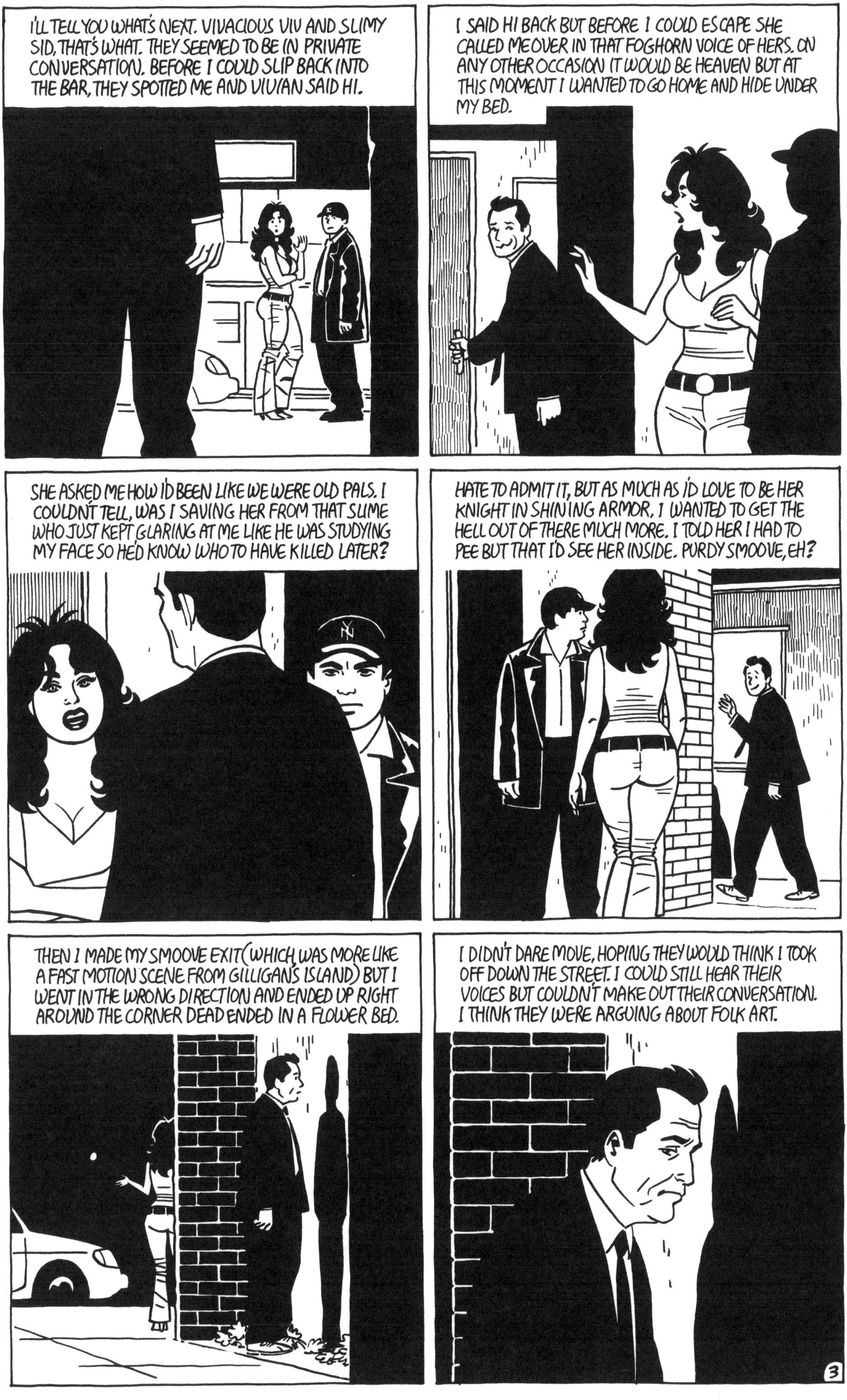
I'LL TELL YOU WHAT'S NEXT. VIVACIOUS VIV AND SLIMY SID, THAT'S WHAT. THEY SEEMED TO BE IN PRIVATE CONVERSATION. BEFORE I COULD SLIP BACK INTO THE BAR, THEY SPOTTED ME AND VIVIAN SAID HI.
I SAID HI BACK BUT BEFORE I COULD ESCAPE SHE CALLED ME OVER IN THAT FOGHORN VOICE OF HERS. ON ANY OTHER OCCASION IT WOULD BE HEAVEN BUT AT THIS MOMENT I WANTED TO GO HOME AND HIDE UNDER MY BED.
SHE ASKED ME HOW I'D BEEN LIKE WE WERE OLD PALS. I COULDN'T TELL, WAS I SAVING HER FROM THAT SLIME WHO JUST KEPT GLARING AT ME LIKE HE WAS STUDYING MY FACE SO HE'D KNOW WHO TO HAVE KILLED LATER?
NY
HATE TO ADMIT IT, BUT AS MUCH AS I'D LOVE TO BE HER KNIGHT IN SHINING ARMOR, I WANTED TO GET THE HELL OUT OF THERE MUCH MORE. I TOLD HER I HAD TO PEE BUT THAT I'D SEE HER INSIDE. PURDY SMOOVE, EH?
THEN I MADE MY SMOOVE EXIT (WHICH WAS MORE LIKE A FAST MOTION SCENE FROM GILLIGAN'S ISLAND) BUT I WENT IN THE WRONG DIRECTION AND ENDED UP RIGHT AROUND THE CORNER DEAD ENDED IN A FLOWER BED.
I DIDN'T DARE MOVE, HOPING THEY WOULD THINK I TOOK OFF DOWN THE STREET. I COULD STILL HEAR THEIR VOICES BUT COULDN'T MAKE OUT THEIR CONVERSATION. I THINK THEY WERE ARGUING ABOUT FOLK ART.
3

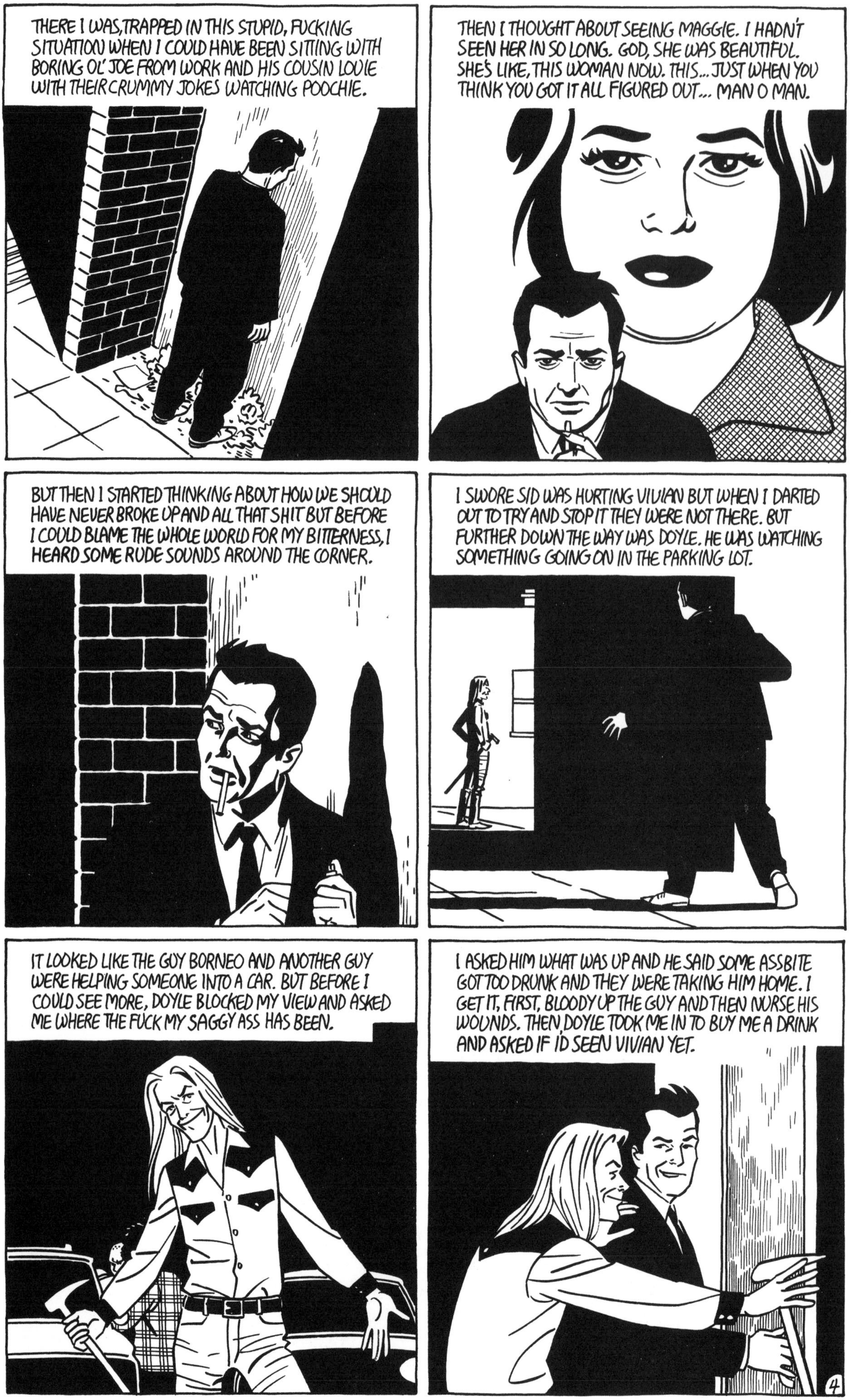
THERE I WAS, TRAPPED IN THIS STUPID, FUCKING SITUATION WHEN I COULD HAVE BEEN SITTING WITH BORING OL' JOE FROM WORK AND HIS COUSIN LOUIE WITH THEIR CRUMMY JOKES WATCHING POOCHIE.
THEN I THOUGHT ABOUT SEEING MAGGIE. I HADN'T SEEN HER IN SO LONG. GOD, SHE WAS BEAUTIFUL. SHE'S LIKE, THIS WOMAN NOW. THIS... JUST WHEN YOU THINK YOU GOT IT ALL FIGURED OUT... MAN O MAN.
BUT THEN I STARTED THINKING ABOUT HOW WE SHOULD HAVE NEVER BROKE UP AND ALL THAT SHIT BUT BEFORE I COULD BLAME THE WHOLE WORLD FOR MY BITTERNESS, I HEARD SOME RUDE SOUNDS AROUND THE CORNER.
I SWORE SID WAS HURTING VIVIAN BUT WHEN I DARTED OUT TO TRY AND STOP IT THEY WERE NOT THERE. BUT FURTHER DOWN THE WAY WAS DOYLE. HE WAS WATCHING SOMETHING GOING ON IN THE PARKING LOT.
IT LOOKED LIKE THE GUY BORNEO AND ANOTHER GUY WERE HELPING SOMEONE INTO A CAR. BUT BEFORE I COULD SEE MORE, DOYLE BLOCKED MY VIEW AND ASKED ME WHERE THE FUCK MY SAGGY ASS HAS BEEN.
I ASKED HIM WHAT WAS UP AND HE SAID SOME ASSBITE GOT TOO DRUNK AND THEY WERE TAKING HIM HOME. I GET IT, FIRST, BLOODY UP THE GUY AND THEN NURSE HIS WOUNDS. THEN, DOYLE TOOK ME IN TO BUY ME A DRINK AND ASKED IF I'D SEEN VIVIAN YET.
4

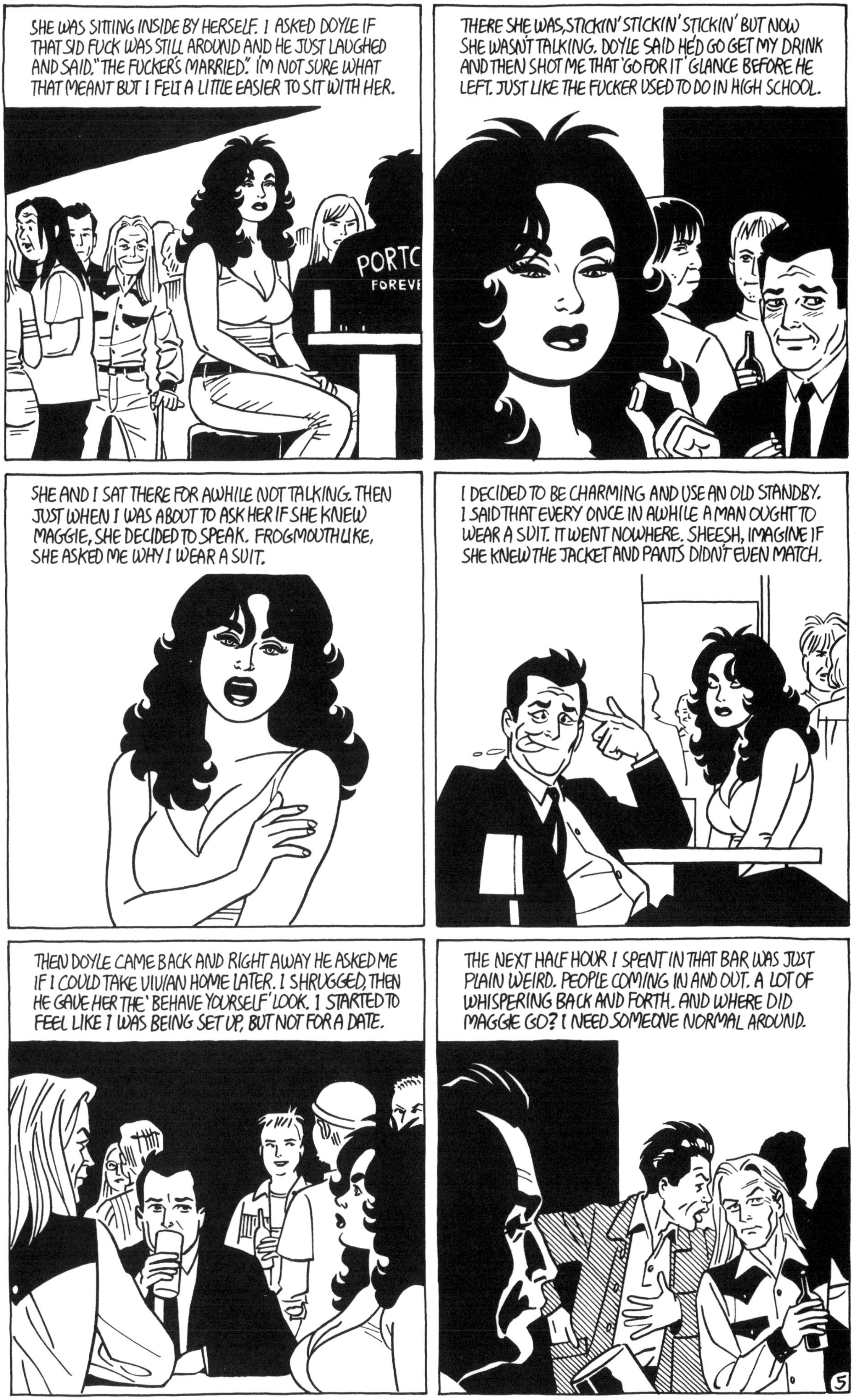
SHE WAS SITTING INSIDE BY HERSELF. I ASKED DOYLE IF THAT SID FUCK WAS STILL AROUND AND HE JUST LAUGHED AND SAID, "THE FUCKER'S MARRIED". I'M NOT SURE WHAT THAT MEANT BUT I FELT A LITTLE EASIER TO SIT WITH HER.
THERE SHE WAS, STICKIN' STICKIN' STICKIN' BUT NOW SHE WASN'T TALKING. DOYLE SAID HE'D GO GET MY DRINK AND THEN SHOT ME THAT 'GO FOR IT' GLANCE BEFORE HE LEFT. JUST LIKE THE FUCKER USED TO DO IN HIGH SCHOOL.
SHE AND I SAT THERE FOR AWHILE NOT TALKING. THEN JUST WHEN I WAS ABOUT TO ASK HER IF SHE KNEW MAGGIE, SHE DECIDED TO SPEAK. FROGMOUTHLIKE, SHE ASKED ME WHY I WEAR A SUIT.
I DECIDED TO BE CHARMING AND USE AN OLD STANDBY. I SAID THAT EVERY ONCE IN AWHILE A MAN OUGHT TO WEAR A SUIT. IT WENT NOWHERE. SHEESH, IMAGINE IF SHE KNEW THE JACKET AND PANTS DIDN'T EVEN MATCH.
THEN DOYLE CAME BACK AND RIGHT AWAY HE ASKED ME IF I COULD TAKE VIVIAN HOME LATER. I SHRUGGED, THEN HE GAVE HER THE 'BEHAVE YOURSELF' LOOK. I STARTED TO FEEL LIKE I WAS BEING SET UP, BUT NOT FOR A DATE.
THE NEXT HALF HOUR I SPENT IN THAT BAR WAS JUST PLAIN WEIRD. PEOPLE COMING IN AND OUT. A LOT OF WHISPERING BACK AND FORTH. AND WHERE DID MAGGIE GO? I NEED SOMEONE NORMAL AROUND.
5

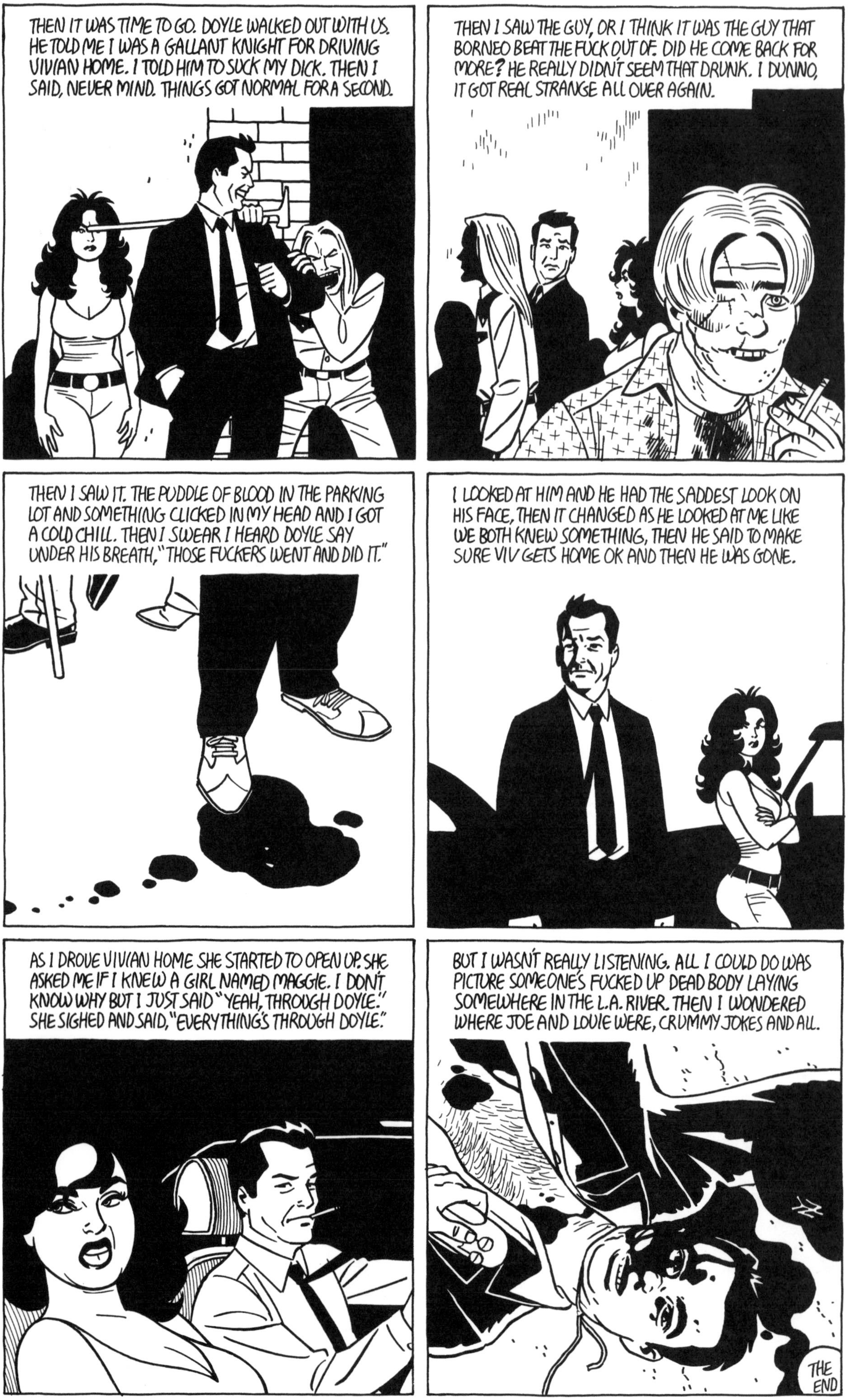
THEN IT WAS TIME TO GO. DOYLE WALKED OUT WITH US. HE TOLD ME I WAS A GALLANT KNIGHT FOR DRIVING VIVIAN HOME. I TOLD HIM TO SUCK MY DICK. THEN I SAID, NEVER MIND. THINGS GOT NORMAL FOR A SECOND.
THEN I SAW THE GUY, OR I THINK IT WAS THE GUY THAT BORNEO BEAT THE FUCK OUT OF. DID HE COME BACK FOR MORE? HE REALLY DIDN'T SEEM THAT DRUNK. I DUNNO, IT GOT REAL STRANGE ALL OVER AGAIN.
THEN I SAW IT. THE PUDDLE OF BLOOD IN THE PARKING LOT AND SOMETHING CLICKED IN MY HEAD AND I GOT A COLD CHILL. THEN I SWEAR I HEARD DOYLE SAY UNDER HIS BREATH, "THOSE FUCKERS WENT AND DID IT."
I LOOKED AT HIM AND HE HAD THE SADDEST LOOK ON HIS FACE, THEN IT CHANGED AS HE LOOKED AT ME LIKE WE BOTH KNEW SOMETHING, THEN HE SAID TO MAKE SURE VIV GETS HOME OK AND THEN HE WAS GONE.
AS I DROVE VIVIAN HOME SHE STARTED TO OPEN UP. SHE ASKED ME IF I KNEW A GIRL NAMED MAGGIE. I DON'T KNOW WHY BUT I JUST SAID "YEAH, THROUGH DOYLE." SHE SIGHED AND SAID, "EVERYTHING'S THROUGH DOYLE."
BUT I WASN'T REALLY LISTENING. ALL I COULD DO WAS PICTURE SOMEONE'S FUCKED UP DEAD BODY LAYING SOMEWHERE IN THE L.A. RIVER. THEN I WONDERED WHERE JOE AND LOUIE WERE, CRUMMY JOKES AND ALL.
THE END

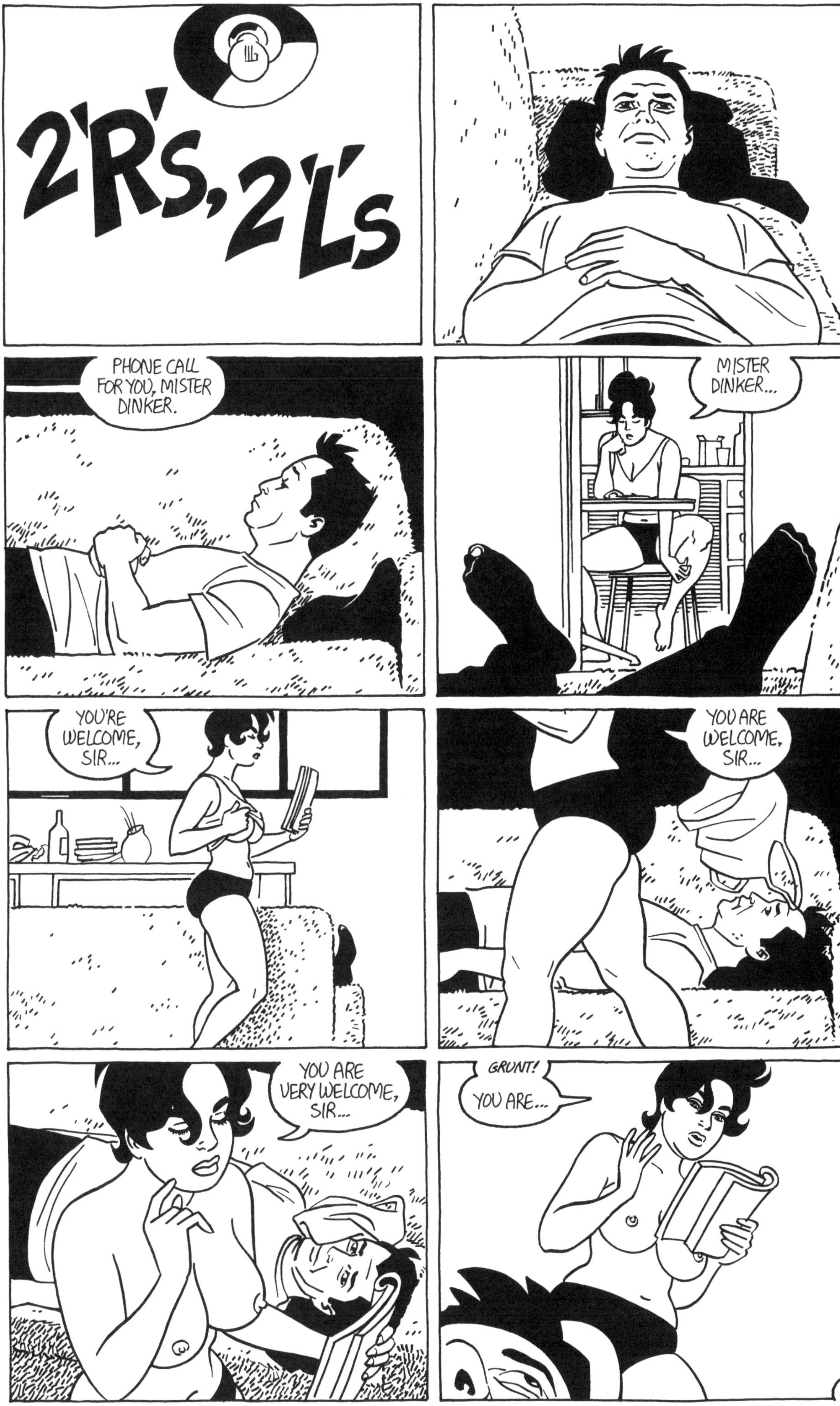
2 'R'S, 2 'L'S
PHONE CALL FOR YOU, MISTER DINKER.
MISTER DINKER...
YOU'RE WELCOME, SIR...
YOU ARE WELCOME, SIR...
YOU ARE VERY WELCOME, SIR...
GRUNT!
YOU ARE...

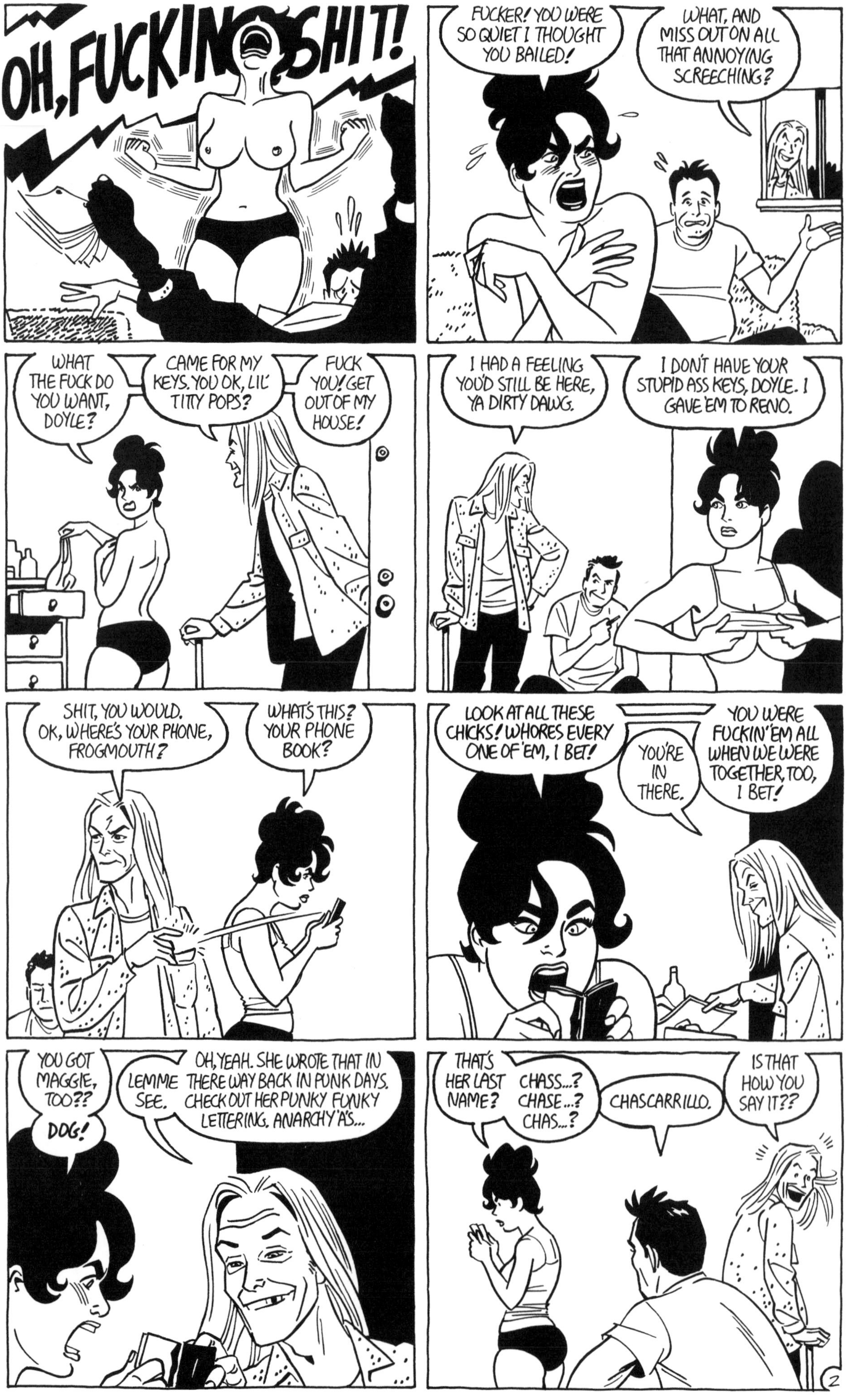
OH, FUCKING SHIT!
FUCKER! YOU WERE SO QUIET I THOUGHT YOU BAILED!
WHAT, AND MISS OUT ON ALL THAT ANNOYING SCREECHING?
WHAT THE FUCK DO YOU WANT, DOYLE?
CAME FOR MY KEYS. YOU OK, LIL' TITTY POPS?
FUCK YOU! GET OUT OF MY HOUSE!
I HAD A FEELING YOU'D STILL BE HERE, YA DIRTY DAWG.
I DON'T HAVE YOUR STUPID ASS KEYS, DOYLE. I GAVE 'EM TO RENO.
SHIT, YOU WOULD. OK, WHERE'S YOUR PHONE, FROGMOUTH?
WHAT'S THIS? YOUR PHONE BOOK?
LOOK AT ALL THESE CHICKS! WHORES EVERY ONE OF 'EM, I BET!
YOU'RE IN THERE.
YOU WERE FUCKIN' 'EM ALL WHEN WE WERE TOGETHER, TOO, I BET!
YOU GOT MAGGIE, TOO??
DOG!
LEMME SEE.
OH, YEAH. SHE WROTE THAT IN THERE WAY BACK IN PUNK DAYS. CHECK OUT HER PUNKY FUNKY LETTERING. ANARCHY 'A'S...
THAT'S HER LAST NAME?
CHASS...? CHASE...? CHAS...?
CHASCARRILLO.
IS THAT HOW YOU SAY IT??
2

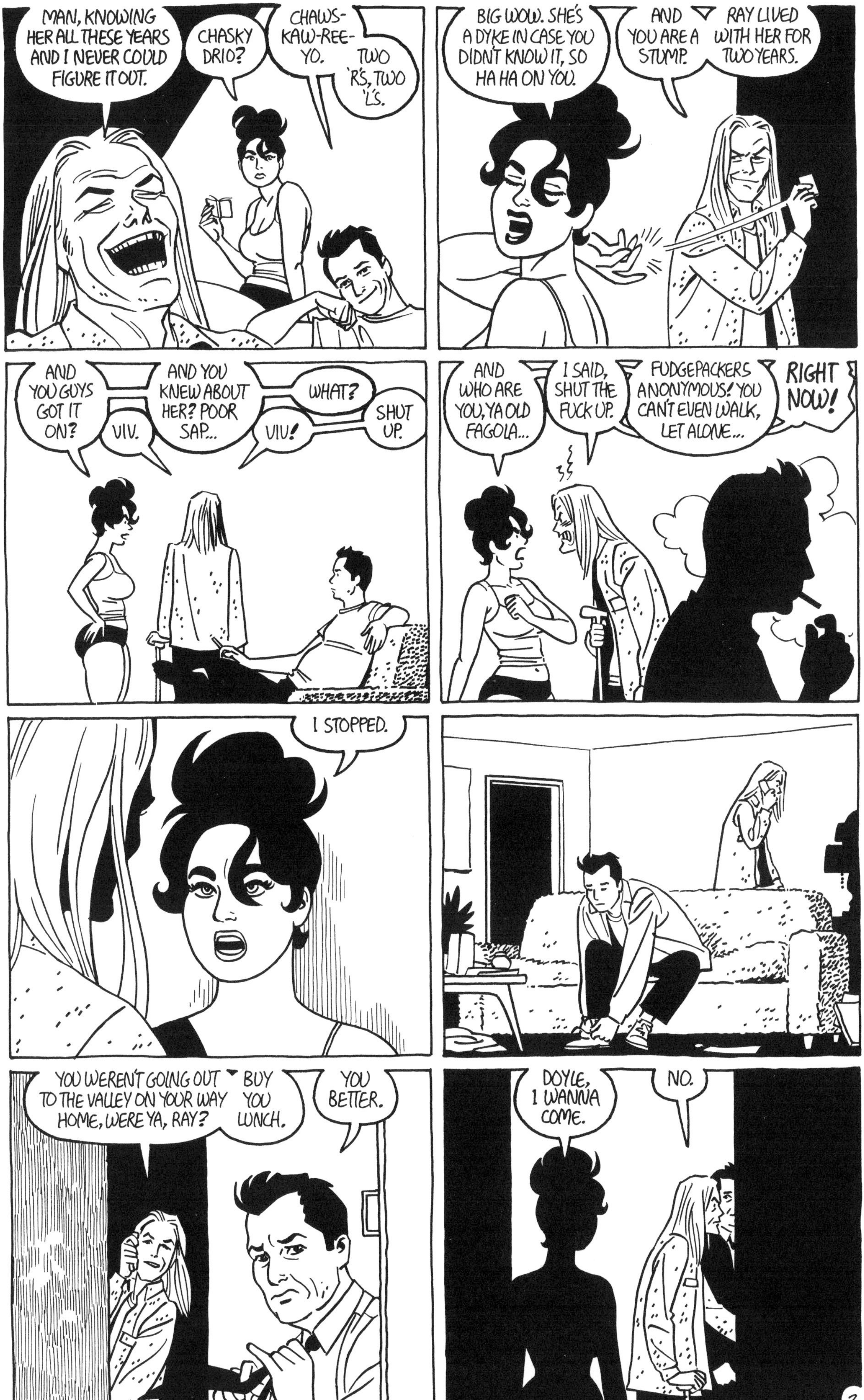
MAN, KNOWING HER ALL THESE YEARS AND I NEVER COULD FIGURE IT OUT.
CHASKY DRIO?
CHAWS-KAW-REE-YO.
TWO 'R'S, TWO 'L'S.
BIG WOW. SHE'S A DYKE IN CASE YOU DIDN'T KNOW IT, SO HA HA ON YOU.
AND YOU ARE A STUMP.
RAY LIVED WITH HER FOR TWO YEARS.
AND YOU GUYS GOT IT ON?
VIV.
AND YOU KNEW ABOUT HER? POOR SAP...
WHAT?
VIV!
SHUT UP.
AND WHO ARE YOU, YA OLD FAGOLA...
I SAID, SHUT THE FUCK UP.
FUDGEPACKERS ANONYMOUS! YOU CAN'T EVEN WALK, LET ALONE...
RIGHT NOW!
I STOPPED.
YOU WEREN'T GOING OUT TO THE VALLEY ON YOUR WAY HOME, WERE YA, RAY?
BUY YOU LUNCH.
YOU BETTER.
DOYLE, I WANNA COME.
NO.
3

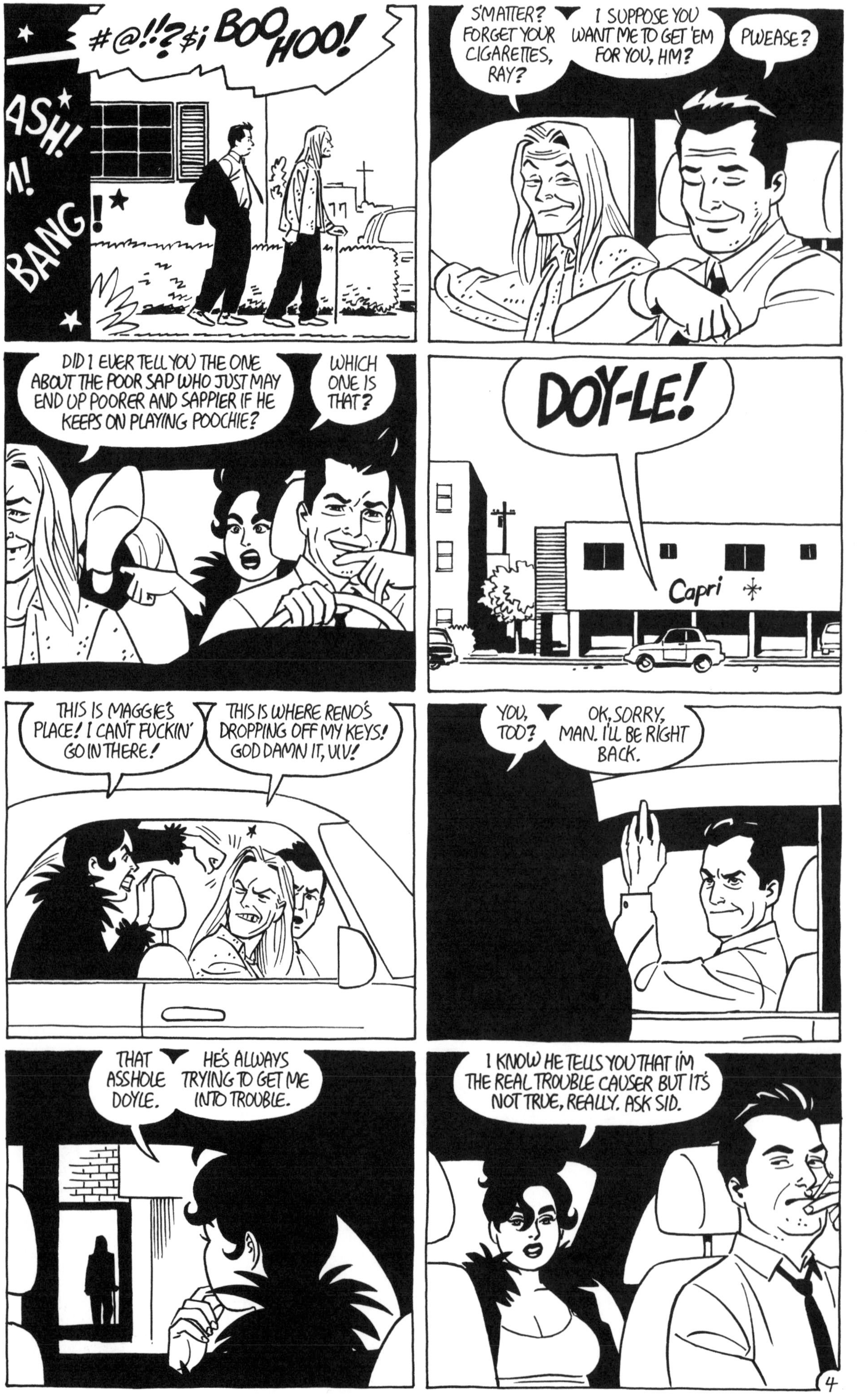
#@!!?$¡ BOO HOO!
ASH!
N!
BANG!
S'MATTER? FORGET YOUR CIGARETTES, RAY?
I SUPPOSE YOU WANT ME TO GET 'EM FOR YOU, HM?
PWEASE?
DID I EVER TELL YOU THE ONE ABOUT THE POOR SAP WHO JUST MAY END UP POORER AND SAPPIER IF HE KEEPS ON PLAYING POOCHIE?
WHICH ONE IS THAT?
DOY-LE!
Capri
THIS IS MAGGIE'S PLACE! I CAN'T FUCKIN' GO IN THERE!
THIS IS WHERE RENO'S DROPPING OFF MY KEYS! GOD DAMN IT, VIV!
YOU, TOO?
OK, SORRY, MAN. I'LL BE RIGHT BACK.
THAT ASSHOLE DOYLE.
HE'S ALWAYS TRYING TO GET ME INTO TROUBLE.
I KNOW HE TELLS YOU THAT I'M THE REAL TROUBLE CAUSER BUT IT'S NOT TRUE, REALLY. ASK SID.
4

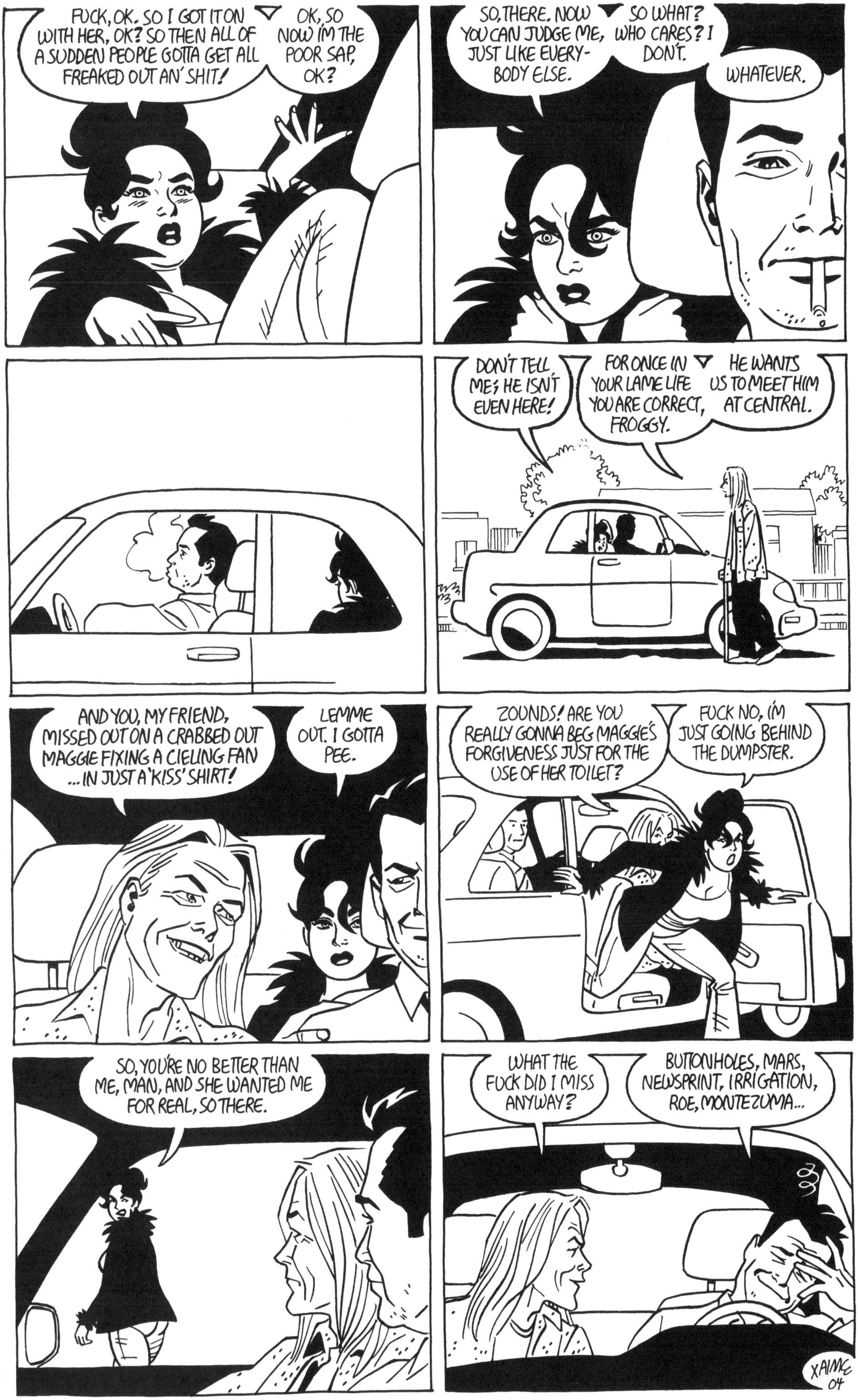
FUCK, OK. SO I GOT IT ON WITH HER, OK? SO THEN ALL OF A SUDDEN PEOPLE GOTTA GET ALL FREAKED OUT AN' SHIT!
OK, SO NOW I'M THE POOR SAP, OK?
SO, THERE. NOW YOU CAN JUDGE ME, JUST LIKE EVERY-BODY ELSE.
SO WHAT? WHO CARES? I DON'T.
WHATEVER.
DON'T TELL ME; HE ISN'T EVEN HERE!
FOR ONCE IN YOUR LAME LIFE YOU ARE CORRECT, FROGGY.
HE WANTS US TO MEET HIM AT CENTRAL.
AND YOU, MY FRIEND, MISSED OUT ON A CRABBED OUT MAGGIE FIXING A CIELING FAN ...IN JUST A 'KISS' SHIRT!
LEMME OUT. I GOTTA PEE.
ZOUNDS! ARE YOU REALLY GONNA BEG MAGGIE'S FORGIVENESS JUST FOR THE USE OF HER TOILET?
FUCK NO, I'M JUST GOING BEHIND THE DUMPSTER.
SO, YOU'RE NO BETTER THAN ME, MAN, AND SHE WANTED ME FOR REAL, SO THERE.
WHAT THE FUCK DID I MISS ANYWAY?
BUTTONHOLES, MARS, NEWSPRINT, IRRIGATION, ROE, MONTEZUMA...
XAIME 04

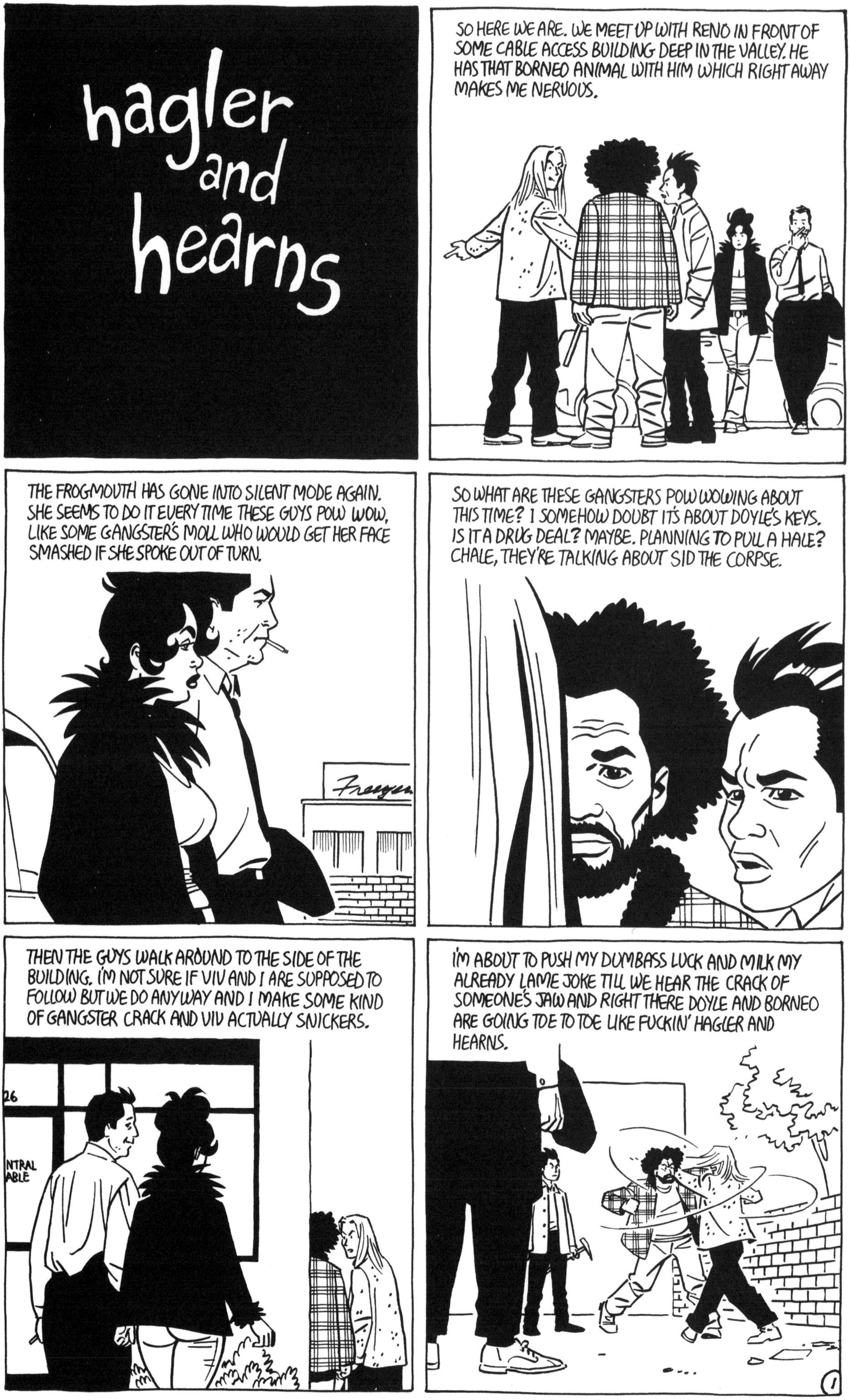
hagler and hearns
SO HERE WE ARE. WE MEET UP WITH RENO IN FRONT OF SOME CABLE ACCESS BUILDING DEEP IN THE VALLEY. HE HAS THAT BORNEO ANIMAL WITH HIM WHICH RIGHT AWAY MAKES ME NERVOUS.
THE FROGMOUTH HAS GONE INTO SILENT MODE AGAIN. SHE SEEMS TO DO IT EVERY TIME THESE GUYS POW WOW, LIKE SOME GANGSTER'S MOLL WHO WOULD GET HER FACE SMASHED IF SHE SPOKE OUT OF TURN.
SO WHAT ARE THESE GANGSTERS POW WOWING ABOUT THIS TIME? I SOMEHOW DOUBT IT'S ABOUT DOYLE'S KEYS. IS IT A DRUG DEAL? MAYBE. PLANNING TO PULL A HALE? CHALE, THEY'RE TALKING ABOUT SID THE CORPSE.
THEN THE GUYS WALK AROUND TO THE SIDE OF THE BUILDING. I'M NOT SURE IF VIV AND I ARE SUPPOSED TO FOLLOW BUT WE DO ANYWAY AND I MAKE SOME KIND OF GANGSTER CRACK AND VIV ACTUALLY SNICKERS.
I'M ABOUT TO PUSH MY DUMBASS LUCK AND MILK MY ALREADY LAME JOKE TILL WE HEAR THE CRACK OF SOMEONE'S JAW AND RIGHT THERE DOYLE AND BORNEO ARE GOING TOE TO TOE LIKE FUCKIN' HAGLER AND HEARNS.

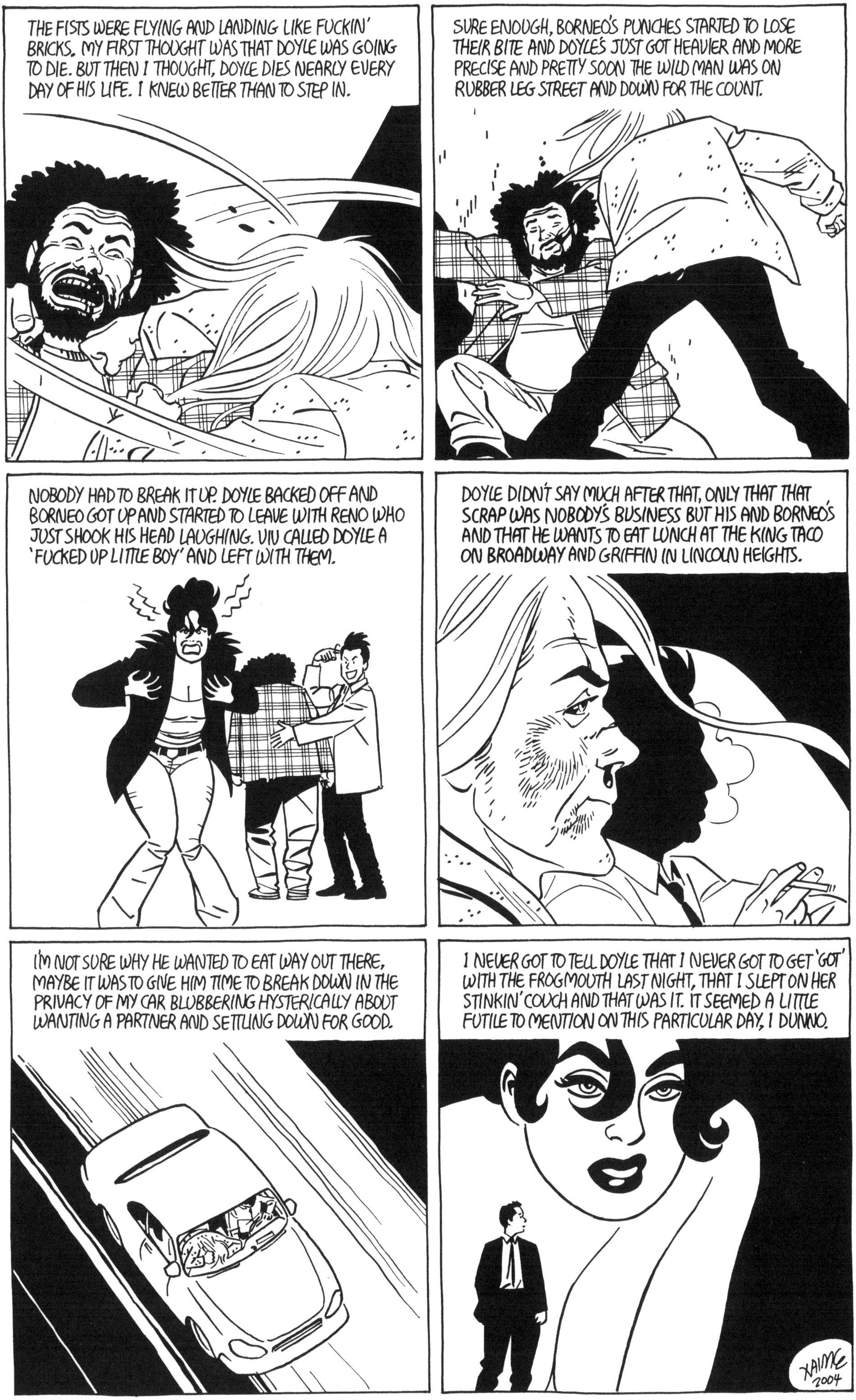
THE FISTS WERE FLYING AND LANDING LIKE FUCKIN' BRICKS. MY FIRST THOUGHT WAS THAT DOYLE WAS GOING TO DIE. BUT THEN I THOUGHT, DOYLE DIES NEARLY EVERY DAY OF HIS LIFE. I KNEW BETTER THAN TO STEP IN.
SURE ENOUGH, BORNEO'S PUNCHES STARTED TO LOSE THEIR BITE AND DOYLE'S JUST GOT HEAVIER AND MORE PRECISE AND PRETTY SOON THE WILD MAN WAS ON RUBBER LEG STREET AND DOWN FOR THE COUNT.
NOBODY HAD TO BREAK IT UP. DOYLE BACKED OFF AND BORNEO GOT UP AND STARTED TO LEAVE WITH RENO WHO JUST SHOOK HIS HEAD LAUGHING. VIV CALLED DOYLE A 'FUCKED UP LITTLE BOY' AND LEFT WITH THEM.
DOYLE DIDN'T SAY MUCH AFTER THAT, ONLY THAT THAT SCRAP WAS NOBODY'S BUSINESS BUT HIS AND BORNEO'S AND THAT HE WANTS TO EAT LUNCH AT THE KING TACO ON BROADWAY AND GRIFFIN IN LINCOLN HEIGHTS.
I'M NOT SURE WHY HE WANTED TO EAT WAY OUT THERE, MAYBE IT WAS TO GIVE HIM TIME TO BREAK DOWN IN THE PRIVACY OF MY CAR BLUBBERING HYSTERICALLY ABOUT WANTING A PARTNER AND SETTLING DOWN FOR GOOD.
I NEVER GOT TO TELL DOYLE THAT I NEVER GOT TO GET 'GOT' WITH THE FROGMOUTH LAST NIGHT, THAT I SLEPT ON HER STINKIN' COUCH AND THAT WAS IT. IT SEEMED A LITTLE FUTILE TO MENTION ON THIS PARTICULAR DAY, I DUNNO.
XAIME 2004

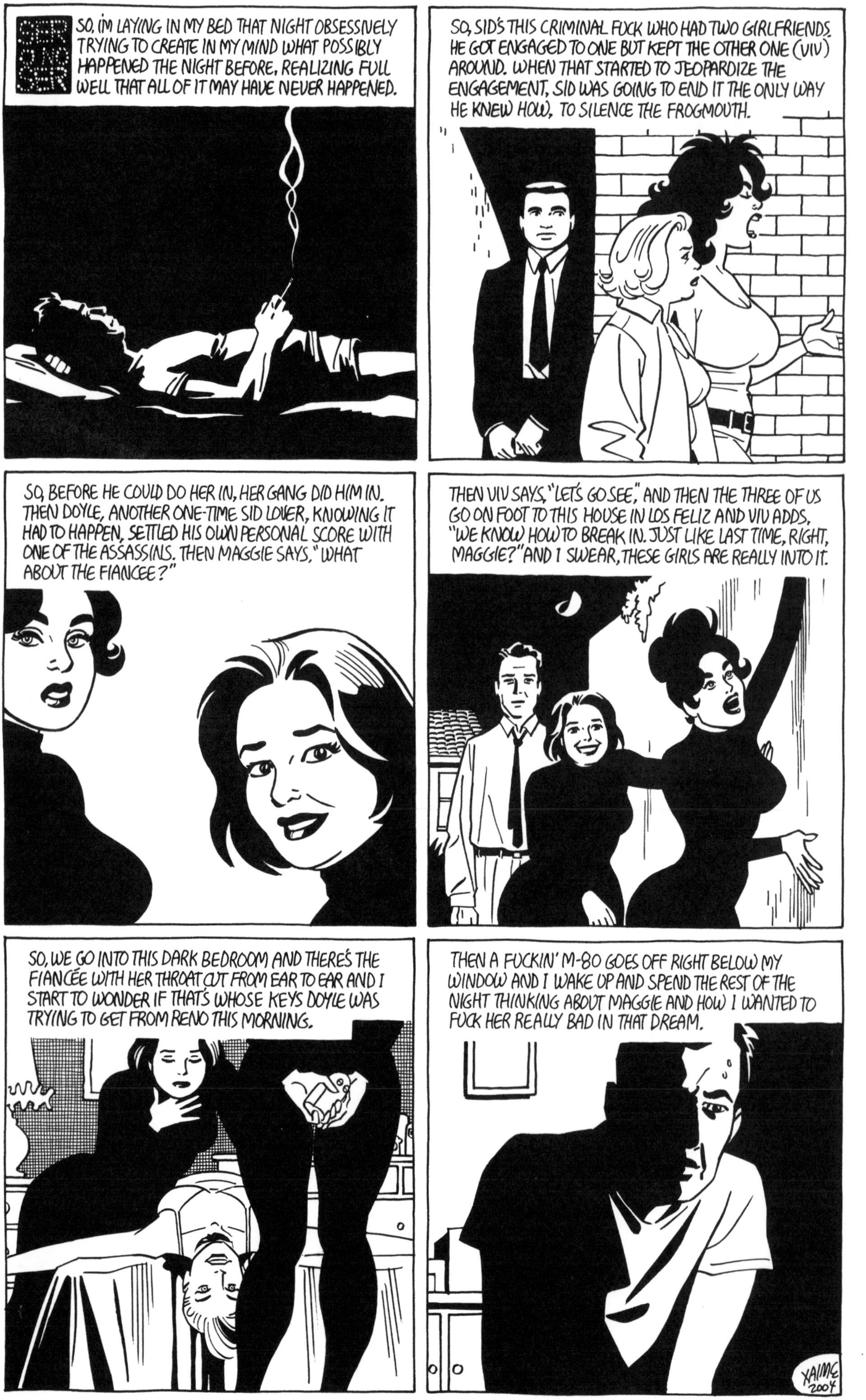
SO, I'M LAYING IN MY BED THAT NIGHT OBSESSIVELY TRYING TO CREATE IN MY MIND WHAT POSSIBLY HAPPENED THE NIGHT BEFORE, REALIZING FULL WELL THAT ALL OF IT MAY HAVE NEVER HAPPENED.
SO, SID'S THIS CRIMINAL FUCK WHO HAD TWO GIRLFRIENDS. HE GOT ENGAGED TO ONE BUT KEPT THE OTHER ONE (VIV) AROUND. WHEN THAT STARTED TO JEOPARDIZE THE ENGAGEMENT, SID WAS GOING TO END IT THE ONLY WAY HE KNEW HOW, TO SILENCE THE FROGMOUTH.
SO, BEFORE HE COULD DO HER IN, HER GANG DID HIM IN. THEN DOYLE, ANOTHER ONE-TIME SID LOVER, KNOWING IT HAD TO HAPPEN, SETTLED HIS OWN PERSONAL SCORE WITH ONE OF THE ASSASSINS. THEN MAGGIE SAYS, "WHAT ABOUT THE FIANCEE?"
THEN VIV SAYS, "LET'S GO SEE," AND THEN THE THREE OF US GO ON FOOT TO THIS HOUSE IN LOS FELIZ AND VIV ADDS, "WE KNOW HOW TO BREAK IN. JUST LIKE LAST TIME, RIGHT, MAGGIE?" AND I SWEAR, THESE GIRLS ARE REALLY INTO IT.
SO, WE GO INTO THIS DARK BEDROOM AND THERE'S THE FIANCÉE WITH HER THROAT CUT FROM EAR TO EAR AND I START TO WONDER IF THAT'S WHOSE KEYS DOYLE WAS TRYING TO GET FROM RENO THIS MORNING.
THEN A FUCKIN' M-80 GOES OFF RIGHT BELOW MY WINDOW AND I WAKE UP AND SPEND THE REST OF THE NIGHT THINKING ABOUT MAGGIE AND HOW I WANTED TO FUCK HER REALLY BAD IN THAT DREAM.
XAIME 2004

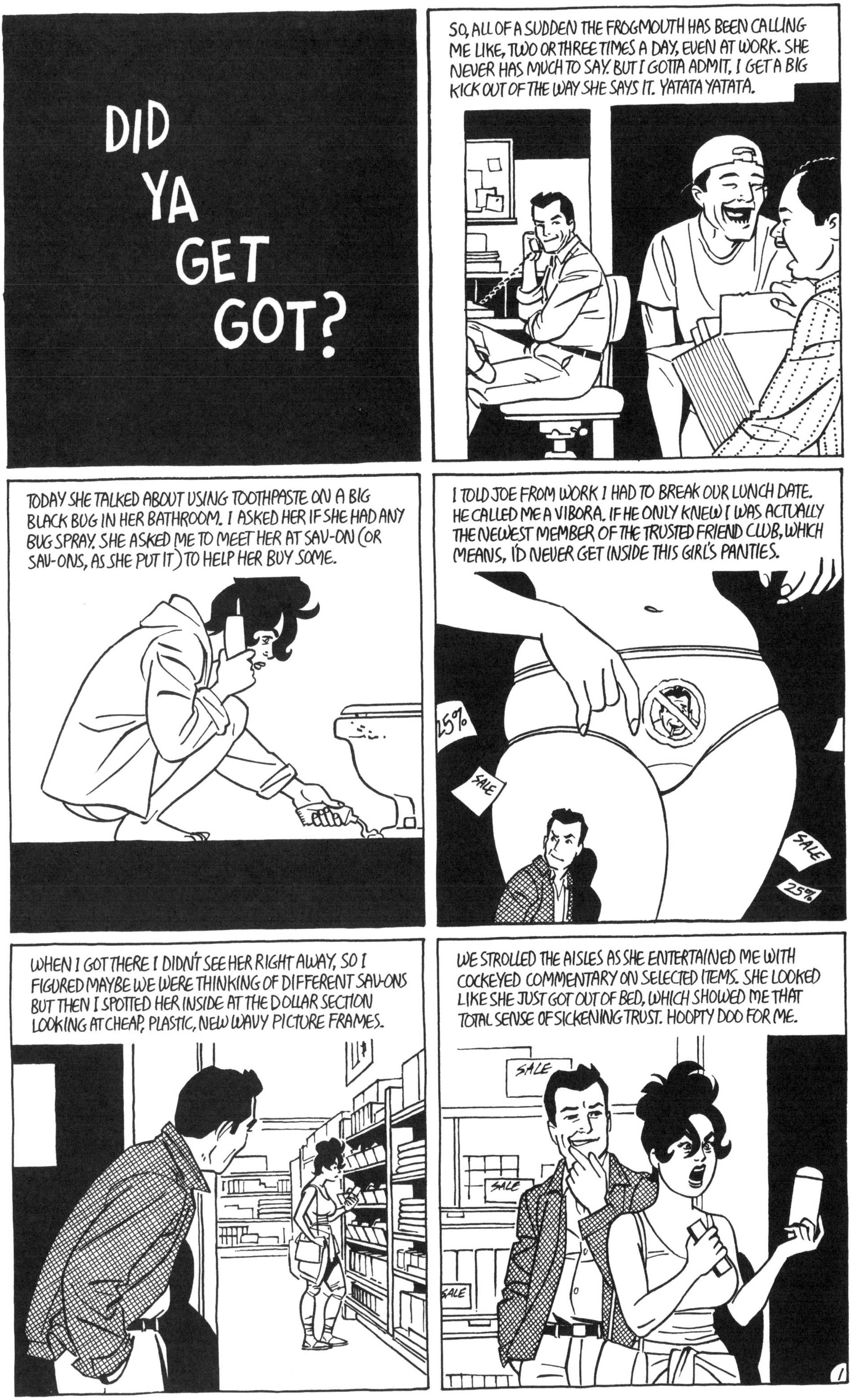
DID YA GET GOT?
SO, ALL OF A SUDDEN THE FROGMOUTH HAS BEEN CALLING ME LIKE, TWO OR THREE TIMES A DAY, EVEN AT WORK. SHE NEVER HAS MUCH TO SAY. BUT I GOTTA ADMIT, I GET A BIG KICK OUT OF THE WAY SHE SAYS IT. YATATA YATATA.
TODAY SHE TALKED ABOUT USING TOOTHPASTE ON A BIG BLACK BUG IN HER BATHROOM. I ASKED HER IF SHE HAD ANY BUG SPRAY. SHE ASKED ME TO MEET HER AT SAV-ON (OR SAV-ONS, AS SHE PUT IT) TO HELP HER BUY SOME.
I TOLD JOE FROM WORK I HAD TO BREAK OUR LUNCH DATE. HE CALLED ME A VIBORA. IF HE ONLY KNEW I WAS ACTUALLY THE NEWEST MEMBER OF THE TRUSTED FRIEND CLUB, WHICH MEANS, I'D NEVER GET INSIDE THIS GIRL'S PANTIES.
25%
SALE
SALE
25%
WHEN I GOT THERE I DIDN'T SEE HER RIGHT AWAY, SO I FIGURED MAYBE WE WERE THINKING OF DIFFERENT SAV-ONS BUT THEN I SPOTTED HER INSIDE AT THE DOLLAR SECTION LOOKING AT CHEAP, PLASTIC, NEW WAVY PICTURE FRAMES.
WE STROLLED THE AISLES AS SHE ENTERTAINED ME WITH COCKEYED COMMENTARY ON SELECTED ITEMS. SHE LOOKED LIKE SHE JUST GOT OUT OF BED, WHICH SHOWED ME THAT TOTAL SENSE OF SICKENING TRUST. HOOPTY DOO FOR ME.
SALE
SALE
SALE
1

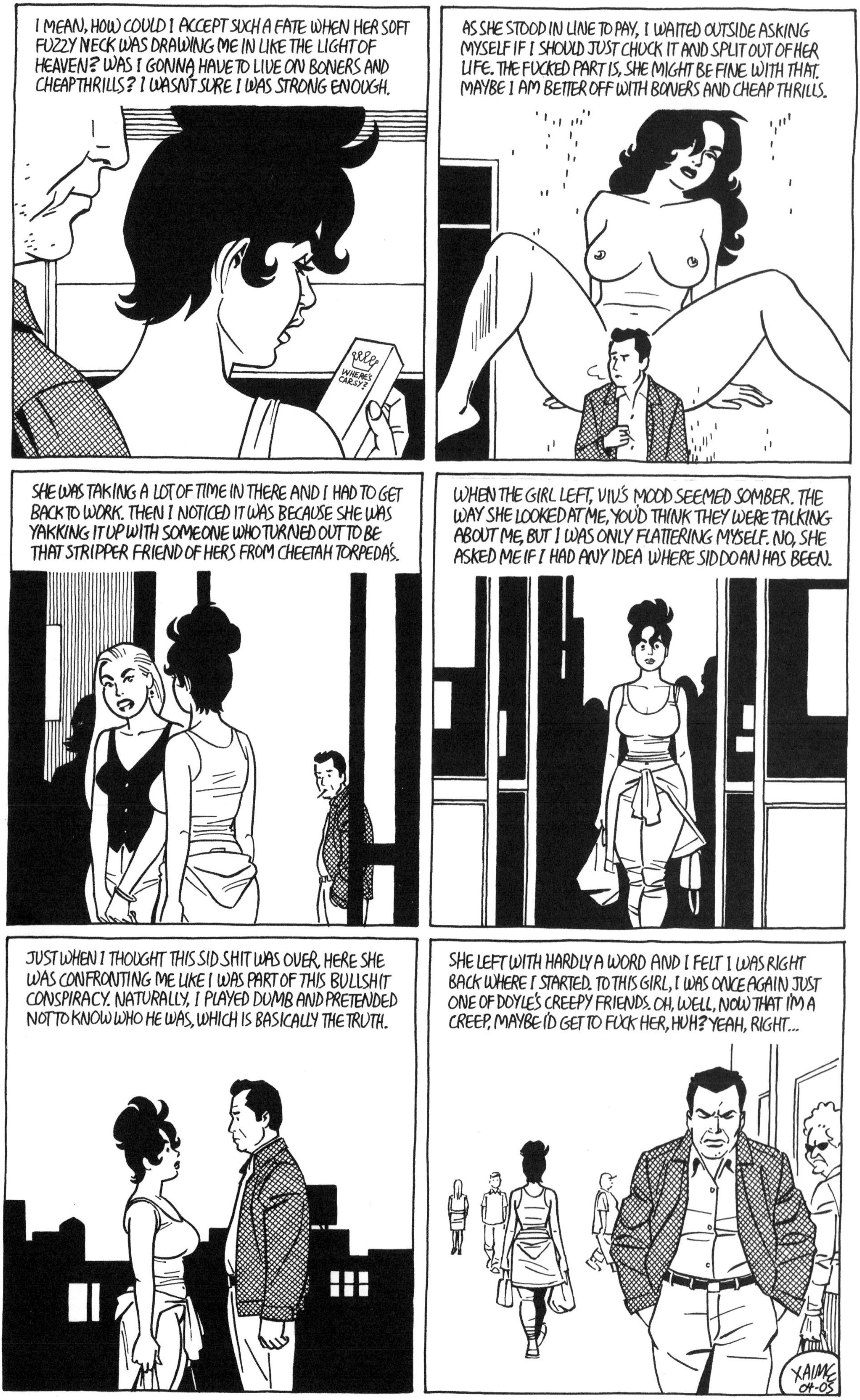
I MEAN, HOW COULD I ACCEPT SUCH A FATE WHEN HER SOFT FUZZY NECK WAS DRAWING ME IN LIKE THE LIGHT OF HEAVEN? WAS I GONNA HAVE TO LIVE ON BONERS AND CHEAP THRILLS? I WASN'T SURE I WAS STRONG ENOUGH.
WHERE'S CARSY?
AS SHE STOOD IN LINE TO PAY, I WAITED OUTSIDE ASKING MYSELF IF I SHOULD JUST CHUCK IT AND SPLIT OUT OF HER LIFE. THE FUCKED PART IS, SHE MIGHT BE FINE WITH THAT. MAYBE I AM BETTER OFF WITH BONERS AND CHEAP THRILLS.
SHE WAS TAKING A LOT OF TIME IN THERE AND I HAD TO GET BACK TO WORK. THEN I NOTICED IT WAS BECAUSE SHE WAS YAKKING IT UP WITH SOMEONE WHO TURNED OUT TO BE THAT STRIPPER FRIEND OF HERS FROM CHEETAH TORPEDA'S.
WHEN THE GIRL LEFT, VIV'S MOOD SEEMED SOMBER. THE WAY SHE LOOKED AT ME, YOU'D THINK THEY WERE TALKING ABOUT ME, BUT I WAS ONLY FLATTERING MYSELF. NO, SHE ASKED ME IF I HAD ANY IDEA WHERE SID DOAN HAS BEEN.
JUST WHEN I THOUGHT THIS SID SHIT WAS OVER, HERE SHE WAS CONFRONTING ME LIKE I WAS PART OF THIS BULLSHIT CONSPIRACY. NATURALLY, I PLAYED DUMB AND PRETENDED NOT TO KNOW WHO HE WAS, WHICH IS BASICALLY THE TRUTH.
SHE LEFT WITH HARDLY A WORD AND I FELT I WAS RIGHT BACK WHERE I STARTED. TO THIS GIRL, I WAS ONCE AGAIN JUST ONE OF DOYLE'S CREEPY FRIENDS. OH, WELL, NOW THAT I'M A CREEP, MAYBE I'D GET TO FUCK HER, HUH? YEAH, RIGHT...
XAIME
04-05

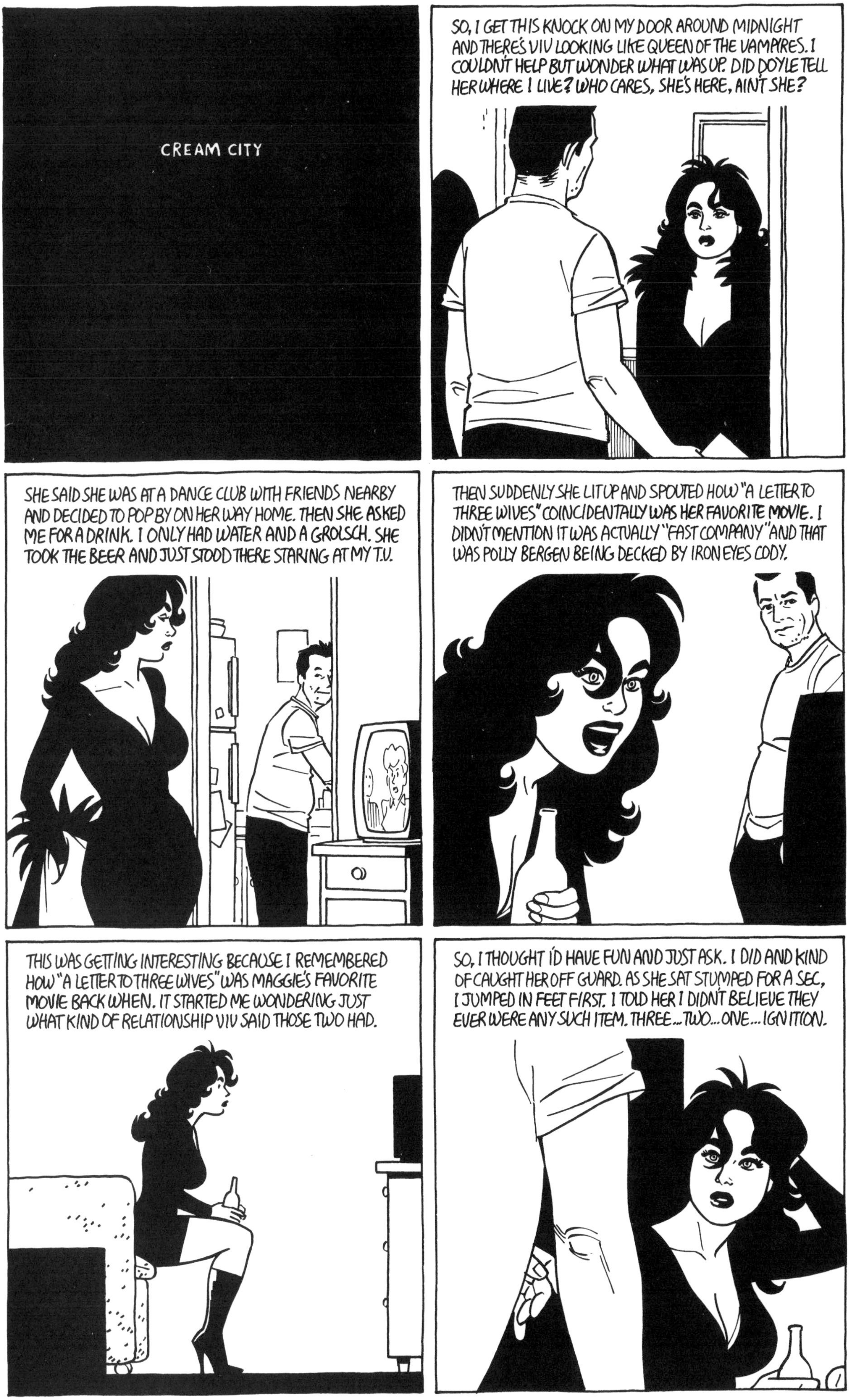
CREAM CITY
SO, I GET THIS KNOCK ON MY DOOR AROUND MIDNIGHT AND THERE'S VIV LOOKING LIKE QUEEN OF THE VAMPIRES. I COULDN'T HELP BUT WONDER WHAT WAS UP. DID DOYLE TELL HER WHERE I LIVE? WHO CARES, SHE'S HERE, AIN'T SHE?
SHE SAID SHE WAS AT A DANCE CLUB WITH FRIENDS NEARBY AND DECIDED TO POP BY ON HER WAY HOME. THEN SHE ASKED ME FOR A DRINK. I ONLY HAD WATER AND A GROLSCH. SHE TOOK THE BEER AND JUST STOOD THERE STARING AT MY T.V.
THEN SUDDENLY SHE LIT UP AND SPOUTED HOW "A LETTER TO THREE WIVES" COINCIDENTALLY WAS HER FAVORITE MOVIE. I DIDN'T MENTION IT WAS ACTUALLY "FAST COMPANY" AND THAT WAS POLLY BERGEN BEING DECKED BY IRON EYES CODY.
THIS WAS GETTING INTERESTING BECAUSE I REMEMBERED HOW "A LETTER TO THREE WIVES" WAS MAGGIE'S FAVORITE MOVIE BACK WHEN. IT STARTED ME WONDERING JUST WHAT KIND OF RELATIONSHIP VIV SAID THOSE TWO HAD.
SO, I THOUGHT I'D HAVE FUN AND JUST ASK. I DID AND KIND OF CAUGHT HER OFF GUARD. AS SHE SAT STUMPED FOR A SEC, I JUMPED IN FEET FIRST. I TOLD HER I DIDN'T BELIEVE THEY EVER WERE ANY SUCH ITEM. THREE... TWO... ONE... IGNITION.

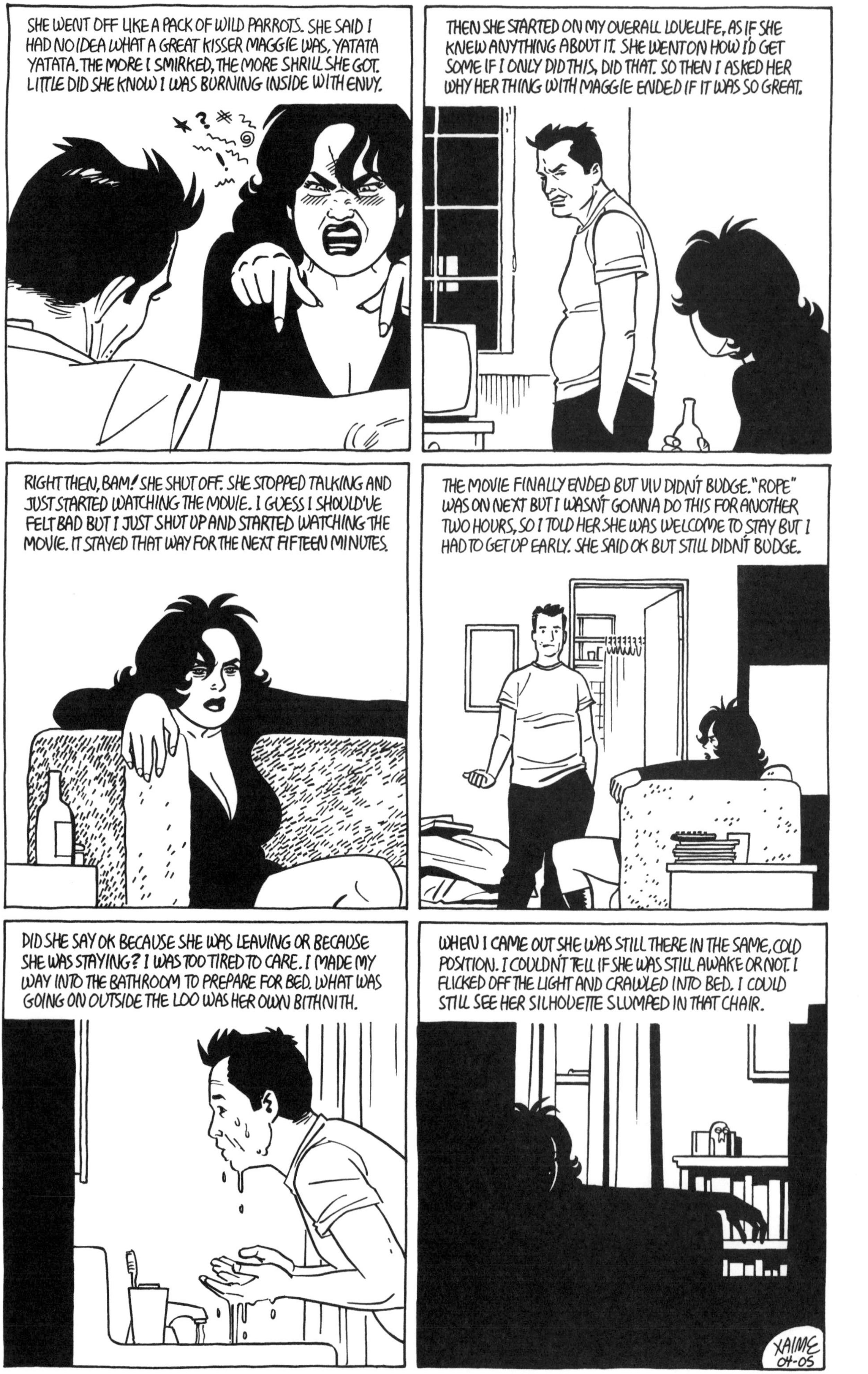
SHE WENT OFF LIKE A PACK OF WILD PARROTS. SHE SAID I HAD NO IDEA WHAT A GREAT KISSER MAGGIE WAS, YATATA YATATA. THE MORE I SMIRKED, THE MORE SHRILL SHE GOT. LITTLE DID SHE KNOW I WAS BURNING INSIDE WITH ENVY.
THEN SHE STARTED ON MY OVERALL LOVELIFE, AS IF SHE KNEW ANYTHING ABOUT IT. SHE WENT ON HOW I'D GET SOME IF I ONLY DID THIS, DID THAT. SO THEN I ASKED HER WHY HER THING WITH MAGGIE ENDED IF IT WAS SO GREAT.
RIGHT THEN, BAM! SHE SHUT OFF. SHE STOPPED TALKING AND JUST STARTED WATCHING THE MOVIE. I GUESS I SHOULD'VE FELT BAD BUT I JUST SHUT UP AND STARTED WATCHING THE MOVIE. IT STAYED THAT WAY FOR THE NEXT FIFTEEN MINUTES.
THE MOVIE FINALLY ENDED BUT VIV DIDN'T BUDGE. "ROPE" WAS ON NEXT BUT I WASN'T GONNA DO THIS FOR ANOTHER TWO HOURS, SO I TOLD HER SHE WAS WELCOME TO STAY BUT I HAD TO GET UP EARLY. SHE SAID OK BUT STILL DIDN'T BUDGE.
DID SHE SAY OK BECAUSE SHE WAS LEAVING OR BECAUSE SHE WAS STAYING? I WAS TOO TIRED TO CARE. I MADE MY WAY INTO THE BATHROOM TO PREPARE FOR BED. WHAT WAS GOING ON OUTSIDE THE LOO WAS HER OWN BITHNITH.
WHEN I CAME OUT SHE WAS STILL THERE IN THE SAME, COLD POSITION. I COULDN'T TELL IF SHE WAS STILL AWAKE OR NOT. I FLICKED OFF THE LIGHT AND CRAWLED INTO BED. I COULD STILL SEE HER SILHOUETTE SLUMPED IN THAT CHAIR.
XAIME 04-05

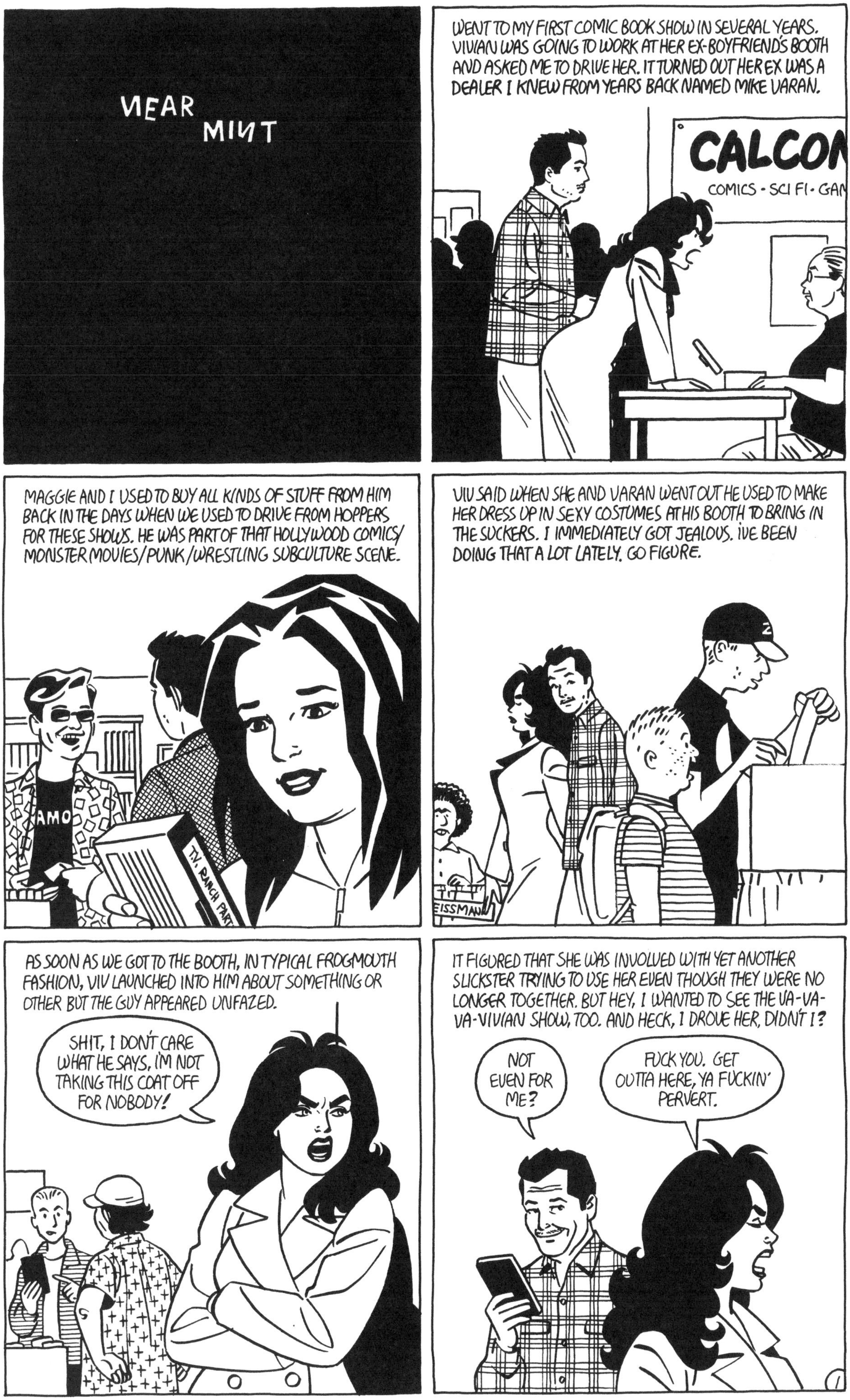
NEAR MINT
WENT TO MY FIRST COMIC BOOK SHOW IN SEVERAL YEARS. VIVIAN WAS GOING TO WORK AT HER EX-BOYFRIEND'S BOOTH AND ASKED ME TO DRIVE HER. IT TURNED OUT HER EX WAS A DEALER I KNEW FROM YEARS BACK NAMED MIKE VARAN.
CALCON
COMICS • SCI FI • GAM
MAGGIE AND I USED TO BUY ALL KINDS OF STUFF FROM HIM BACK IN THE DAYS WHEN WE USED TO DRIVE FROM HOPPERS FOR THESE SHOWS. HE WAS PART OF THAT HOLLYWOOD COMICS/ MONSTER MOVIES/PUNK/WRESTLING SUBCULTURE SCENE.
AMO
T.V. RANCH PART
VIV SAID WHEN SHE AND VARAN WENT OUT HE USED TO MAKE HER DRESS UP IN SEXY COSTUMES AT HIS BOOTH TO BRING IN THE SUCKERS. I IMMEDIATELY GOT JEALOUS. I'VE BEEN DOING THAT A LOT LATELY. GO FIGURE.
EISSMAN
AS SOON AS WE GOT TO THE BOOTH, IN TYPICAL FROGMOUTH FASHION, VIV LAUNCHED INTO HIM ABOUT SOMETHING OR OTHER BUT THE GUY APPEARED UNFAZED.
SHIT, I DON'T CARE WHAT HE SAYS, I'M NOT TAKING THIS COAT OFF FOR NOBODY!
IT FIGURED THAT SHE WAS INVOLVED WITH YET ANOTHER SLICKSTER TRYING TO USE HER EVEN THOUGH THEY WERE NO LONGER TOGETHER. BUT HEY, I WANTED TO SEE THE VA-VA-VA-VIVIAN SHOW, TOO. AND HECK, I DROVE HER, DIDN'T I?
NOT EVEN FOR ME?
FUCK YOU. GET OUTTA HERE, YA FUCKIN' PERVERT.
1

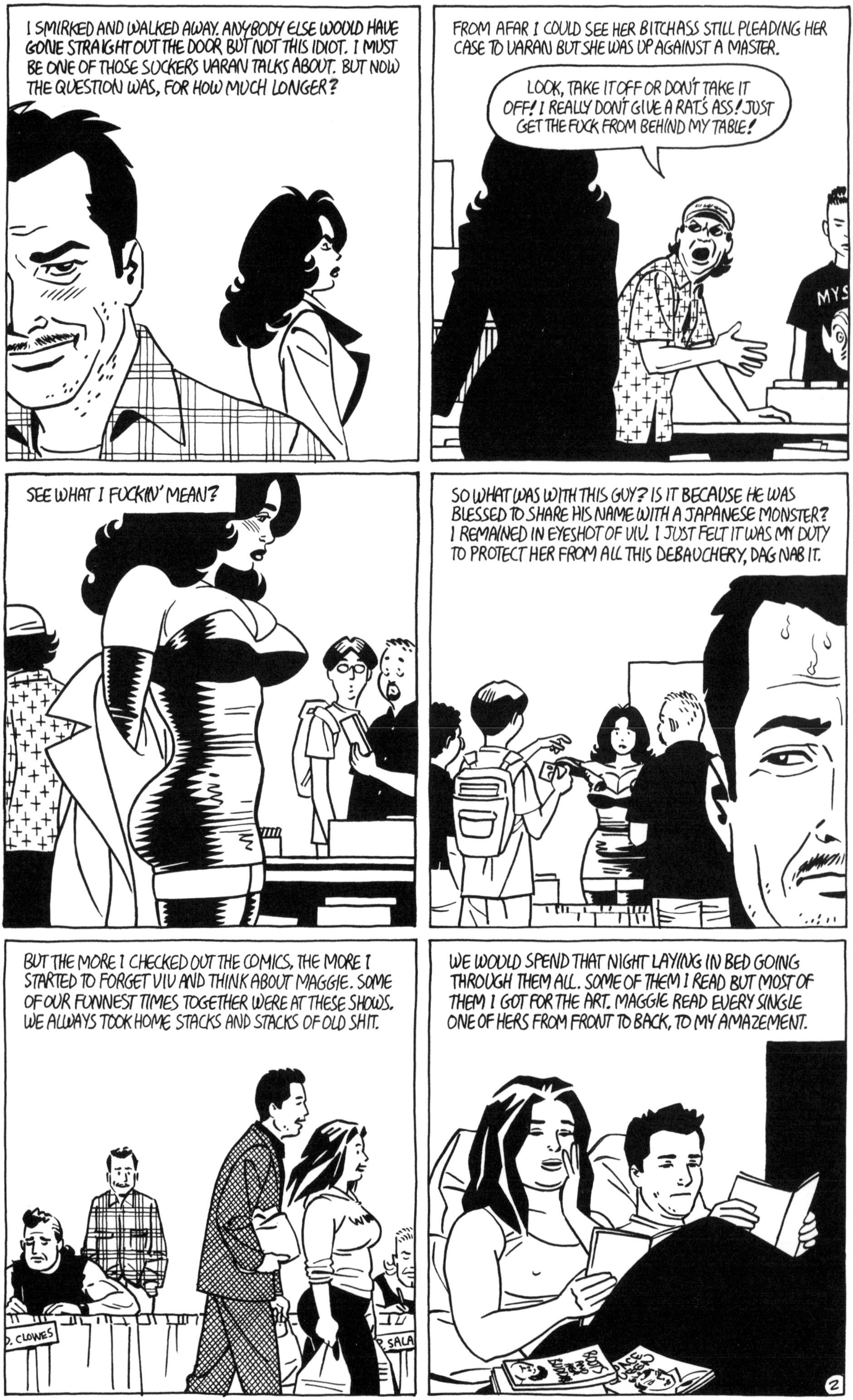
I SMIRKED AND WALKED AWAY. ANYBODY ELSE WOULD HAVE GONE STRAIGHT OUT THE DOOR BUT NOT THIS IDIOT. I MUST BE ONE OF THOSE SUCKERS VARAN TALKS ABOUT. BUT NOW THE QUESTION WAS, FOR HOW MUCH LONGER?
FROM AFAR I COULD SEE HER BITCHASS STILL PLEADING HER CASE TO VARAN BUT SHE WAS UP AGAINST A MASTER.
LOOK, TAKE IT OFF OR DON'T TAKE IT OFF! I REALLY DON'T GIVE A RAT'S ASS! JUST GET THE FUCK FROM BEHIND MY TABLE!
MYS
SEE WHAT I FUCKIN' MEAN?
SO WHAT WAS WITH THIS GUY? IS IT BECAUSE HE WAS BLESSED TO SHARE HIS NAME WITH A JAPANESE MONSTER? I REMAINED IN EYESHOT OF VIV. I JUST FELT IT WAS MY DUTY TO PROTECT HER FROM ALL THIS DEBAUCHERY, DAG NAB IT.
BUT THE MORE I CHECKED OUT THE COMICS, THE MORE I STARTED TO FORGET VIV AND THINK ABOUT MAGGIE. SOME OF OUR FUNNEST TIMES TOGETHER WERE AT THESE SHOWS. WE ALWAYS TOOK HOME STACKS AND STACKS OF OLD SHIT.
D. CLOWES
SALA
WE WOULD SPEND THAT NIGHT LAYING IN BED GOING THROUGH THEM ALL. SOME OF THEM I READ BUT MOST OF THEM I GOT FOR THE ART. MAGGIE READ EVERY SINGLE ONE OF HERS FROM FRONT TO BACK, TO MY AMAZEMENT.
2

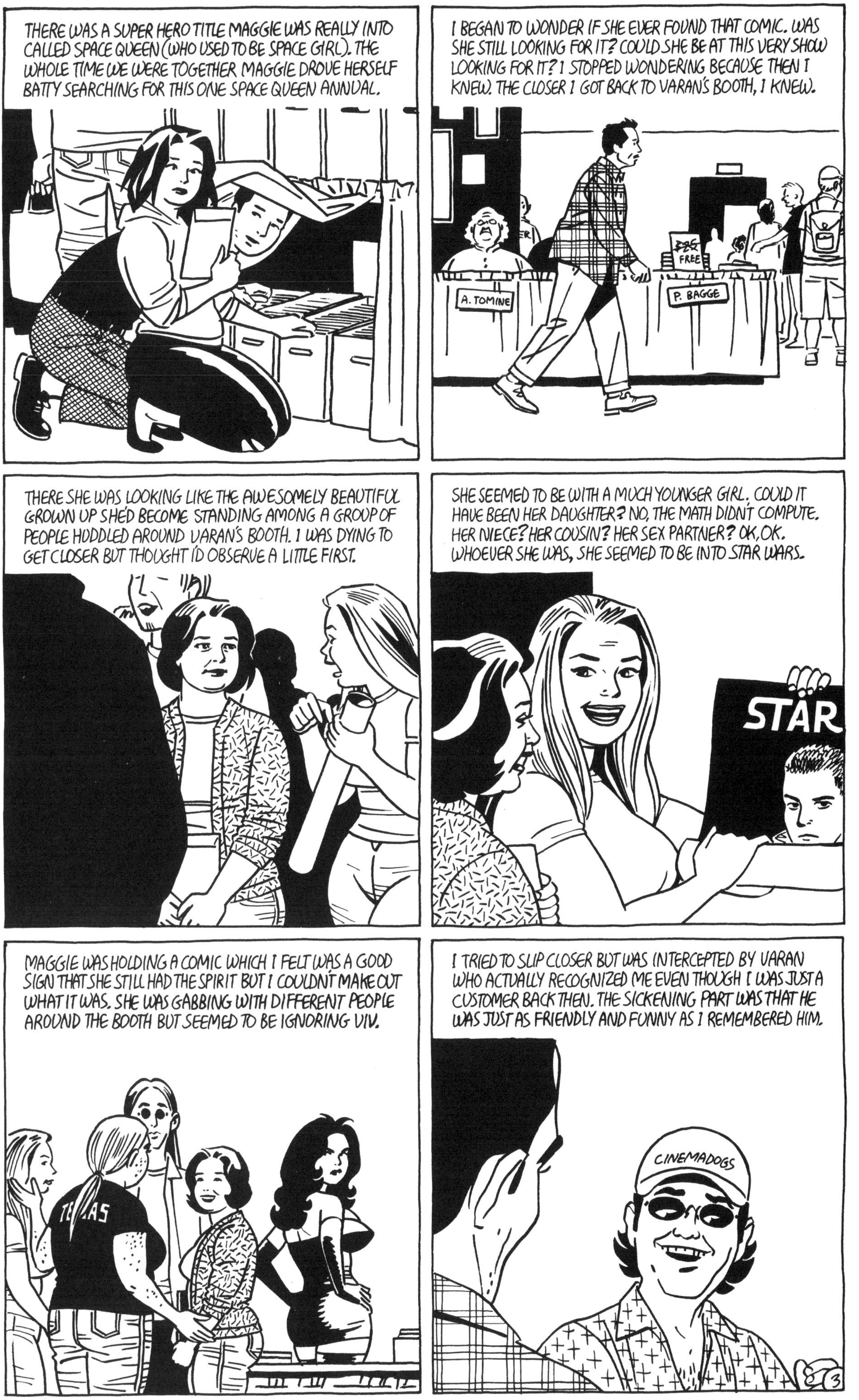
THERE WAS A SUPER HERO TITLE MAGGIE WAS REALLY INTO CALLED SPACE QUEEN (WHO USED TO BE SPACE GIRL). THE WHOLE TIME WE WERE TOGETHER MAGGIE DROVE HERSELF BATTY SEARCHING FOR THIS ONE SPACE QUEEN ANNUAL.
I BEGAN TO WONDER IF SHE EVER FOUND THAT COMIC. WAS SHE STILL LOOKING FOR IT? COULD SHE BE AT THIS VERY SHOW LOOKING FOR IT? I STOPPED WONDERING BECAUSE THEN I KNEW. THE CLOSER I GOT BACK TO VARAN'S BOOTH, I KNEW.
FREE
A. TOMINE
P. BAGGE
THERE SHE WAS LOOKING LIKE THE AWESOMELY BEAUTIFUL GROWN UP SHE'D BECOME STANDING AMONG A GROUP OF PEOPLE HUDDLED AROUND VARAN'S BOOTH. I WAS DYING TO GET CLOSER BUT THOUGHT I'D OBSERVE A LITTLE FIRST.
SHE SEEMED TO BE WITH A MUCH YOUNGER GIRL. COULD IT HAVE BEEN HER DAUGHTER? NO, THE MATH DIDN'T COMPUTE. HER NIECE? HER COUSIN? HER SEX PARTNER? OK, OK. WHOEVER SHE WAS, SHE SEEMED TO BE INTO STAR WARS.
STÄR
MAGGIE WAS HOLDING A COMIC WHICH I FELT WAS A GOOD SIGN THAT SHE STILL HAD THE SPIRIT BUT I COULDN'T MAKE OUT WHAT IT WAS. SHE WAS GABBING WITH DIFFERENT PEOPLE AROUND THE BOOTH BUT SEEMED TO BE IGNORING VIV.
I TRIED TO SLIP CLOSER BUT WAS INTERCEPTED BY VARAN WHO ACTUALLY RECOGNIZED ME EVEN THOUGH I WAS JUST A CUSTOMER BACK THEN. THE SICKENING PART WAS THAT HE WAS JUST AS FRIENDLY AND FUNNY AS I REMEMBERED HIM.
CINEMADOGS

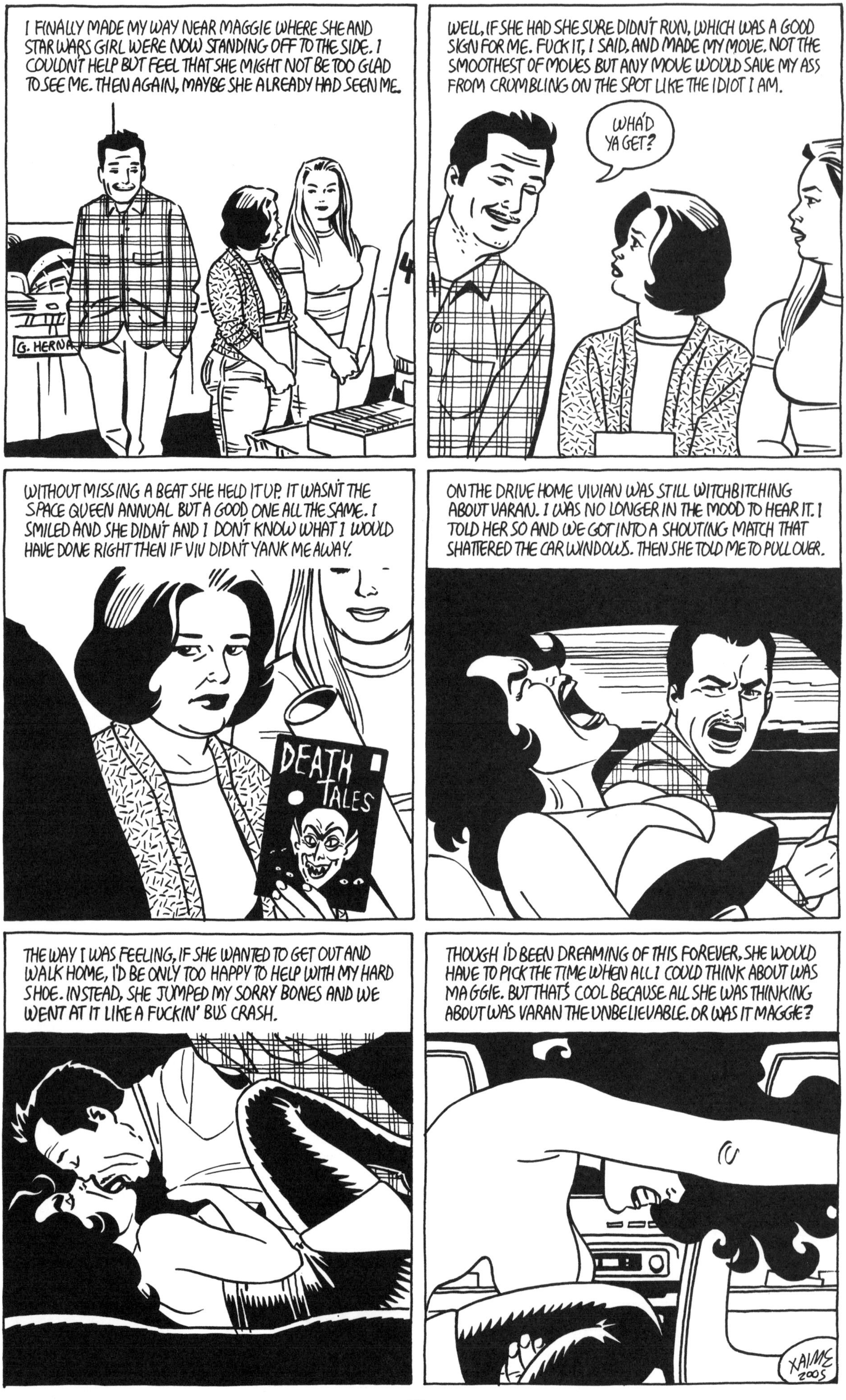
I FINALLY MADE MY WAY NEAR MAGGIE WHERE SHE AND STAR WARS GIRL WERE NOW STANDING OFF TO THE SIDE. I COULDN'T HELP BUT FEEL THAT SHE MIGHT NOT BE TOO GLAD TO SEE ME. THEN AGAIN, MAYBE SHE ALREADY HAD SEEN ME.
G. HERNA
WELL, IF SHE HAD SHE SURE DIDN'T RUN, WHICH WAS A GOOD SIGN FOR ME. FUCK IT, I SAID, AND MADE MY MOVE. NOT THE SMOOTHEST OF MOVES BUT ANY MOVE WOULD SAVE MY ASS FROM CRUMBLING ON THE SPOT LIKE THE IDIOT I AM.
WHA'D YA GET?
WITHOUT MISSING A BEAT SHE HELD IT UP. IT WASN'T THE SPACE QUEEN ANNUAL BUT A GOOD ONE ALL THE SAME. I SMILED AND SHE DIDN'T AND I DON'T KNOW WHAT I WOULD HAVE DONE RIGHT THEN IF VIV DIDN'T YANK ME AWAY.
DEATH TALES
ON THE DRIVE HOME VIVIAN WAS STILL WITCHBITCHING ABOUT VARAN. I WAS NO LONGER IN THE MOOD TO HEAR IT. I TOLD HER SO AND WE GOT INTO A SHOUTING MATCH THAT SHATTERED THE CAR WINDOWS. THEN SHE TOLD ME TO PULL OVER.
THE WAY I WAS FEELING, IF SHE WANTED TO GET OUT AND WALK HOME, I'D BE ONLY TOO HAPPY TO HELP WITH MY HARD SHOE. INSTEAD, SHE JUMPED MY SORRY BONES AND WE WENT AT IT LIKE A FUCKIN' BUS CRASH.
THOUGH I'D BEEN DREAMING OF THIS FOREVER, SHE WOULD HAVE TO PICK THE TIME WHEN ALL I COULD THINK ABOUT WAS MAGGIE. BUT THAT'S COOL BECAUSE ALL SHE WAS THINKING ABOUT WAS VARAN THE UNBELIEVABLE. OR WAS IT MAGGIE?
XAIME 2005

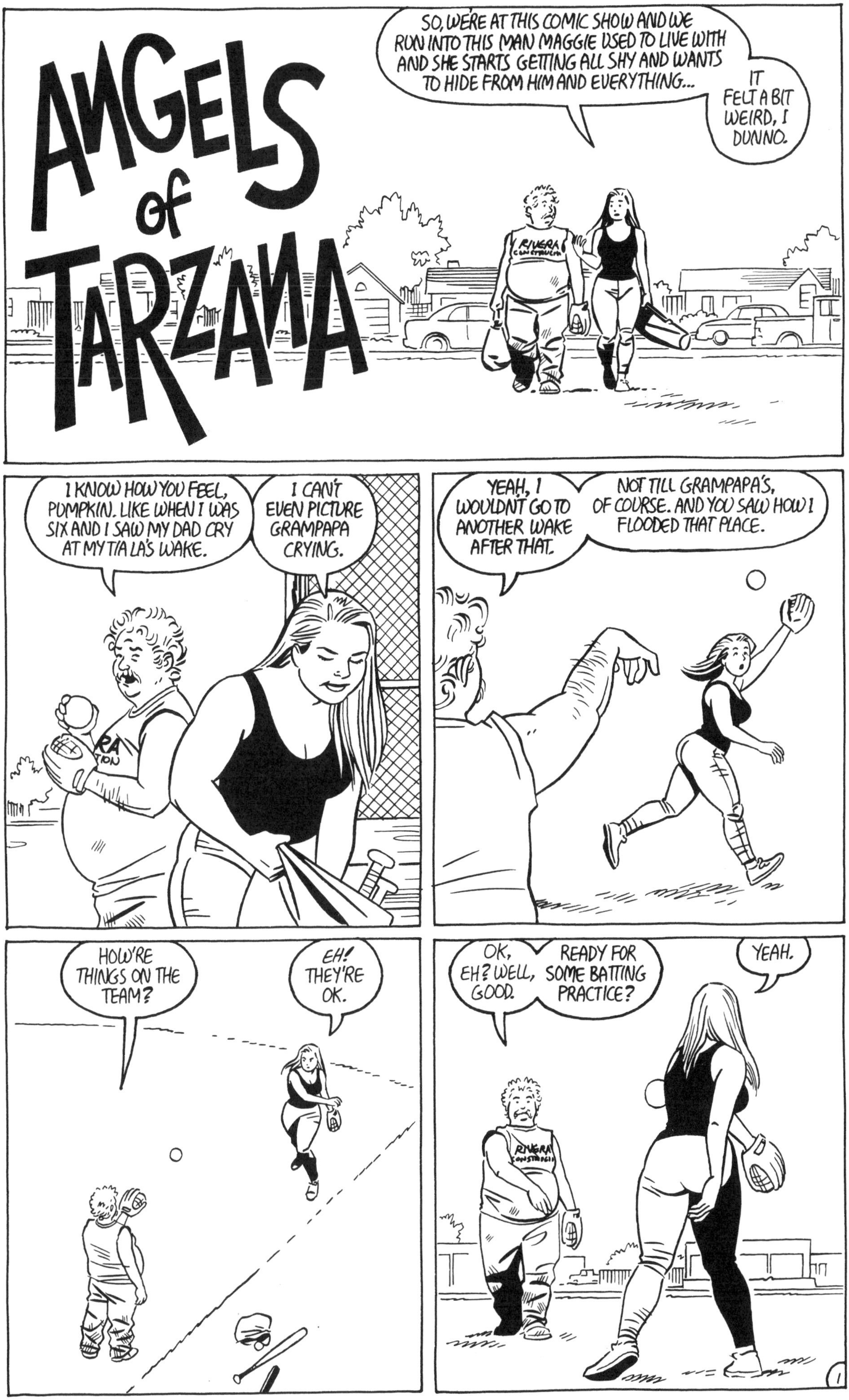
ANGELS of TARZANA
SO, WE'RE AT THIS COMIC SHOW AND WE RUN INTO THIS MAN MAGGIE USED TO LIVE WITH AND SHE STARTS GETTING ALL SHY AND WANTS TO HIDE FROM HIM AND EVERYTHING...
IT FELT A BIT WEIRD, I DUNNO.
RIVERA
I KNOW HOW YOU FEEL, PUMPKIN. LIKE WHEN I WAS SIX AND I SAW MY DAD CRY AT MY TIA LA'S WAKE.
I CAN'T EVEN PICTURE GRAMPAPA CRYING.
YEAH, I WOULDN'T GO TO ANOTHER WAKE AFTER THAT.
NOT TILL GRAMPAPA'S, OF COURSE. AND YOU SAW HOW I FLOODED THAT PLACE.
HOW'RE THINGS ON THE TEAM?
EH! THEY'RE OK.
OK, EH? WELL, GOOD.
READY FOR SOME BATTING PRACTICE?
YEAH.
RIVERA
1

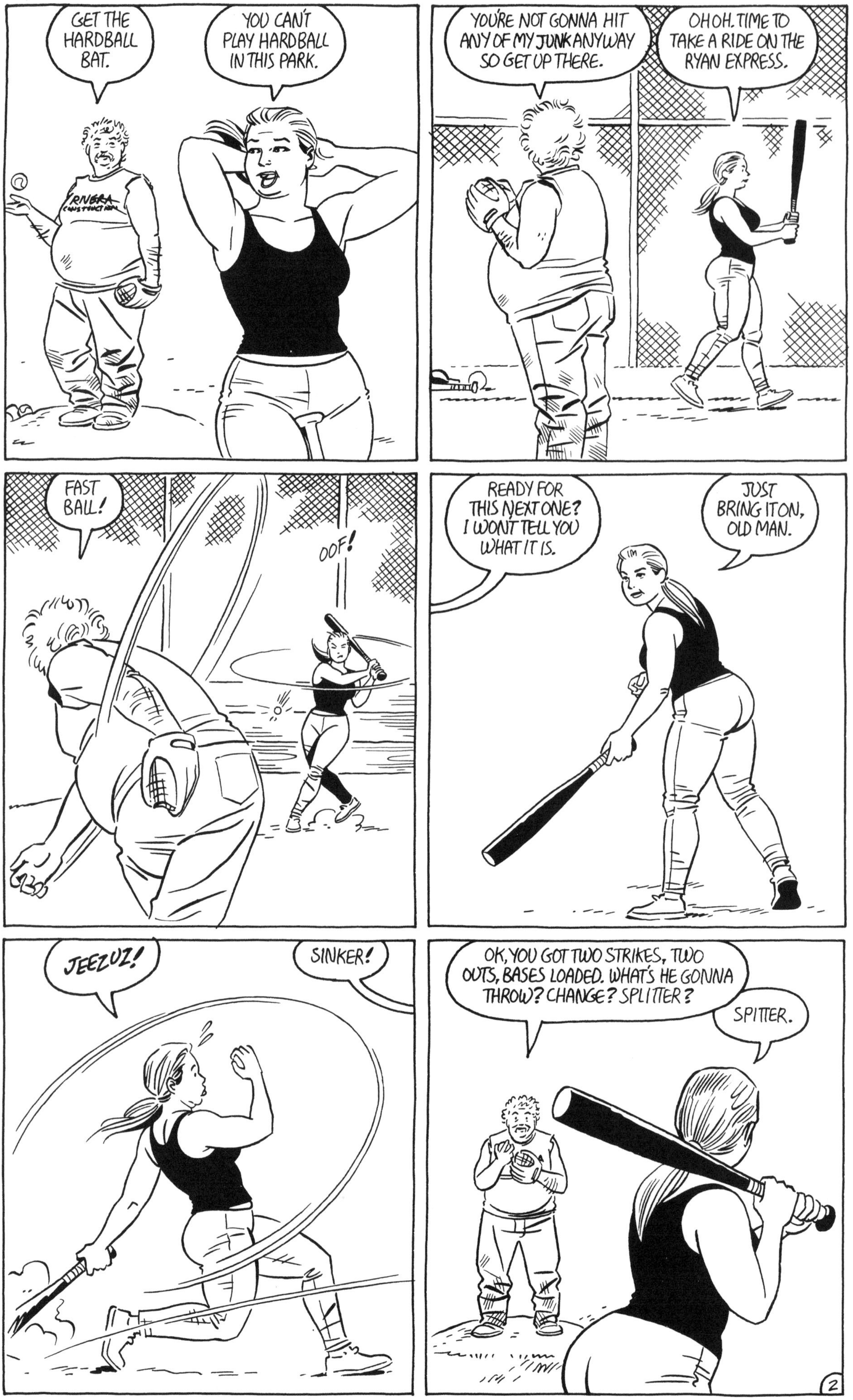
GET THE HARDBALL BAT.
YOU CAN'T PLAY HARDBALL IN THIS PARK.
RIVERA CONSTRUCTION
YOU'RE NOT GONNA HIT ANY OF MY JUNK ANYWAY SO GET UP THERE.
OH OH. TIME TO TAKE A RIDE ON THE RYAN EXPRESS.
FAST BALL!
OOF!
READY FOR THIS NEXT ONE? I WON'T TELL YOU WHAT IT IS.
JUST BRING IT ON, OLD MAN.
JEEZUZ!
SINKER!
OK, YOU GOT TWO STRIKES, TWO OUTS, BASES LOADED. WHAT'S HE GONNA THROW? CHANGE? SPLITTER?
SPITTER.
2

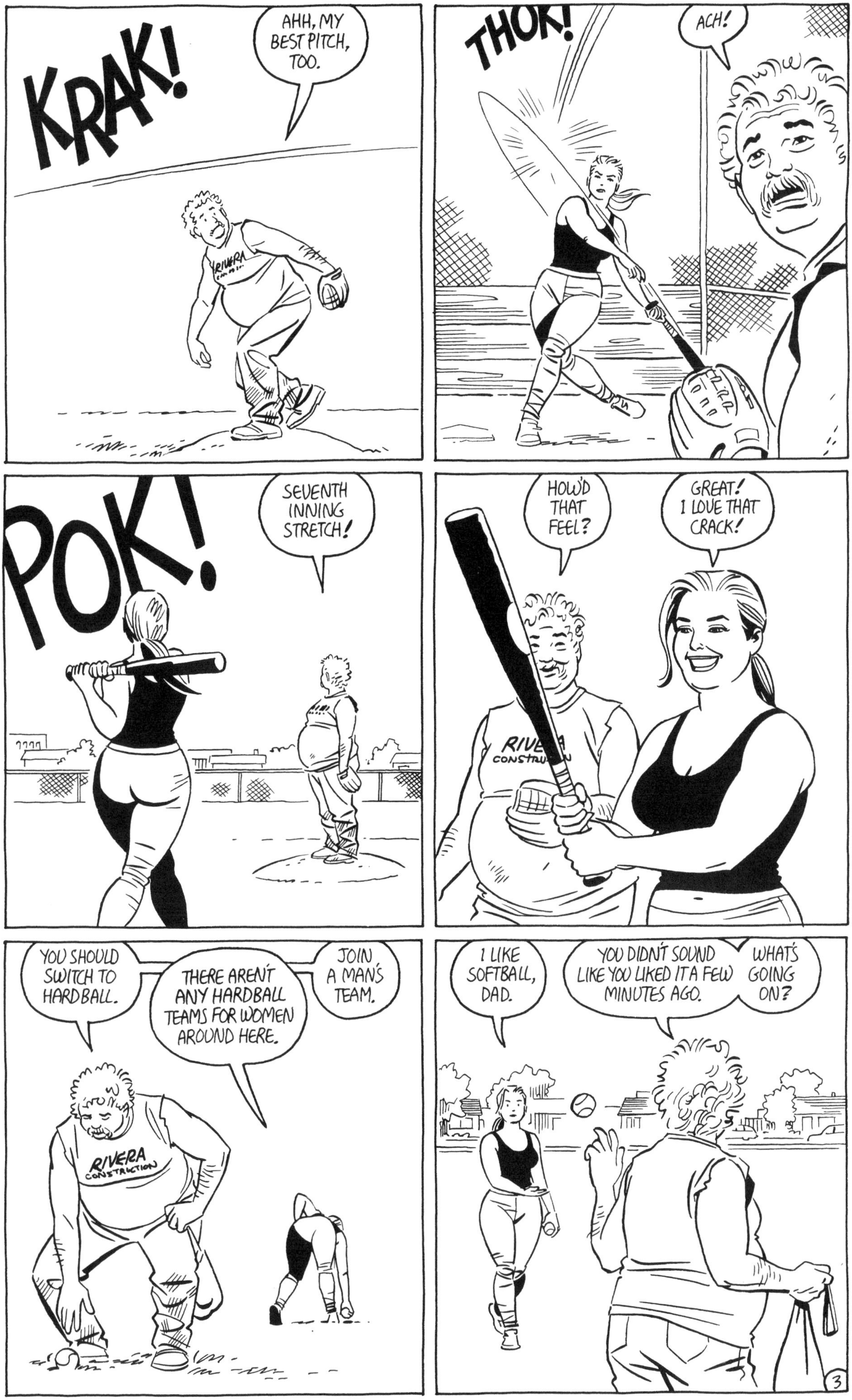
KRAK!
AHH, MY BEST PITCH, TOO.
THOK!
ACH!
RIVERA
POK!
SEVENTH INNING STRETCH!
HOW'D THAT FEEL?
GREAT! I LOVE THAT CRACK!
YOU SHOULD SWITCH TO HARDBALL.
THERE AREN'T ANY HARDBALL TEAMS FOR WOMEN AROUND HERE.
JOIN A MAN'S TEAM.
RIVERA CONSTRUCTION
I LIKE SOFTBALL, DAD.
YOU DIDN'T SOUND LIKE YOU LIKED IT A FEW MINUTES AGO.
WHAT'S GOING ON?
3

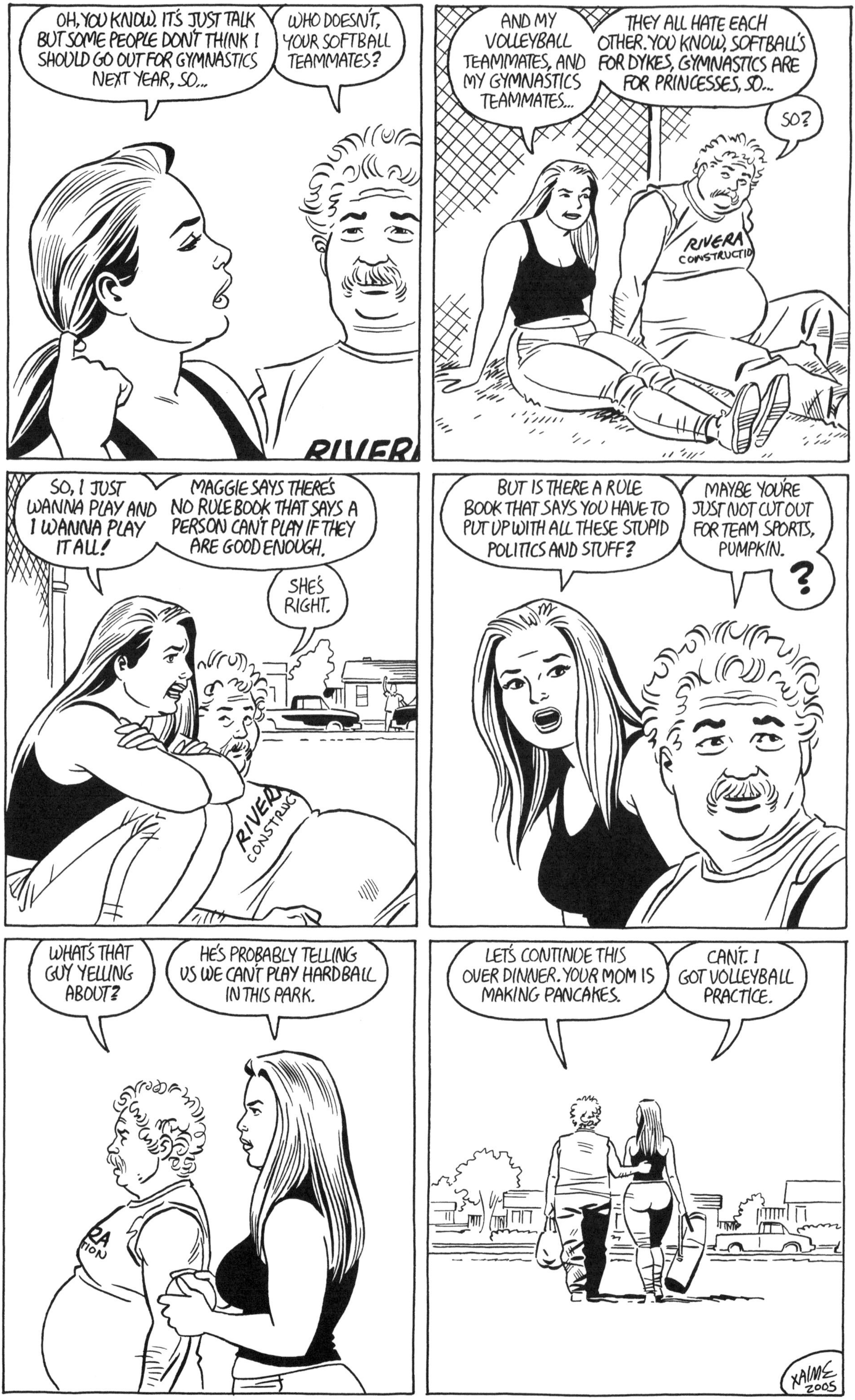
OH, YOU KNOW. IT'S JUST TALK BUT SOME PEOPLE DON'T THINK I SHOULD GO OUT FOR GYMNASTICS NEXT YEAR, SO...
WHO DOESN'T, YOUR SOFTBALL TEAMMATES?
RIVERA
AND MY VOLLEYBALL TEAMMATES, AND MY GYMNASTICS TEAMMATES...
THEY ALL HATE EACH OTHER. YOU KNOW, SOFTBALL'S FOR DYKES, GYMNASTICS ARE FOR PRINCESSES, SO...
SO?
RIVERA CONSTRUCTIO
SO, I JUST WANNA PLAY AND I WANNA PLAY IT ALL!
MAGGIE SAYS THERE'S NO RULE BOOK THAT SAYS A PERSON CAN'T PLAY IF THEY ARE GOOD ENOUGH.
SHE'S RIGHT.
BUT IS THERE A RULE BOOK THAT SAYS YOU HAVE TO PUT UP WITH ALL THESE STUPID POLITICS AND STUFF?
MAYBE YOU'RE JUST NOT CUT OUT FOR TEAM SPORTS, PUMPKIN.
?
WHAT'S THAT GUY YELLING ABOUT?
HE'S PROBABLY TELLING US WE CAN'T PLAY HARDBALL IN THIS PARK.
LET'S CONTINUE THIS OVER DINNER. YOUR MOM IS MAKING PANCAKES.
CAN'T. I GOT VOLLEYBALL PRACTICE.
XAIME 2005

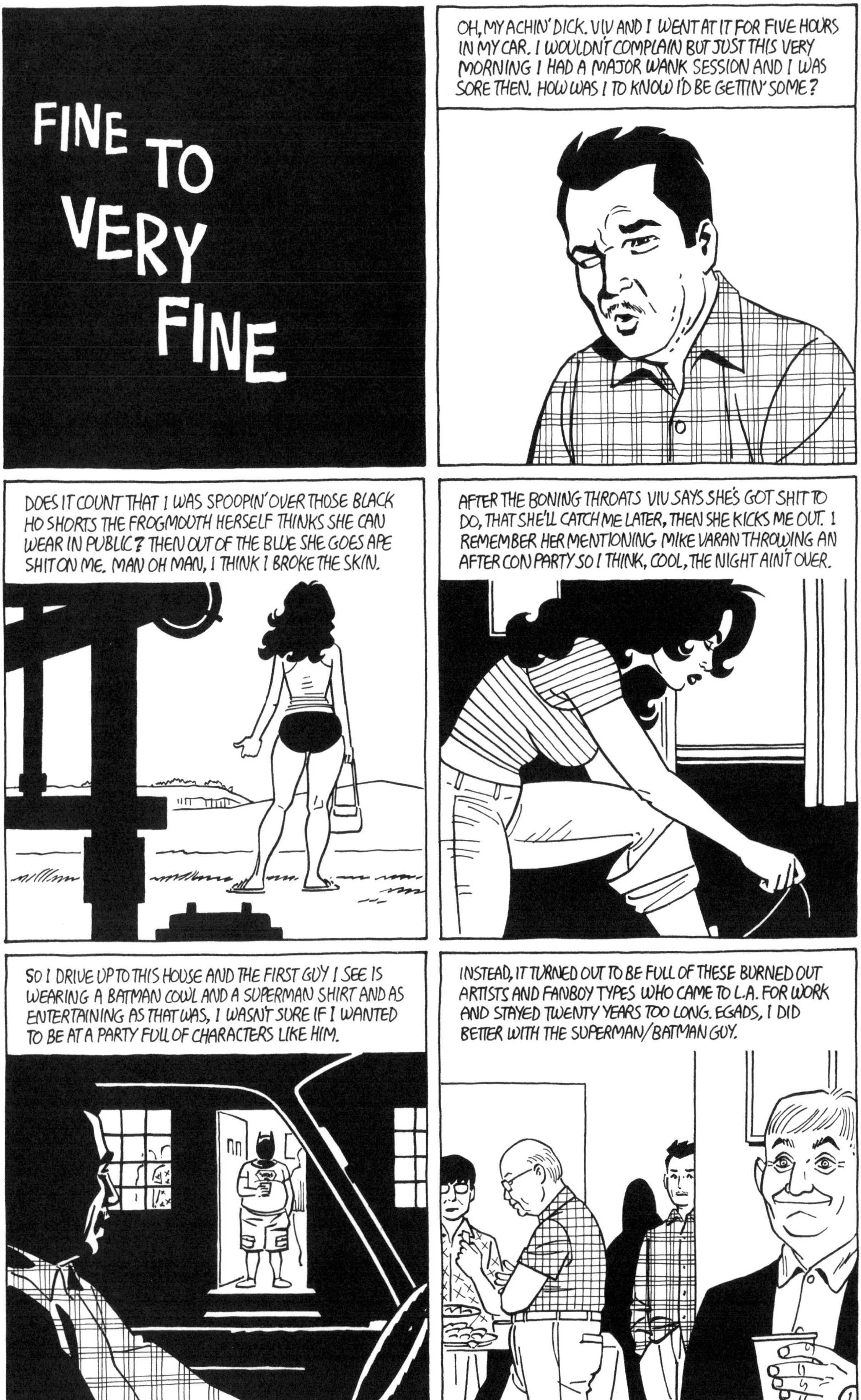
FINE TO VERY FINE
OH, MY ACHIN' DICK. VIV AND I WENT AT IT FOR FIVE HOURS IN MY CAR. I WOULDN'T COMPLAIN BUT JUST THIS VERY MORNING I HAD A MAJOR WANK SESSION AND I WAS SORE THEN. HOW WAS I TO KNOW I'D BE GETTIN' SOME?
DOES IT COUNT THAT I WAS SPOOPIN' OVER THOSE BLACK HO SHORTS THE FROGMOUTH HERSELF THINKS SHE CAN WEAR IN PUBLIC? THEN OUT OF THE BLUE SHE GOES APE SHIT ON ME. MAN OH MAN, I THINK I BROKE THE SKIN.
AFTER THE BONING THROATS VIV SAYS SHE'S GOT SHIT TO DO, THAT SHE'LL CATCH ME LATER, THEN SHE KICKS ME OUT. I REMEMBER HER MENTIONING MIKE VARAN THROWING AN AFTER CON PARTY SO I THINK, COOL, THE NIGHT AIN'T OVER.
SO I DRIVE UP TO THIS HOUSE AND THE FIRST GUY I SEE IS WEARING A BATMAN COWL AND A SUPERMAN SHIRT AND AS ENTERTAINING AS THAT WAS, I WASN'T SURE IF I WANTED TO BE AT A PARTY FULL OF CHARACTERS LIKE HIM.
INSTEAD, IT TURNED OUT TO BE FULL OF THESE BURNED OUT ARTISTS AND FANBOY TYPES WHO CAME TO L.A. FOR WORK AND STAYED TWENTY YEARS TOO LONG. EGADS, I DID BETTER WITH THE SUPERMAN/BATMAN GUY.

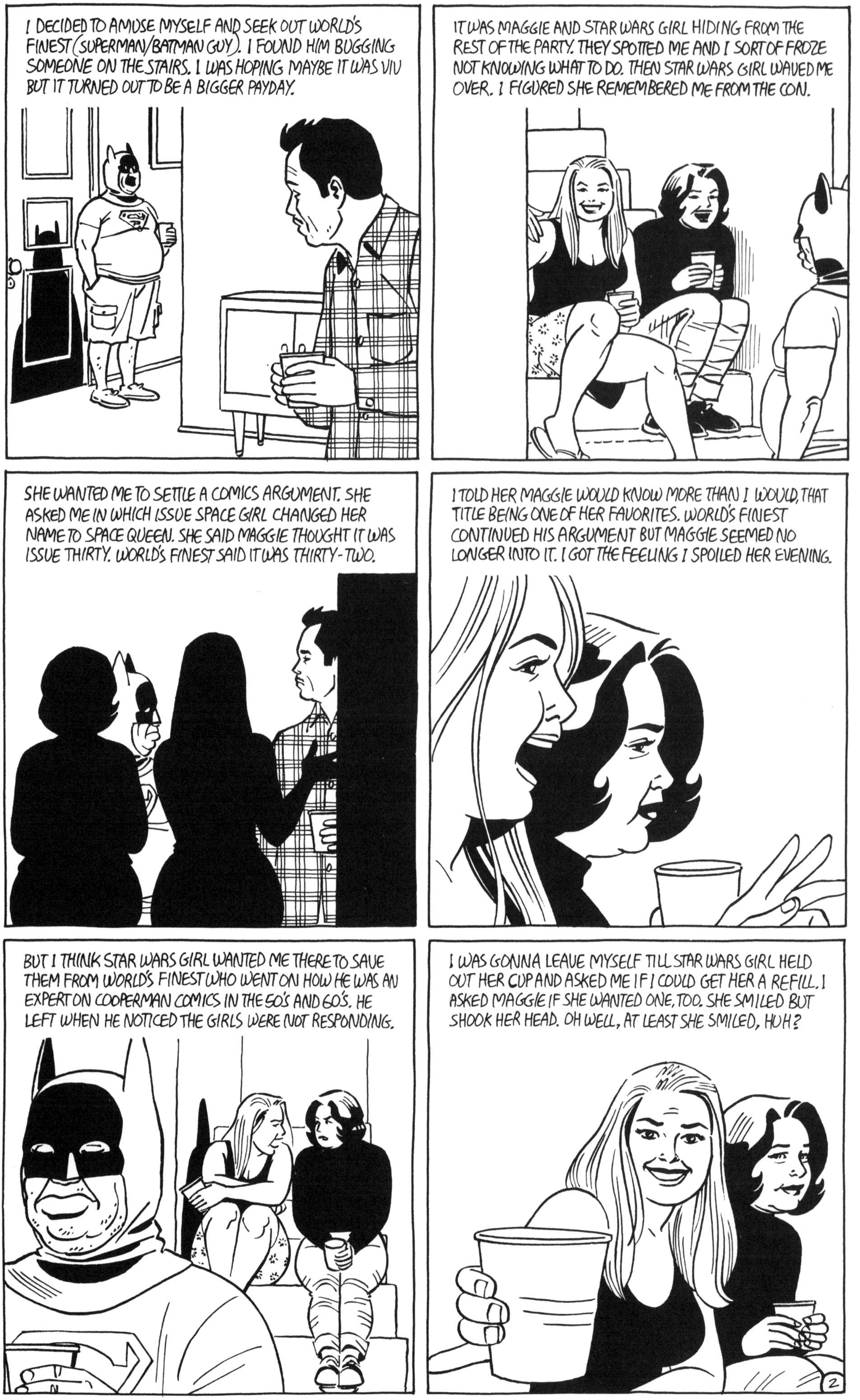
I DECIDED TO AMUSE MYSELF AND SEEK OUT WORLD'S FINEST (SUPERMAN/BATMAN GUY). I FOUND HIM BUGGING SOMEONE ON THE STAIRS. I WAS HOPING MAYBE IT WAS VIV BUT IT TURNED OUT TO BE A BIGGER PAYDAY.
IT WAS MAGGIE AND STAR WARS GIRL HIDING FROM THE REST OF THE PARTY. THEY SPOTTED ME AND I SORT OF FROZE NOT KNOWING WHAT TO DO. THEN STAR WARS GIRL WAVED ME OVER. I FIGURED SHE REMEMBERED ME FROM THE CON.
SHE WANTED ME TO SETTLE A COMICS ARGUMENT. SHE ASKED ME IN WHICH ISSUE SPACE GIRL CHANGED HER NAME TO SPACE QUEEN. SHE SAID MAGGIE THOUGHT IT WAS ISSUE THIRTY. WORLD'S FINEST SAID IT WAS THIRTY-TWO.
I TOLD HER MAGGIE WOULD KNOW MORE THAN I WOULD, THAT TITLE BEING ONE OF HER FAVORITES. WORLD'S FINEST CONTINUED HIS ARGUMENT BUT MAGGIE SEEMED NO LONGER INTO IT. I GOT THE FEELING I SPOILED HER EVENING.
BUT I THINK STAR WARS GIRL WANTED ME THERE TO SAVE THEM FROM WORLD'S FINEST WHO WENT ON HOW HE WAS AN EXPERT ON COOPERMAN COMICS IN THE 50'S AND 60'S. HE LEFT WHEN HE NOTICED THE GIRLS WERE NOT RESPONDING.
I WAS GONNA LEAVE MYSELF TILL STAR WARS GIRL HELD OUT HER CUP AND ASKED ME IF I COULD GET HER A REFILL. I ASKED MAGGIE IF SHE WANTED ONE, TOO. SHE SMILED BUT SHOOK HER HEAD. OH WELL, AT LEAST SHE SMILED, HUH?
2

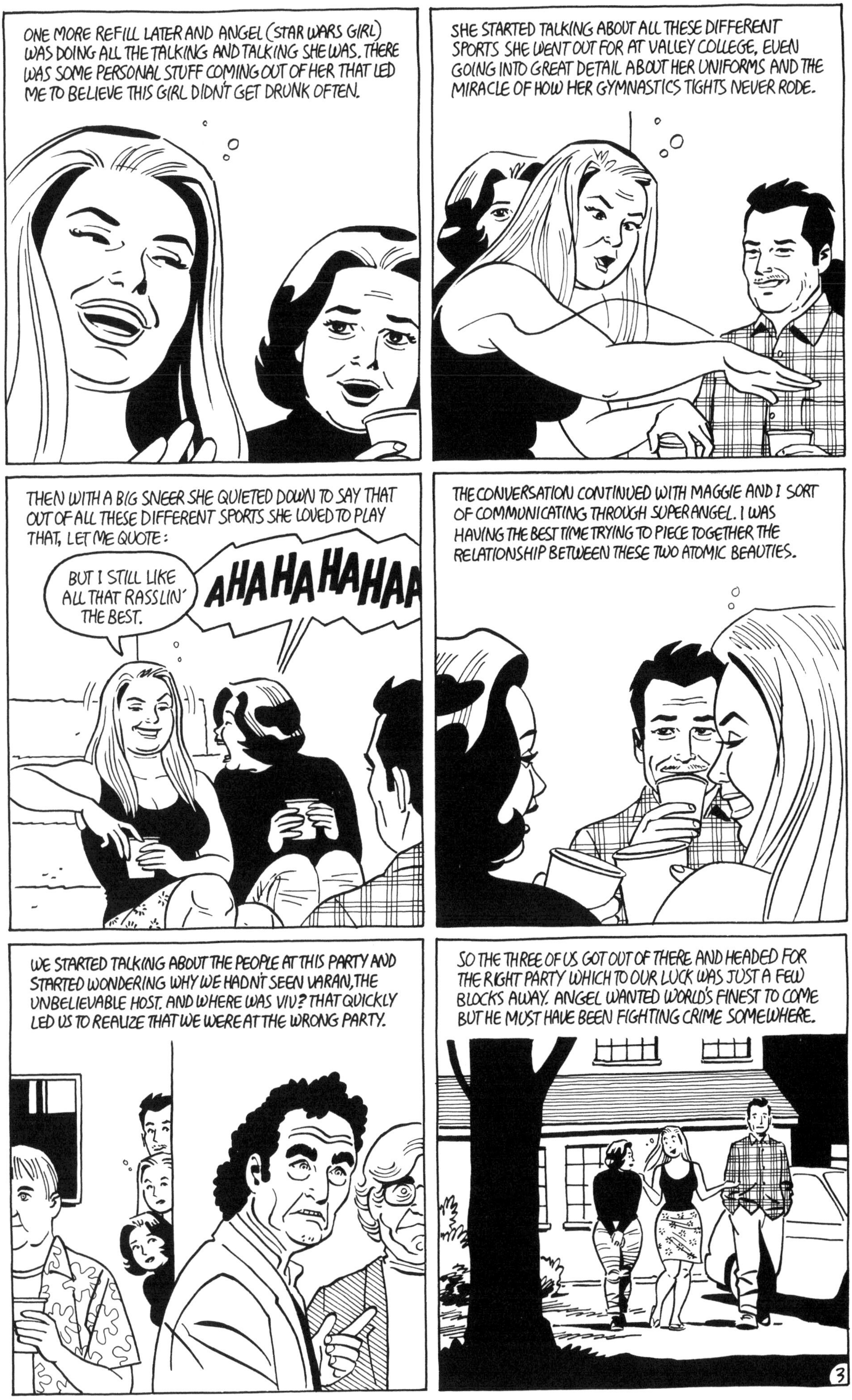
ONE MORE REFILL LATER AND ANGEL (STAR WARS GIRL) WAS DOING ALL THE TALKING AND TALKING SHE WAS. THERE WAS SOME PERSONAL STUFF COMING OUT OF HER THAT LED ME TO BELIEVE THIS GIRL DIDN'T GET DRUNK OFTEN.
SHE STARTED TALKING ABOUT ALL THESE DIFFERENT SPORTS SHE WENT OUT FOR AT VALLEY COLLEGE, EVEN GOING INTO GREAT DETAIL ABOUT HER UNIFORMS AND THE MIRACLE OF HOW HER GYMNASTICS TIGHTS NEVER RODE.
THEN WITH A BIG SNEER SHE QUIETED DOWN TO SAY THAT OUT OF ALL THESE DIFFERENT SPORTS SHE LOVED TO PLAY THAT, LET ME QUOTE:
BUT I STILL LIKE ALL THAT RASSLIN' THE BEST.
AHAHAHAHAHAA
THE CONVERSATION CONTINUED WITH MAGGIE AND I SORT OF COMMUNICATING THROUGH SUPERANGEL. I WAS HAVING THE BEST TIME TRYING TO PIECE TOGETHER THE RELATIONSHIP BETWEEN THESE TWO ATOMIC BEAUTIES.
WE STARTED TALKING ABOUT THE PEOPLE AT THIS PARTY AND STARTED WONDERING WHY WE HADN'T SEEN VARAN, THE UNBELIEVABLE HOST. AND WHERE WAS VIV? THAT QUICKLY LED US TO REALIZE THAT WE WERE AT THE WRONG PARTY.
SO THE THREE OF US GOT OUT OF THERE AND HEADED FOR THE RIGHT PARTY WHICH TO OUR LUCK WAS JUST A FEW BLOCKS AWAY. ANGEL WANTED WORLD'S FINEST TO COME BUT HE MUST HAVE BEEN FIGHTING CRIME SOMEWHERE.
3

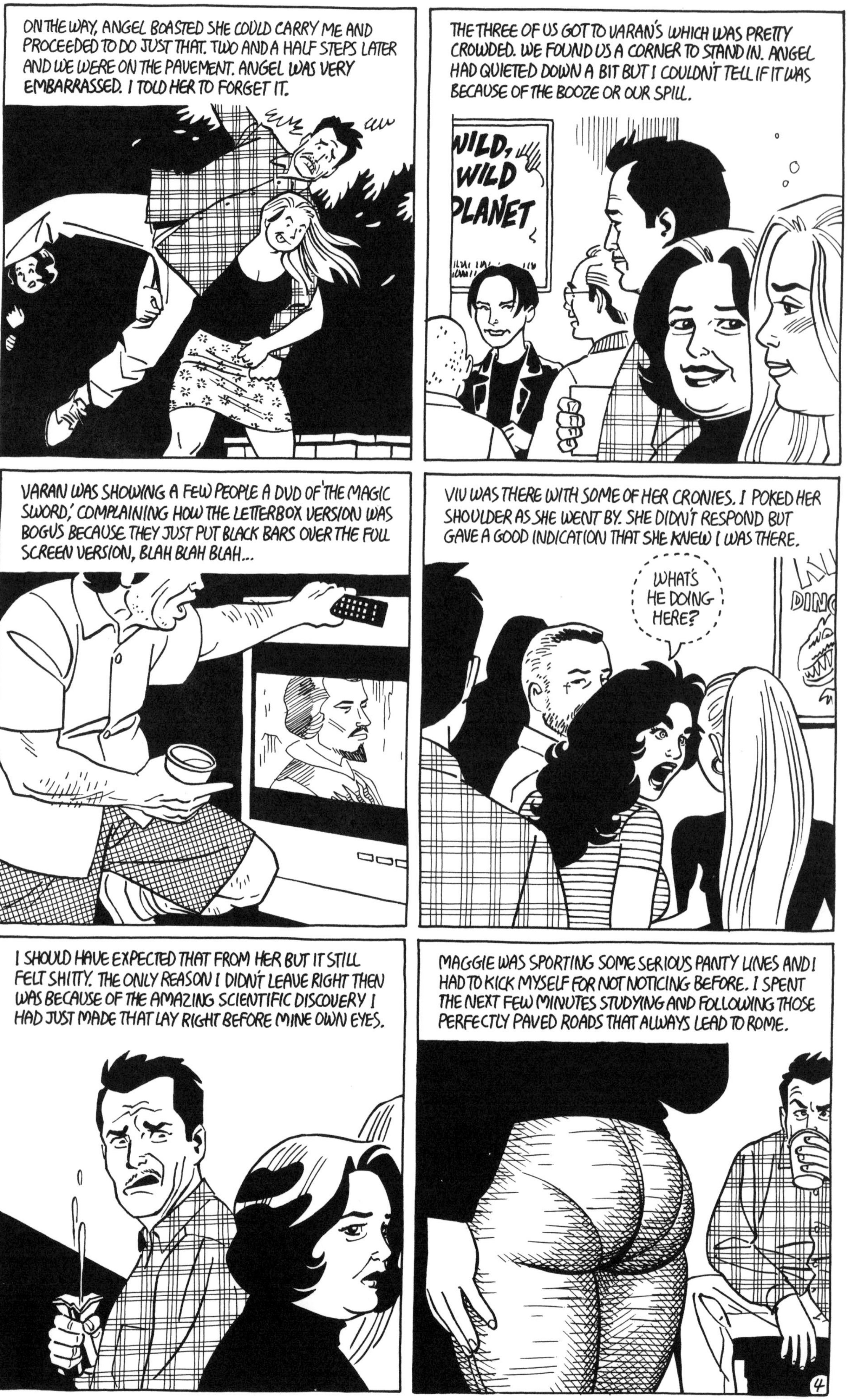
ON THE WAY, ANGEL BOASTED SHE COULD CARRY ME AND PROCEEDED TO DO JUST THAT. TWO AND A HALF STEPS LATER AND WE WERE ON THE PAVEMENT. ANGEL WAS VERY EMBARRASSED. I TOLD HER TO FORGET IT.
THE THREE OF US GOT TO VARAN'S WHICH WAS PRETTY CROWDED. WE FOUND US A CORNER TO STAND IN. ANGEL HAD QUIETED DOWN A BIT BUT I COULDN'T TELL IF IT WAS BECAUSE OF THE BOOZE OR OUR SPILL.
VARAN WAS SHOWING A FEW PEOPLE A DVD OF 'THE MAGIC SWORD,' COMPLAINING HOW THE LETTERBOX VERSION WAS BOGUS BECAUSE THEY JUST PUT BLACK BARS OVER THE FULL SCREEN VERSION, BLAH BLAH BLAH...
VIV WAS THERE WITH SOME OF HER CRONIES. I POKED HER SHOULDER AS SHE WENT BY. SHE DIDN'T RESPOND BUT GAVE A GOOD INDICATION THAT SHE KNEW I WAS THERE.
WHAT'S HE DOING HERE?
I SHOULD HAVE EXPECTED THAT FROM HER BUT IT STILL FELT SHITTY. THE ONLY REASON I DIDN'T LEAVE RIGHT THEN WAS BECAUSE OF THE AMAZING SCIENTIFIC DISCOVERY I HAD JUST MADE THAT LAY RIGHT BEFORE MINE OWN EYES.
MAGGIE WAS SPORTING SOME SERIOUS PANTY LINES AND I HAD TO KICK MYSELF FOR NOT NOTICING BEFORE. I SPENT THE NEXT FEW MINUTES STUDYING AND FOLLOWING THOSE PERFECTLY PAVED ROADS THAT ALWAYS LEAD TO ROME.
4

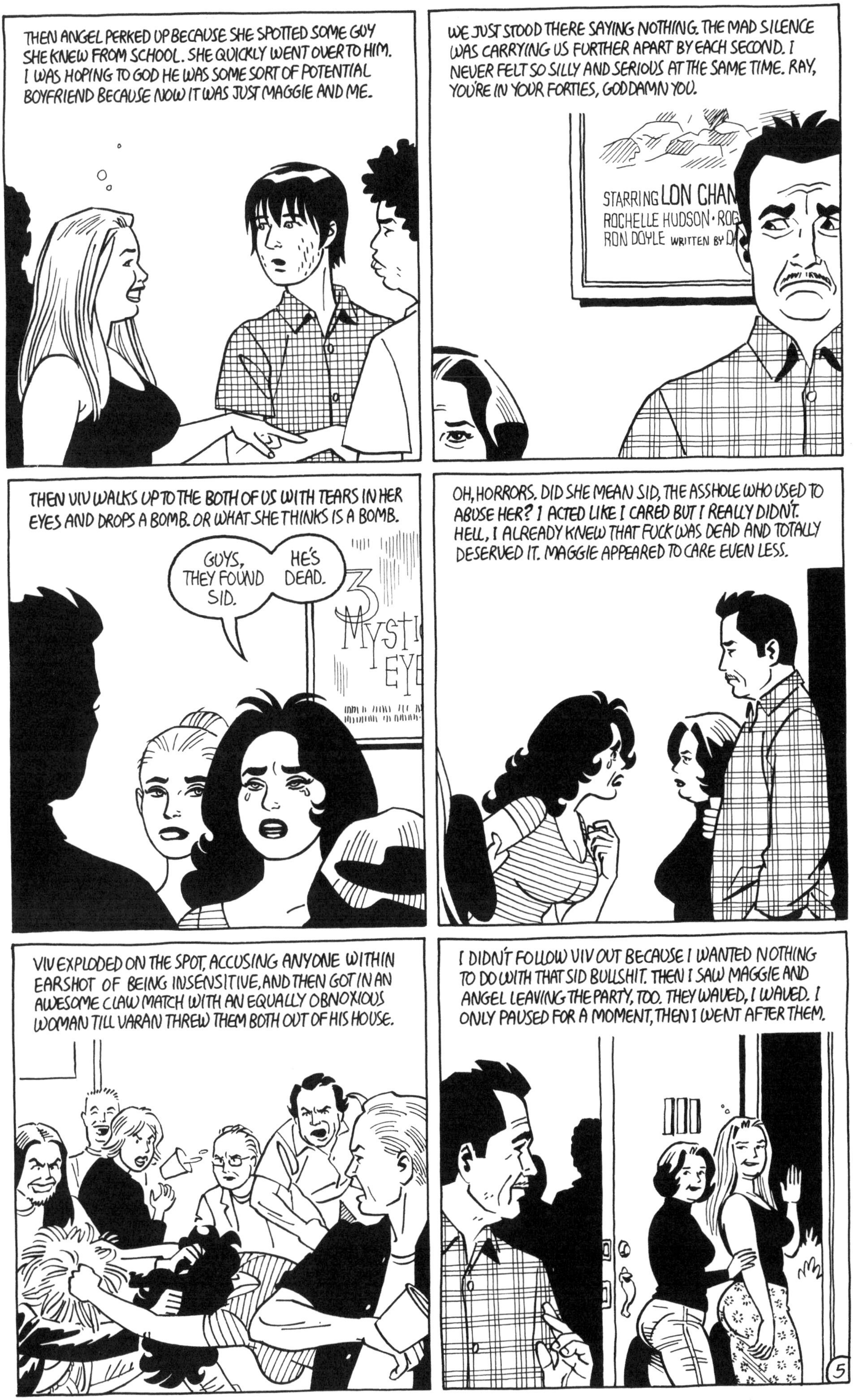
THEN ANGEL PERKED UP BECAUSE SHE SPOTTED SOME GUY SHE KNEW FROM SCHOOL. SHE QUICKLY WENT OVER TO HIM. I WAS HOPING TO GOD HE WAS SOME SORT OF POTENTIAL BOYFRIEND BECAUSE NOW IT WAS JUST MAGGIE AND ME.
WE JUST STOOD THERE SAYING NOTHING. THE MAD SILENCE WAS CARRYING US FURTHER APART BY EACH SECOND. I NEVER FELT SO SILLY AND SERIOUS AT THE SAME TIME. RAY, YOU'RE IN YOUR FORTIES, GODDAMN YOU.
STARRING LON CHAN
ROCHELLE HUDSON · ROG
RON DOYLE WRITTEN BY D
THEN VIV WALKS UP TO THE BOTH OF US WITH TEARS IN HER EYES AND DROPS A BOMB. OR WHAT SHE THINKS IS A BOMB.
GUYS, THEY FOUND SID.
HE'S DEAD.
3 MYSTI EYE
OH, HORRORS. DID SHE MEAN SID, THE ASSHOLE WHO USED TO ABUSE HER? I ACTED LIKE I CARED BUT I REALLY DIDN'T. HELL, I ALREADY KNEW THAT FUCK WAS DEAD AND TOTALLY DESERVED IT. MAGGIE APPEARED TO CARE EVEN LESS.
VIV EXPLODED ON THE SPOT, ACCUSING ANYONE WITHIN EARSHOT OF BEING INSENSITIVE, AND THEN GOT IN AN AWESOME CLAW MATCH WITH AN EQUALLY OBNOXIOUS WOMAN TILL VARAN THREW THEM BOTH OUT OF HIS HOUSE.
I DIDN'T FOLLOW VIV OUT BECAUSE I WANTED NOTHING TO DO WITH THAT SID BULLSHIT. THEN I SAW MAGGIE AND ANGEL LEAVING THE PARTY, TOO. THEY WAVED, I WAVED. I ONLY PAUSED FOR A MOMENT, THEN I WENT AFTER THEM.
5

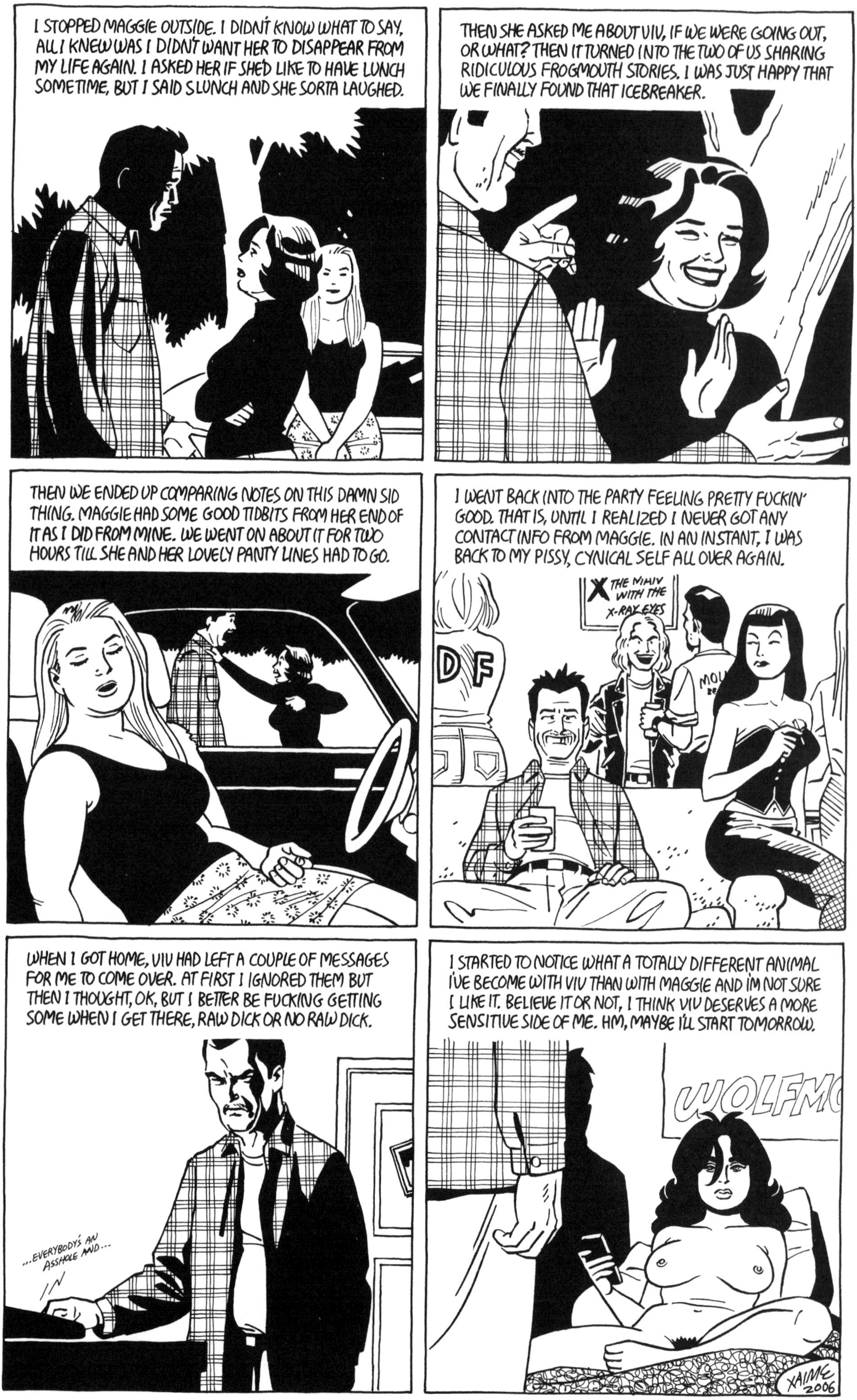
I STOPPED MAGGIE OUTSIDE. I DIDN'T KNOW WHAT TO SAY. ALL I KNEW WAS I DIDN'T WANT HER TO DISAPPEAR FROM MY LIFE AGAIN. I ASKED HER IF SHE'D LIKE TO HAVE LUNCH SOMETIME, BUT I SAID SLUNCH AND SHE SORTA LAUGHED.
THEN SHE ASKED ME ABOUT VIV, IF WE WERE GOING OUT, OR WHAT? THEN IT TURNED INTO THE TWO OF US SHARING RIDICULOUS FROGMOUTH STORIES. I WAS JUST HAPPY THAT WE FINALLY FOUND THAT ICEBREAKER.
THEN WE ENDED UP COMPARING NOTES ON THIS DAMN SID THING. MAGGIE HAD SOME GOOD TIDBITS FROM HER END OF IT AS I DID FROM MINE. WE WENT ON ABOUT IT FOR TWO HOURS TILL SHE AND HER LOVELY PANTY LINES HAD TO GO.
I WENT BACK INTO THE PARTY FEELING PRETTY FUCKIN' GOOD. THAT IS, UNTIL I REALIZED I NEVER GOT ANY CONTACT INFO FROM MAGGIE. IN AN INSTANT, I WAS BACK TO MY PISSY, CYNICAL SELF ALL OVER AGAIN.
X THE MAN WITH THE X-RAY EYES
D F
WHEN I GOT HOME, VIV HAD LEFT A COUPLE OF MESSAGES FOR ME TO COME OVER. AT FIRST I IGNORED THEM BUT THEN I THOUGHT, OK, BUT I BETTER BE FUCKING GETTING SOME WHEN I GET THERE, RAW DICK OR NO RAW DICK.
...EVERYBODY'S AN ASSHOLE AND...
I STARTED TO NOTICE WHAT A TOTALLY DIFFERENT ANIMAL I'VE BECOME WITH VIV THAN WITH MAGGIE AND I'M NOT SURE I LIKE IT. BELIEVE IT OR NOT, I THINK VIV DESERVES A MORE SENSITIVE SIDE OF ME. HM, MAYBE I'LL START TOMORROW.
WOLFMC
XAIME 2006

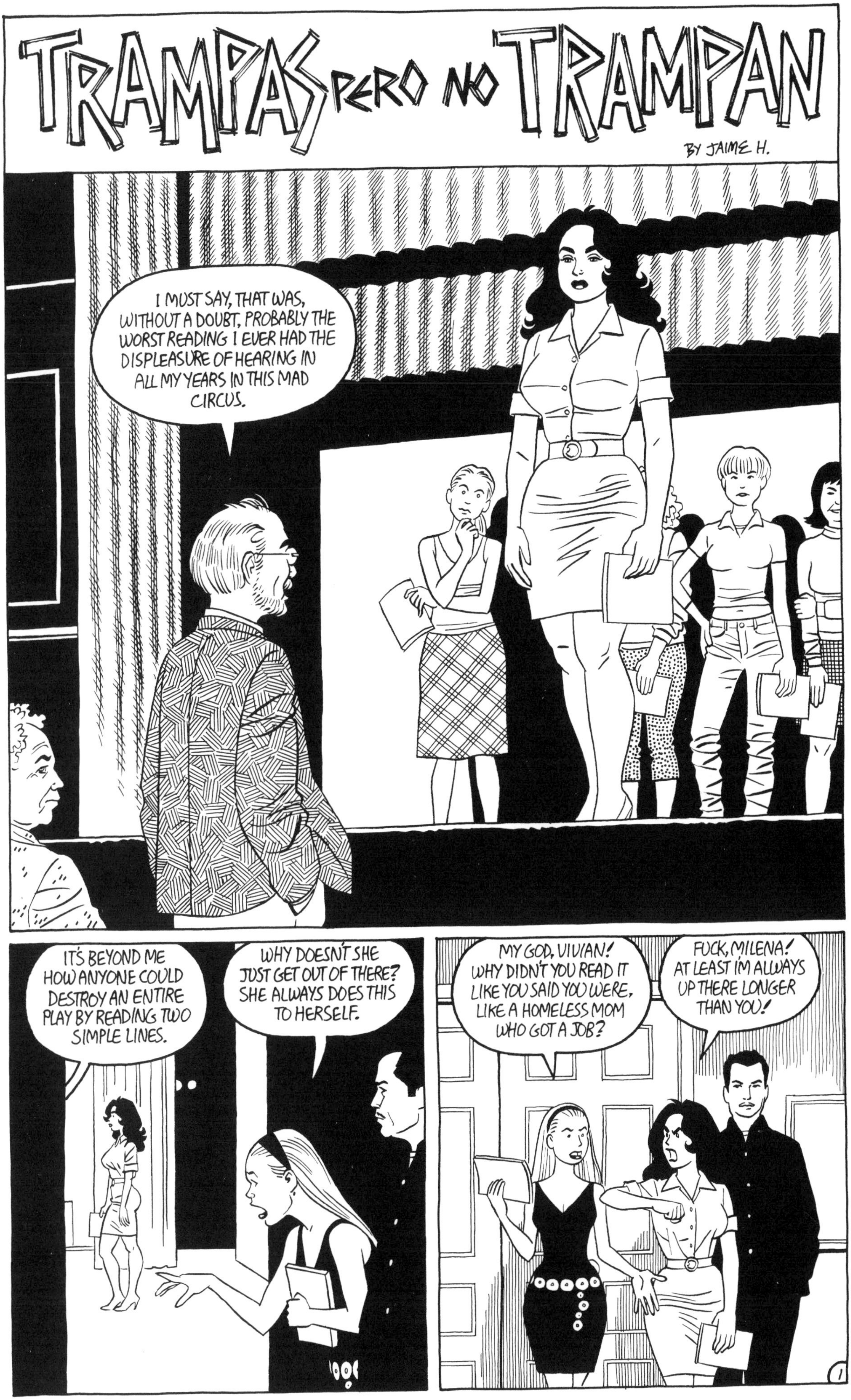
TRAMPAS PERO NO TRAMPAN
BY JAIME H.
I MUST SAY, THAT WAS, WITHOUT A DOUBT, PROBABLY THE WORST READING I EVER HAD THE DISPLEASURE OF HEARING IN ALL MY YEARS IN THIS MAD CIRCUS.
IT'S BEYOND ME HOW ANYONE COULD DESTROY AN ENTIRE PLAY BY READING TWO SIMPLE LINES.
WHY DOESN'T SHE JUST GET OUT OF THERE? SHE ALWAYS DOES THIS TO HERSELF.
MY GOD, VIVIAN! WHY DIDN'T YOU READ IT LIKE YOU SAID YOU WERE, LIKE A HOMELESS MOM WHO GOT A JOB?
FUCK, MILENA! AT LEAST I'M ALWAYS UP THERE LONGER THAN YOU!
1

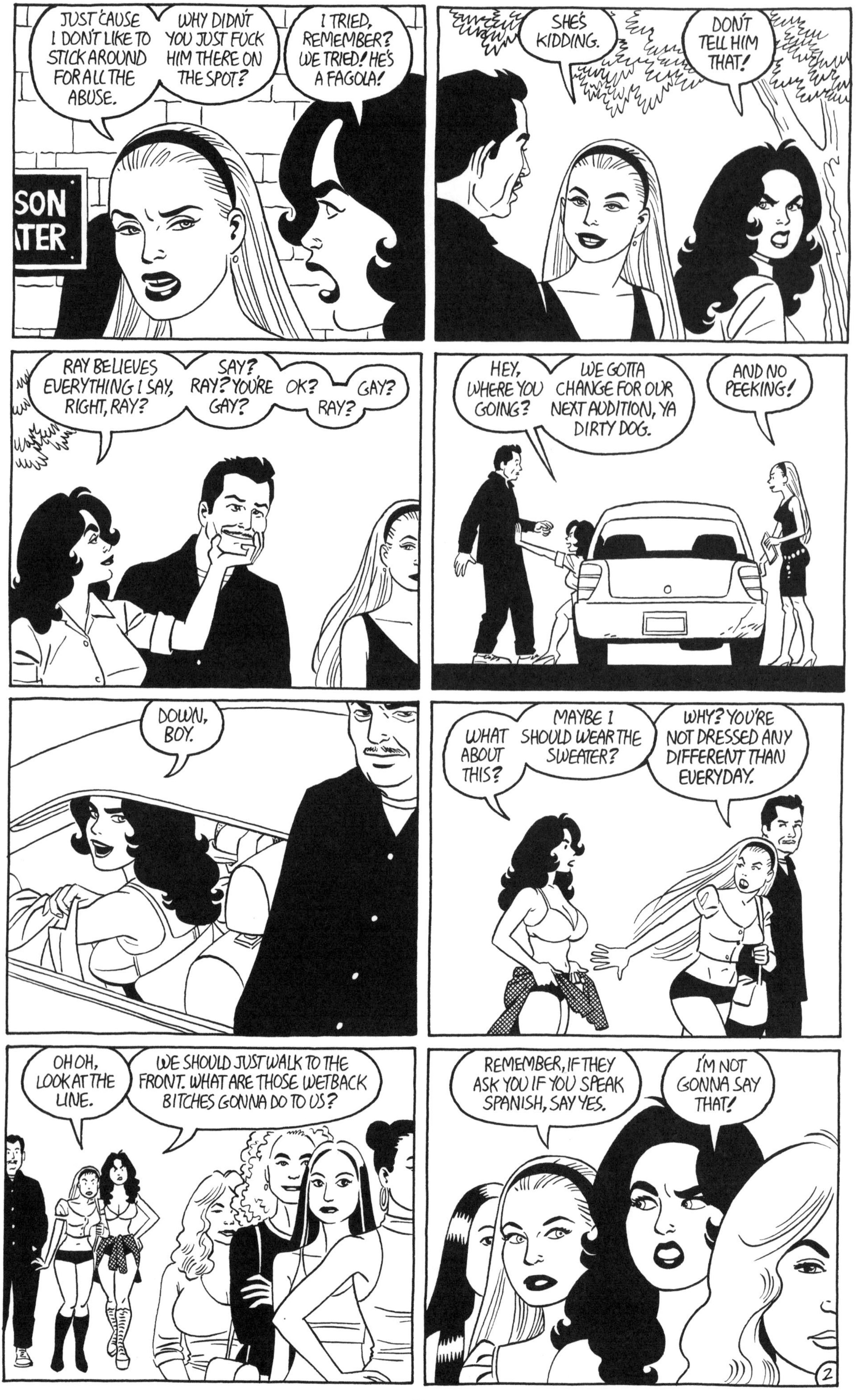
JUST 'CAUSE I DON'T LIKE TO STICK AROUND FOR ALL THE ABUSE.
WHY DIDN'T YOU JUST FUCK HIM THERE ON THE SPOT?
I TRIED, REMEMBER? WE TRIED! HE'S A FAGOLA!
SON
TER
SHE'S KIDDING.
DON'T TELL HIM THAT!
RAY BELIEVES EVERYTHING I SAY, RIGHT, RAY?
SAY? RAY? YOU'RE GAY?
OK? RAY?
GAY?
HEY, WHERE YOU GOING?
WE GOTTA CHANGE FOR OUR NEXT AUDITION, YA DIRTY DOG.
AND NO PEEKING!
DOWN, BOY.
WHAT ABOUT THIS?
MAYBE I SHOULD WEAR THE SWEATER?
WHY? YOU'RE NOT DRESSED ANY DIFFERENT THAN EVERYDAY.
OH OH, LOOK AT THE LINE.
WE SHOULD JUST WALK TO THE FRONT. WHAT ARE THOSE WETBACK BITCHES GONNA DO TO US?
REMEMBER, IF THEY ASK YOU IF YOU SPEAK SPANISH, SAY YES.
I'M NOT GONNA SAY THAT!
2

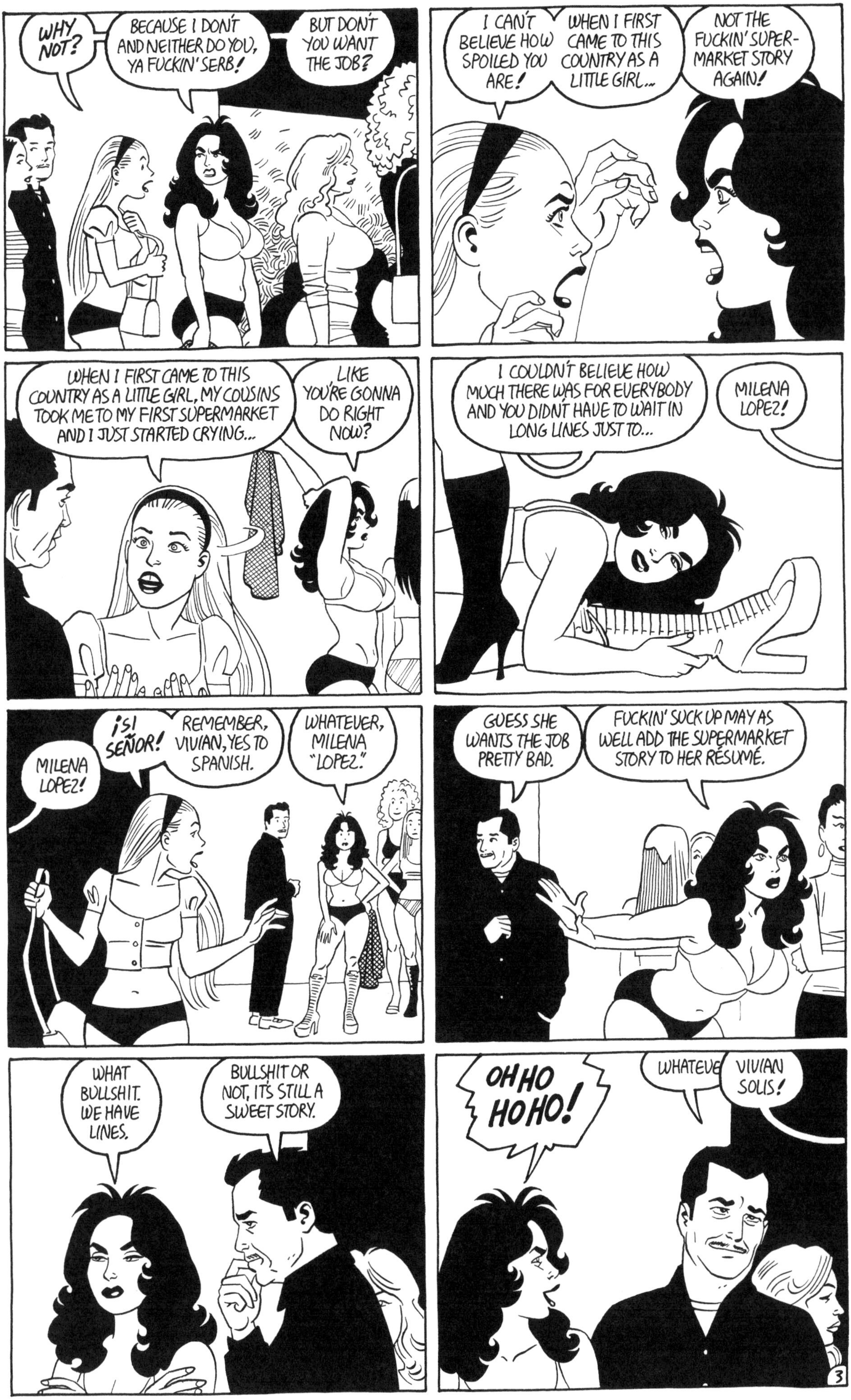
WHY NOT?
BECAUSE I DON'T AND NEITHER DO YOU, YA FUCKIN' SERB!
BUT DON'T YOU WANT THE JOB?
I CAN'T BELIEVE HOW SPOILED YOU ARE!
WHEN I FIRST CAME TO THIS COUNTRY AS A LITTLE GIRL...
NOT THE FUCKIN' SUPER-MARKET STORY AGAIN!
WHEN I FIRST CAME TO THIS COUNTRY AS A LITTLE GIRL, MY COUSINS TOOK ME TO MY FIRST SUPERMARKET AND I JUST STARTED CRYING...
LIKE YOU'RE GONNA DO RIGHT NOW?
I COULDN'T BELIEVE HOW MUCH THERE WAS FOR EVERYBODY AND YOU DIDN'T HAVE TO WAIT IN LONG LINES JUST TO...
MILENA LOPEZ!
MILENA LOPEZ!
¡SI SEÑOR!
REMEMBER, VIVIAN, YES TO SPANISH.
WHATEVER, MILENA "LOPEZ."
GUESS SHE WANTS THE JOB PRETTY BAD.
FUCKIN' SUCK UP MAY AS WELL ADD THE SUPERMARKET STORY TO HER RÉSUMÉ.
WHAT BULLSHIT. WE HAVE LINES.
BULLSHIT OR NOT, IT'S STILL A SWEET STORY.
OH HO HO HO!
WHATEVE
VIVIAN SOLIS!
3

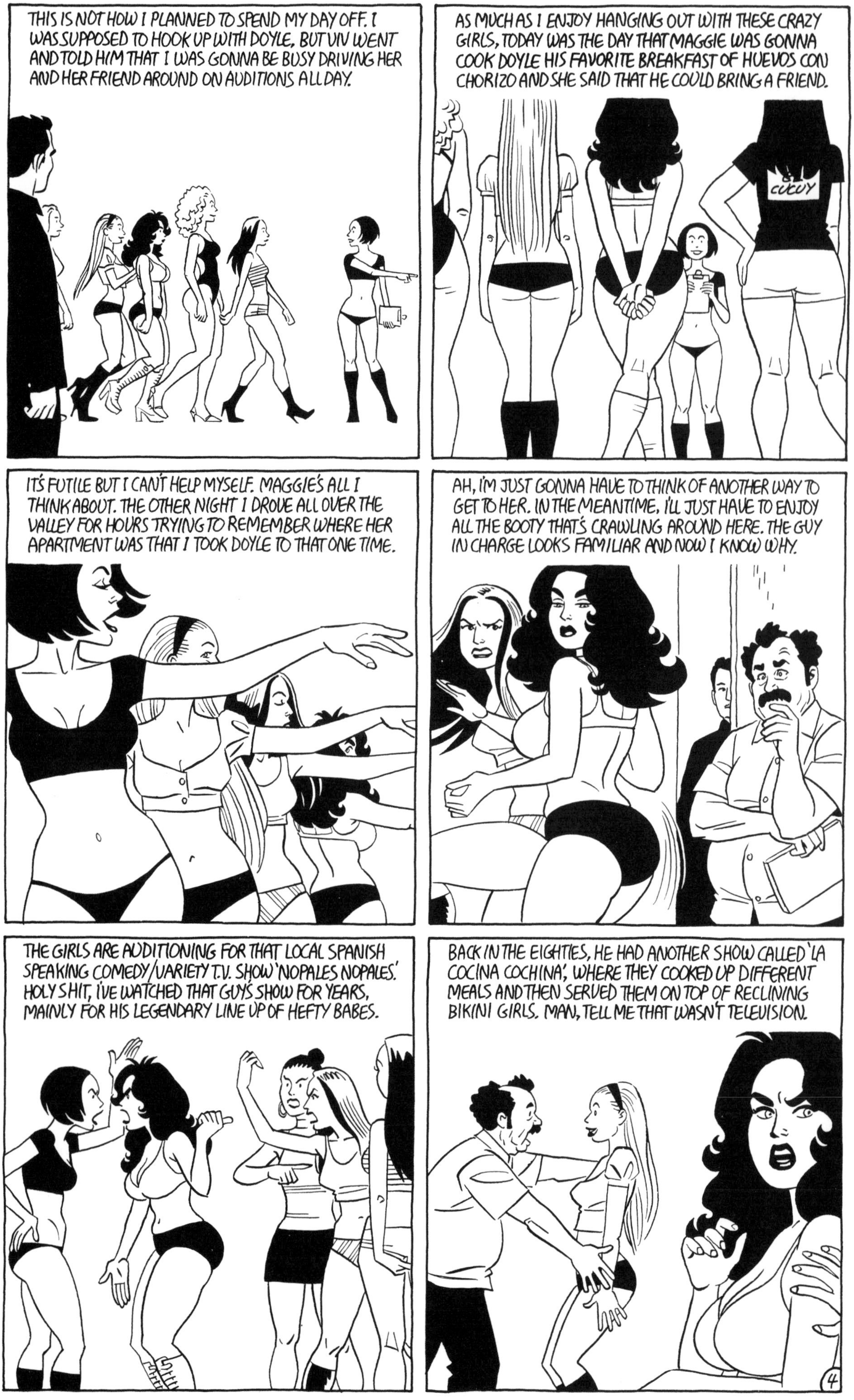
THIS IS NOT HOW I PLANNED TO SPEND MY DAY OFF. I WAS SUPPOSED TO HOOK UP WITH DOYLE, BUT VIV WENT AND TOLD HIM THAT I WAS GONNA BE BUSY DRIVING HER AND HER FRIEND AROUND ON AUDITIONS ALL DAY.
AS MUCH AS I ENJOY HANGING OUT WITH THESE CRAZY GIRLS, TODAY WAS THE DAY THAT MAGGIE WAS GONNA COOK DOYLE HIS FAVORITE BREAKFAST OF HUEVOS CON CHORIZO AND SHE SAID THAT HE COULD BRING A FRIEND.
CUCUY
IT'S FUTILE BUT I CAN'T HELP MYSELF. MAGGIE'S ALL I THINK ABOUT. THE OTHER NIGHT I DROVE ALL OVER THE VALLEY FOR HOURS TRYING TO REMEMBER WHERE HER APARTMENT WAS THAT I TOOK DOYLE TO THAT ONE TIME.
AH, I'M JUST GONNA HAVE TO THINK OF ANOTHER WAY TO GET TO HER. IN THE MEANTIME, I'LL JUST HAVE TO ENJOY ALL THE BOOTY THAT'S CRAWLING AROUND HERE. THE GUY IN CHARGE LOOKS FAMILIAR AND NOW I KNOW WHY.
THE GIRLS ARE AUDITIONING FOR THAT LOCAL SPANISH SPEAKING COMEDY/VARIETY T.V. SHOW 'NOPALES NOPALES.' HOLY SHIT, I'VE WATCHED THAT GUY'S SHOW FOR YEARS, MAINLY FOR HIS LEGENDARY LINE UP OF HEFTY BABES.
BACK IN THE EIGHTIES, HE HAD ANOTHER SHOW CALLED 'LA COCINA COCHINA', WHERE THEY COOKED UP DIFFERENT MEALS AND THEN SERVED THEM ON TOP OF RECLINING BIKINI GIRLS. MAN, TELL ME THAT WASN'T TELEVISION.
4

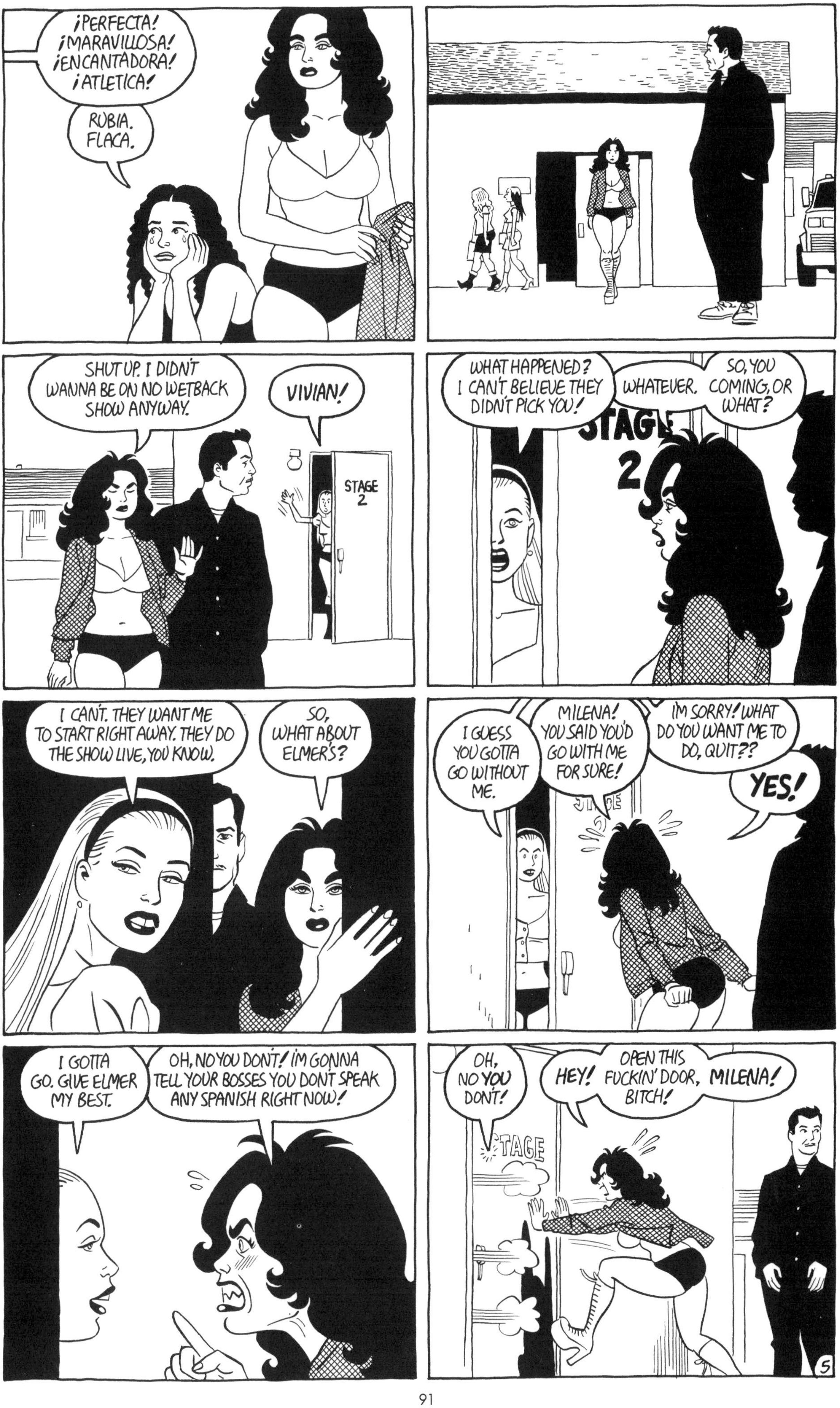
¡PERFECTA! ¡MARAVILLOSA! ¡ENCANTADORA! ¡ATLETICA!
RUBIA. FLACA.
SHUT UP. I DIDN'T WANNA BE ON NO WETBACK SHOW ANYWAY.
VIVIAN!
STAGE 2
WHAT HAPPENED? I CAN'T BELIEVE THEY DIDN'T PICK YOU!
WHATEVER.
SO, YOU COMING, OR WHAT?
STAGE 2
I CAN'T. THEY WANT ME TO START RIGHT AWAY. THEY DO THE SHOW LIVE, YOU KNOW.
SO, WHAT ABOUT ELMER'S?
I GUESS YOU GOTTA GO WITHOUT ME.
MILENA! YOU SAID YOU'D GO WITH ME FOR SURE!
I'M SORRY! WHAT DO YOU WANT ME TO DO, QUIT??
YES!
I GOTTA GO. GIVE ELMER MY BEST.
OH, NO YOU DON'T! I'M GONNA TELL YOUR BOSSES YOU DON'T SPEAK ANY SPANISH RIGHT NOW!
OH, NO YOU DON'T!
HEY! OPEN THIS FUCKIN' DOOR, BITCH! MILENA!
STAGE
5

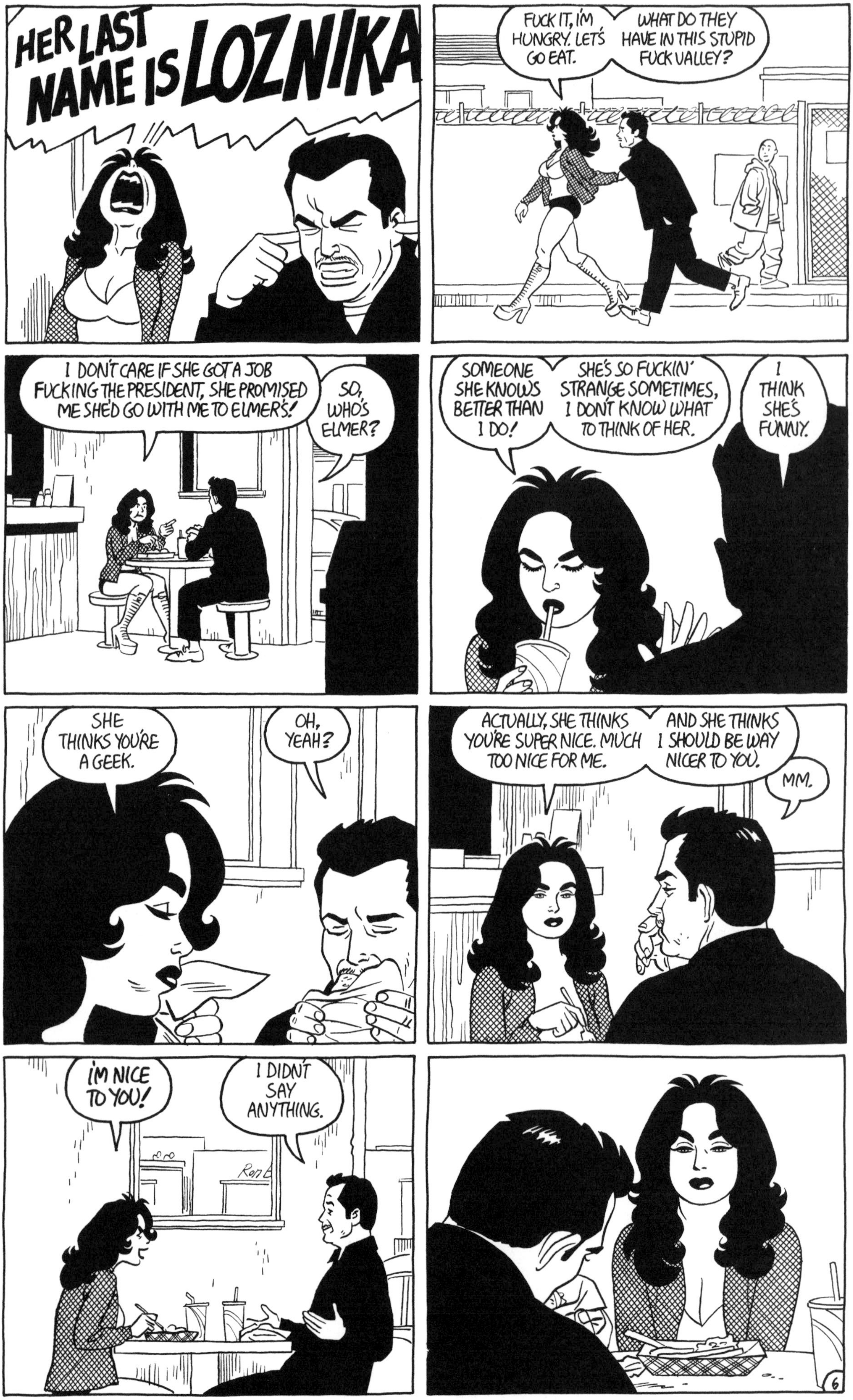
HER LAST NAME IS LOZNIKA
FUCK IT, I'M HUNGRY. LET'S GO EAT.
WHAT DO THEY HAVE IN THIS STUPID FUCK VALLEY?
I DON'T CARE IF SHE GOT A JOB FUCKING THE PRESIDENT, SHE PROMISED ME SHE'D GO WITH ME TO ELMER'S!
SO, WHO'S ELMER?
SOMEONE SHE KNOWS BETTER THAN I DO!
SHE'S SO FUCKIN' STRANGE SOMETIMES, I DON'T KNOW WHAT TO THINK OF HER.
I THINK SHE'S FUNNY.
SHE THINKS YOU'RE A GEEK.
OH, YEAH?
ACTUALLY, SHE THINKS YOU'RE SUPER NICE. MUCH TOO NICE FOR ME.
AND SHE THINKS I SHOULD BE WAY NICER TO YOU.
MM.
I'M NICE TO YOU!
I DIDN'T SAY ANYTHING.
6

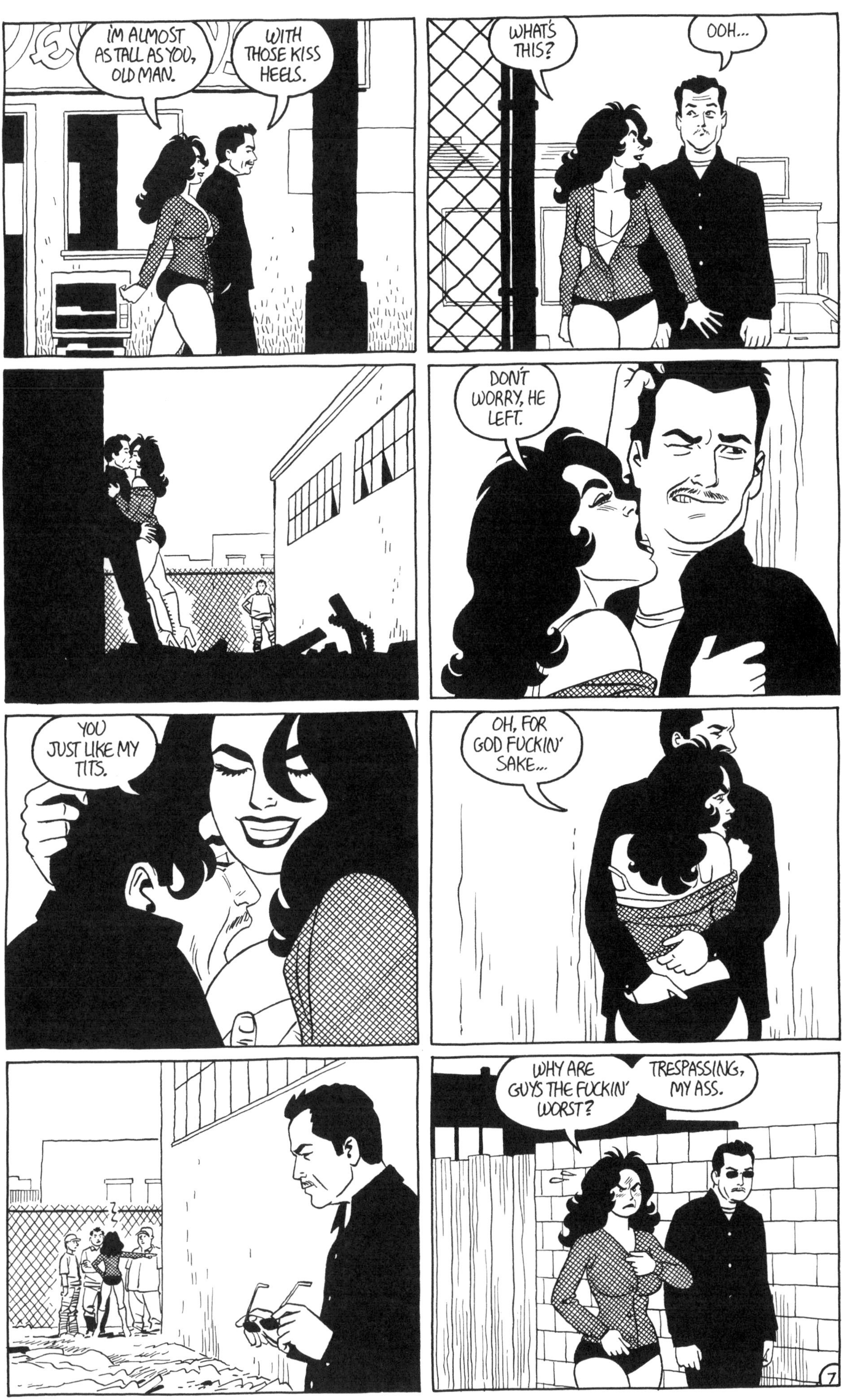

IM ALMOST AS TALL AS YOU, OLD MAN.
WITH THOSE KISS HEELS.
WHAT'S THIS?
OOH...
DON'T WORRY, HE LEFT.
YOU JUST LIKE MY TITS.
OH, FOR GOD FUCKIN' SAKE...
WHY ARE GUYS THE FUCKIN' WORST?
TRESPASSING, MY ASS.
7

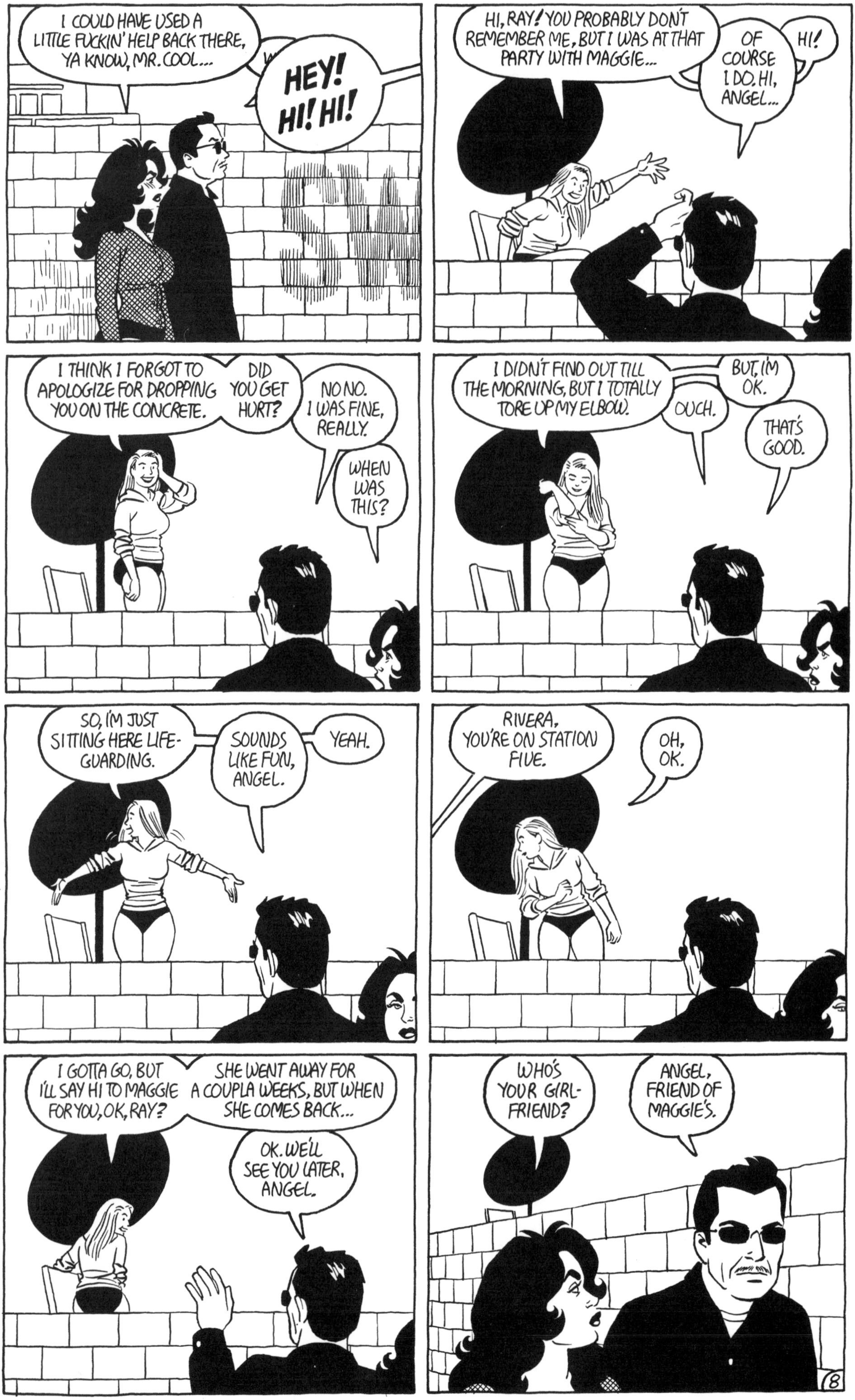
I COULD HAVE USED A LITTLE FUCKIN' HELP BACK THERE, YA KNOW, MR. COOL...
HEY! HI! HI!
HI, RAY! YOU PROBABLY DON'T REMEMBER ME, BUT I WAS AT THAT PARTY WITH MAGGIE...
OF COURSE I DO. HI, ANGEL...
HI!
I THINK I FORGOT TO APOLOGIZE FOR DROPPING YOU ON THE CONCRETE.
DID YOU GET HURT?
NO NO. I WAS FINE, REALLY.
WHEN WAS THIS?
I DIDN'T FIND OUT TILL THE MORNING, BUT I TOTALLY TORE UP MY ELBOW.
BUT, I'M OK.
OUCH.
THAT'S GOOD.
SO, I'M JUST SITTING HERE LIFE-GUARDING.
SOUNDS LIKE FUN, ANGEL.
YEAH.
RIVERA, YOU'RE ON STATION FIVE.
OH, OK.
I GOTTA GO, BUT I'LL SAY HI TO MAGGIE FOR YOU, OK, RAY?
SHE WENT AWAY FOR A COUPLA WEEKS, BUT WHEN SHE COMES BACK...
OK. WE'LL SEE YOU LATER, ANGEL.
WHO'S YOUR GIRL-FRIEND?
ANGEL, FRIEND OF MAGGIE'S.
8

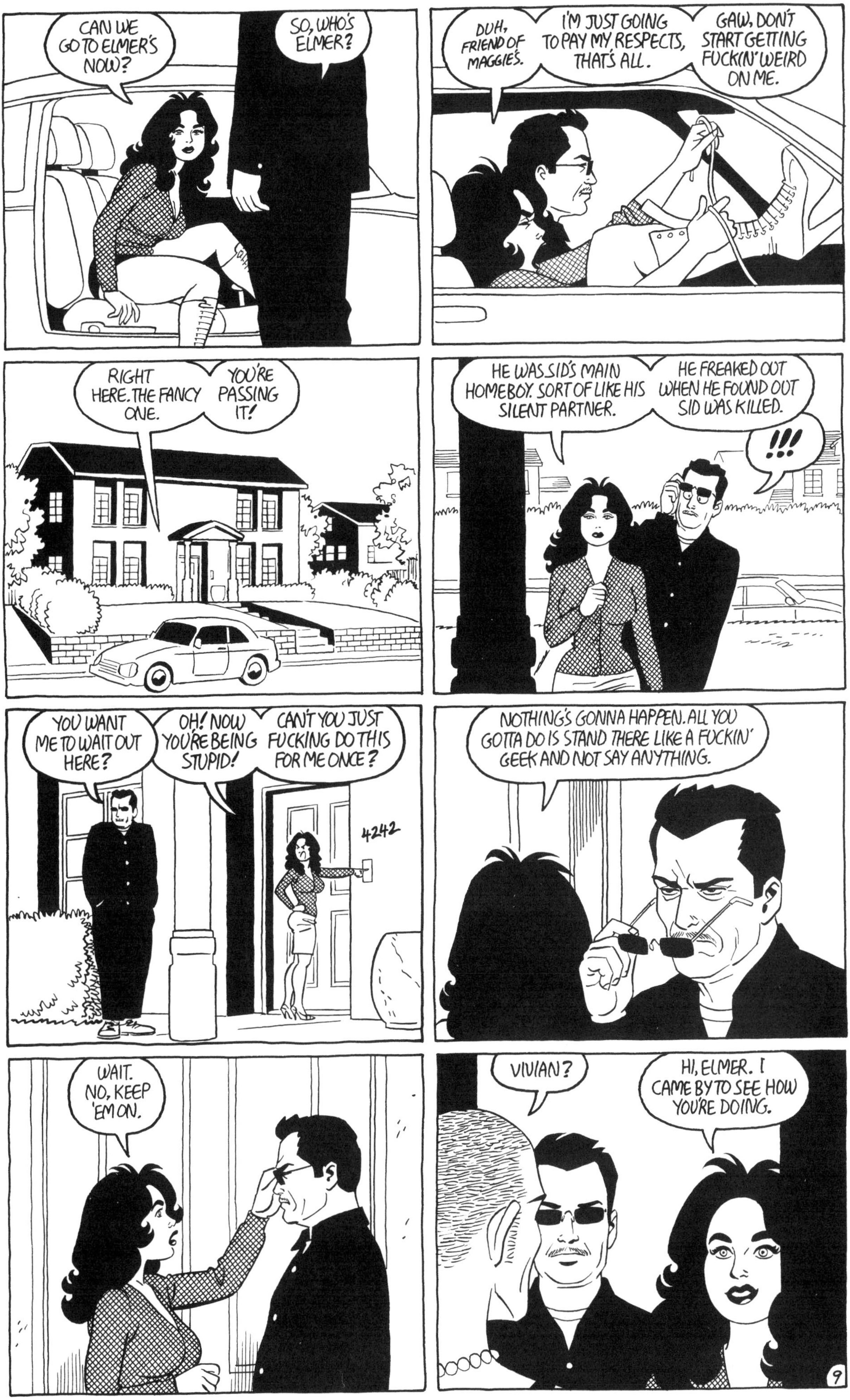
CAN WE GO TO ELMER'S NOW?
SO, WHO'S ELMER?
DUH, FRIEND OF MAGGIE'S.
I'M JUST GOING TO PAY MY RESPECTS, THAT'S ALL.
GAW, DON'T START GETTING FUCKIN' WEIRD ON ME.
RIGHT HERE. THE FANCY ONE.
YOU'RE PASSING IT!
HE WAS SID'S MAIN HOMEBOY. SORT OF LIKE HIS SILENT PARTNER.
HE FREAKED OUT WHEN HE FOUND OUT SID WAS KILLED.
!!!
YOU WANT ME TO WAIT OUT HERE?
OH! NOW YOU'RE BEING STUPID!
CAN'T YOU JUST FUCKING DO THIS FOR ME ONCE?
4242
NOTHING'S GONNA HAPPEN. ALL YOU GOTTA DO IS STAND THERE LIKE A FUCKIN' GEEK AND NOT SAY ANYTHING.
WAIT. NO, KEEP 'EM ON.
VIVIAN?
HI, ELMER. I CAME BY TO SEE HOW YOU'RE DOING.
9

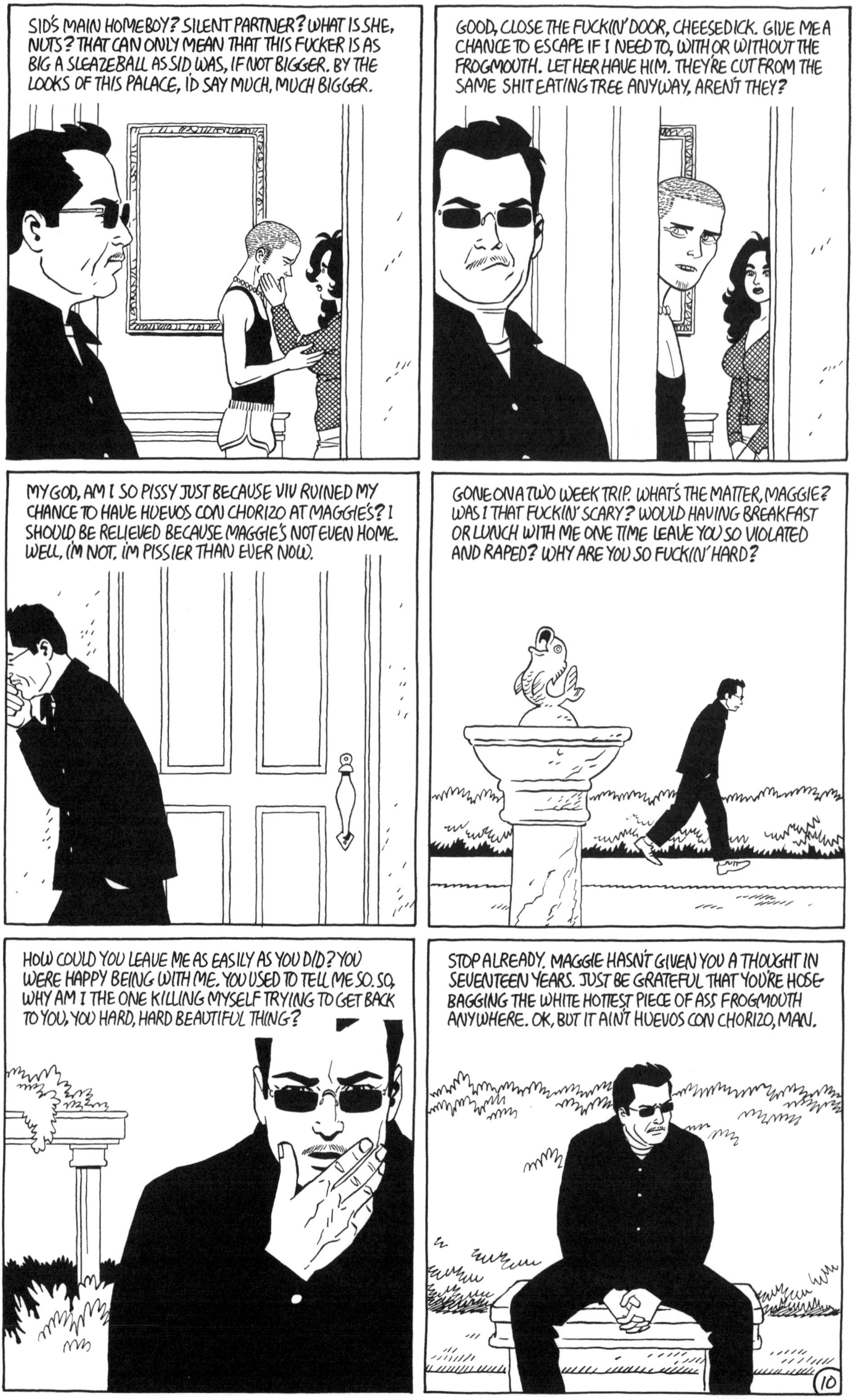
SID'S MAIN HOMEBOY? SILENT PARTNER? WHAT IS SHE, NUTS? THAT CAN ONLY MEAN THAT THIS FUCKER IS AS BIG A SLEAZEBALL AS SID WAS, IF NOT BIGGER. BY THE LOOKS OF THIS PALACE, I'D SAY MUCH, MUCH BIGGER.
GOOD, CLOSE THE FUCKIN' DOOR, CHEESEDICK. GIVE ME A CHANCE TO ESCAPE IF I NEED TO, WITH OR WITHOUT THE FROGMOUTH. LET HER HAVE HIM. THEY'RE CUT FROM THE SAME SHIT EATING TREE ANYWAY, AREN'T THEY?
MY GOD, AM I SO PISSY JUST BECAUSE VIV RUINED MY CHANCE TO HAVE HUEVOS CON CHORIZO AT MAGGIE'S? I SHOULD BE RELIEVED BECAUSE MAGGIE'S NOT EVEN HOME. WELL, I'M NOT. I'M PISSIER THAN EVER NOW.
GONE ON A TWO WEEK TRIP. WHAT'S THE MATTER, MAGGIE? WAS I THAT FUCKIN' SCARY? WOULD HAVING BREAKFAST OR LUNCH WITH ME ONE TIME LEAVE YOU SO VIOLATED AND RAPED? WHY ARE YOU SO FUCKIN' HARD?
HOW COULD YOU LEAVE ME AS EASILY AS YOU DID? YOU WERE HAPPY BEING WITH ME. YOU USED TO TELL ME SO. SO, WHY AM I THE ONE KILLING MYSELF TRYING TO GET BACK TO YOU, YOU HARD, HARD BEAUTIFUL THING?
STOP ALREADY. MAGGIE HASN'T GIVEN YOU A THOUGHT IN SEVENTEEN YEARS. JUST BE GRATEFUL THAT YOU'RE HOSE-BAGGING THE WHITE HOTTEST PIECE OF ASS FROGMOUTH ANYWHERE. OK, BUT IT AIN'T HUEVOS CON CHORIZO, MAN.
10

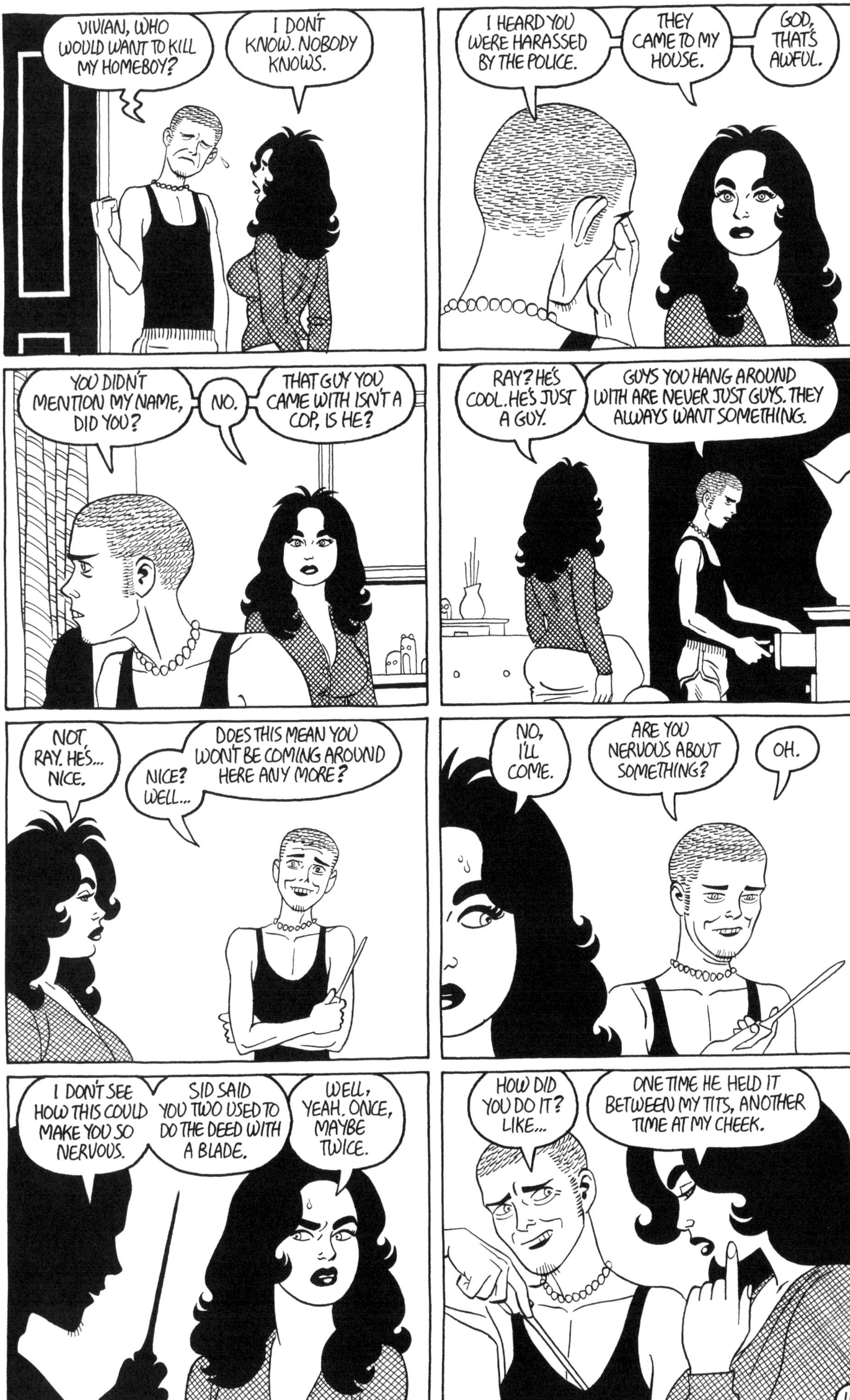
VIVIAN, WHO WOULD WANT TO KILL MY HOMEBOY?
I DON'T KNOW. NOBODY KNOWS.
I HEARD YOU WERE HARASSED BY THE POLICE.
THEY CAME TO MY HOUSE.
GOD, THAT'S AWFUL.
YOU DIDN'T MENTION MY NAME, DID YOU?
NO.
THAT GUY YOU CAME WITH ISN'T A COP, IS HE?
RAY? HE'S COOL. HE'S JUST A GUY.
GUYS YOU HANG AROUND WITH ARE NEVER JUST GUYS. THEY ALWAYS WANT SOMETHING.
NOT, RAY. HE'S... NICE.
NICE? WELL...
DOES THIS MEAN YOU WON'T BE COMING AROUND HERE ANY MORE?
NO, I'LL COME.
ARE YOU NERVOUS ABOUT SOMETHING?
OH.
I DON'T SEE HOW THIS COULD MAKE YOU SO NERVOUS.
SID SAID YOU TWO USED TO DO THE DEED WITH A BLADE.
WELL, YEAH. ONCE, MAYBE TWICE.
HOW DID YOU DO IT? LIKE...
ONE TIME HE HELD IT BETWEEN MY TITS, ANOTHER TIME AT MY CHEEK.
11

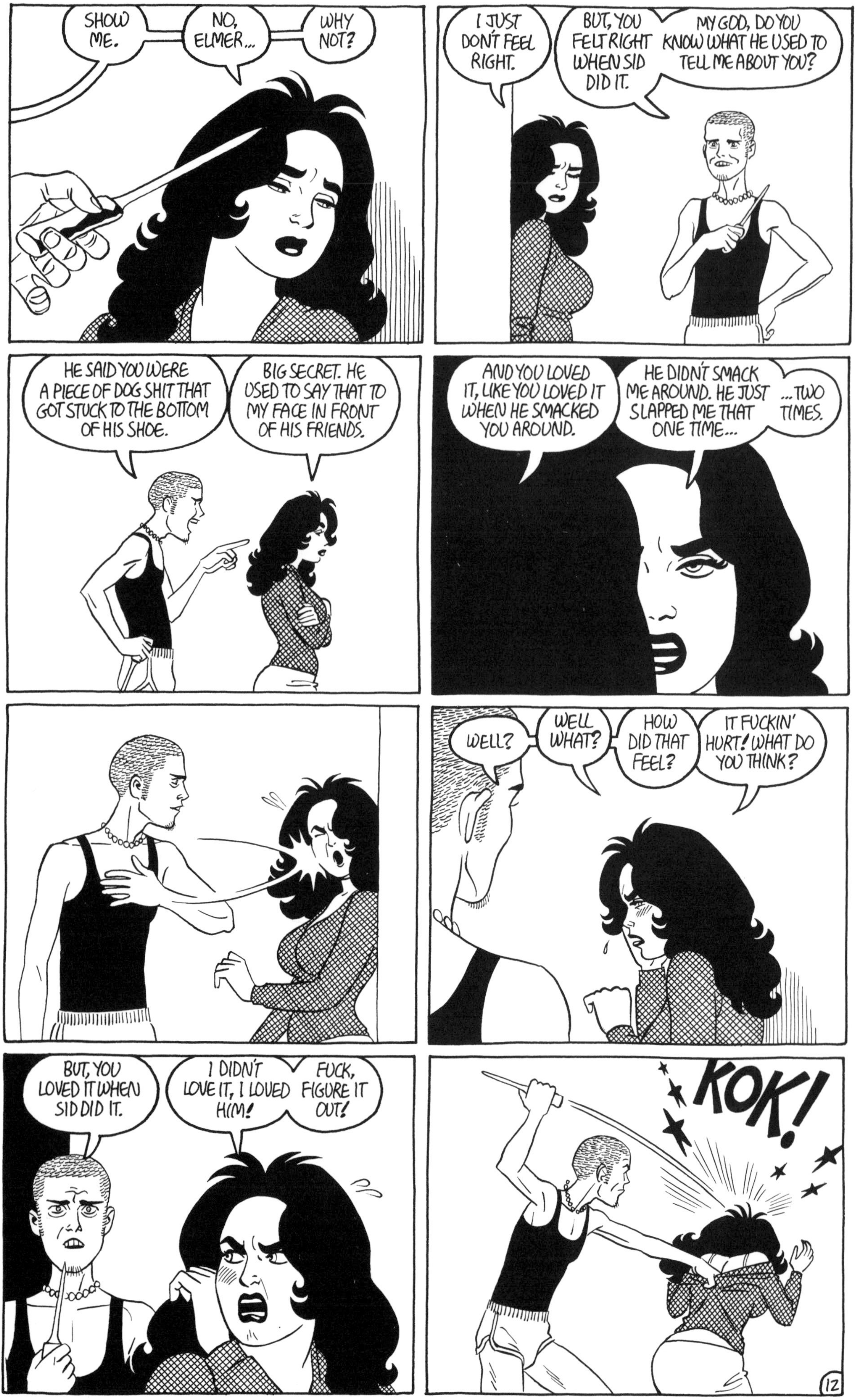
SHOW ME.
NO, ELMER...
WHY NOT?
I JUST DON'T FEEL RIGHT.
BUT, YOU FELT RIGHT WHEN SID DID IT.
MY GOD, DO YOU KNOW WHAT HE USED TO TELL ME ABOUT YOU?
HE SAID YOU WERE A PIECE OF DOG SHIT THAT GOT STUCK TO THE BOTTOM OF HIS SHOE.
BIG SECRET. HE USED TO SAY THAT TO MY FACE IN FRONT OF HIS FRIENDS.
AND YOU LOVED IT, LIKE YOU LOVED IT WHEN HE SMACKED YOU AROUND.
HE DIDN'T SMACK ME AROUND. HE JUST SLAPPED ME THAT ONE TIME...
...TWO TIMES.
WELL?
WELL WHAT?
HOW DID THAT FEEL?
IT FUCKIN' HURT! WHAT DO YOU THINK?
BUT, YOU LOVED IT WHEN SID DID IT.
I DIDN'T LOVE IT, I LOVED HIM!
FUCK, FIGURE IT OUT!
KOK!
12

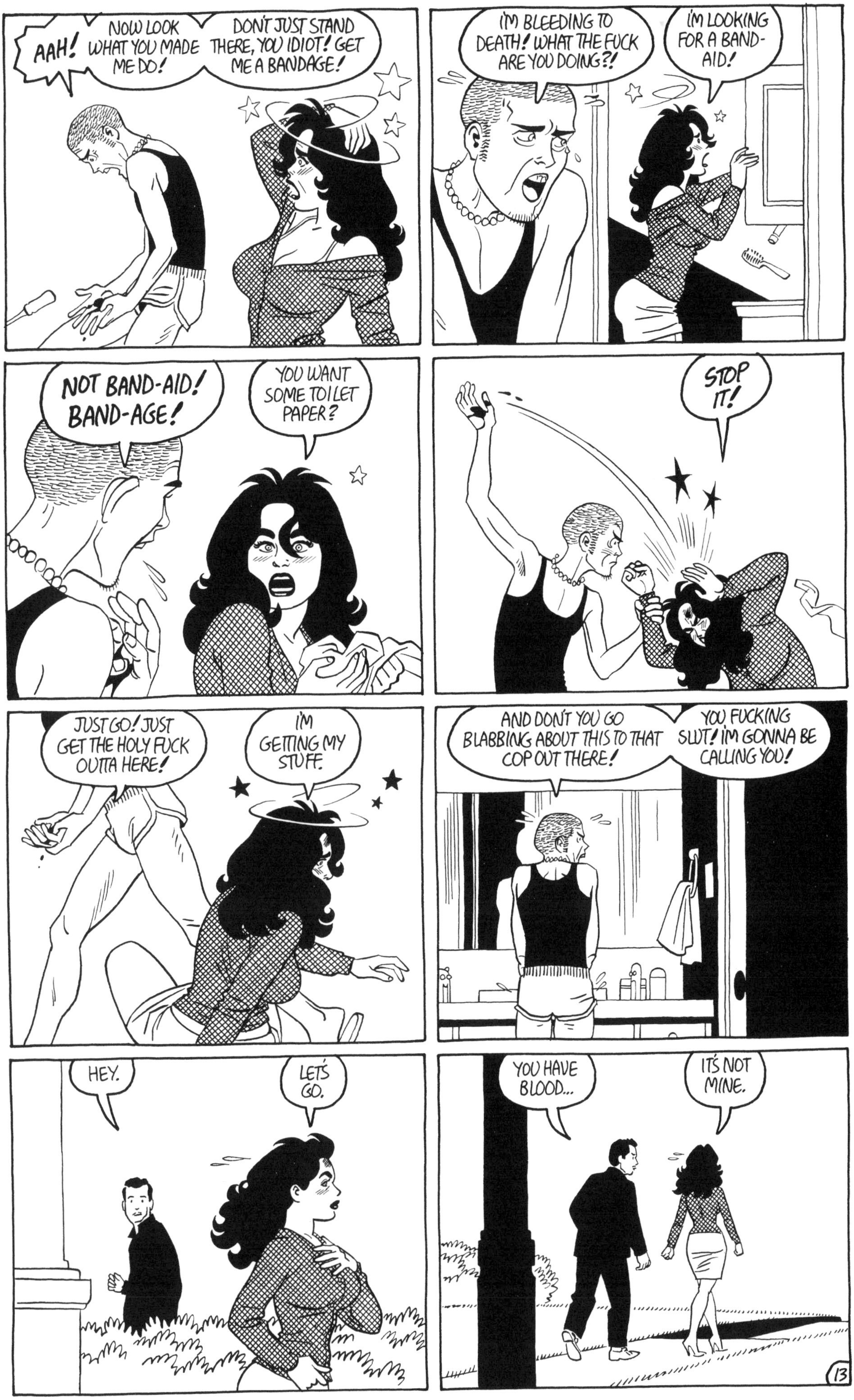
AAH!
NOW LOOK WHAT YOU MADE ME DO!
DON'T JUST STAND THERE, YOU IDIOT! GET ME A BANDAGE!
I'M BLEEDING TO DEATH! WHAT THE FUCK ARE YOU DOING?!
I'M LOOKING FOR A BAND-AID!
NOT BAND-AID! BAND-AGE!
YOU WANT SOME TOILET PAPER?
STOP IT!
JUST GO! JUST GET THE HOLY FUCK OUTTA HERE!
I'M GETTING MY STUFF.
AND DON'T YOU GO BLABBING ABOUT THIS TO THAT COP OUT THERE!
YOU FUCKING SLUT! I'M GONNA BE CALLING YOU!
HEY.
LET'S GO.
YOU HAVE BLOOD...
IT'S NOT MINE.
13

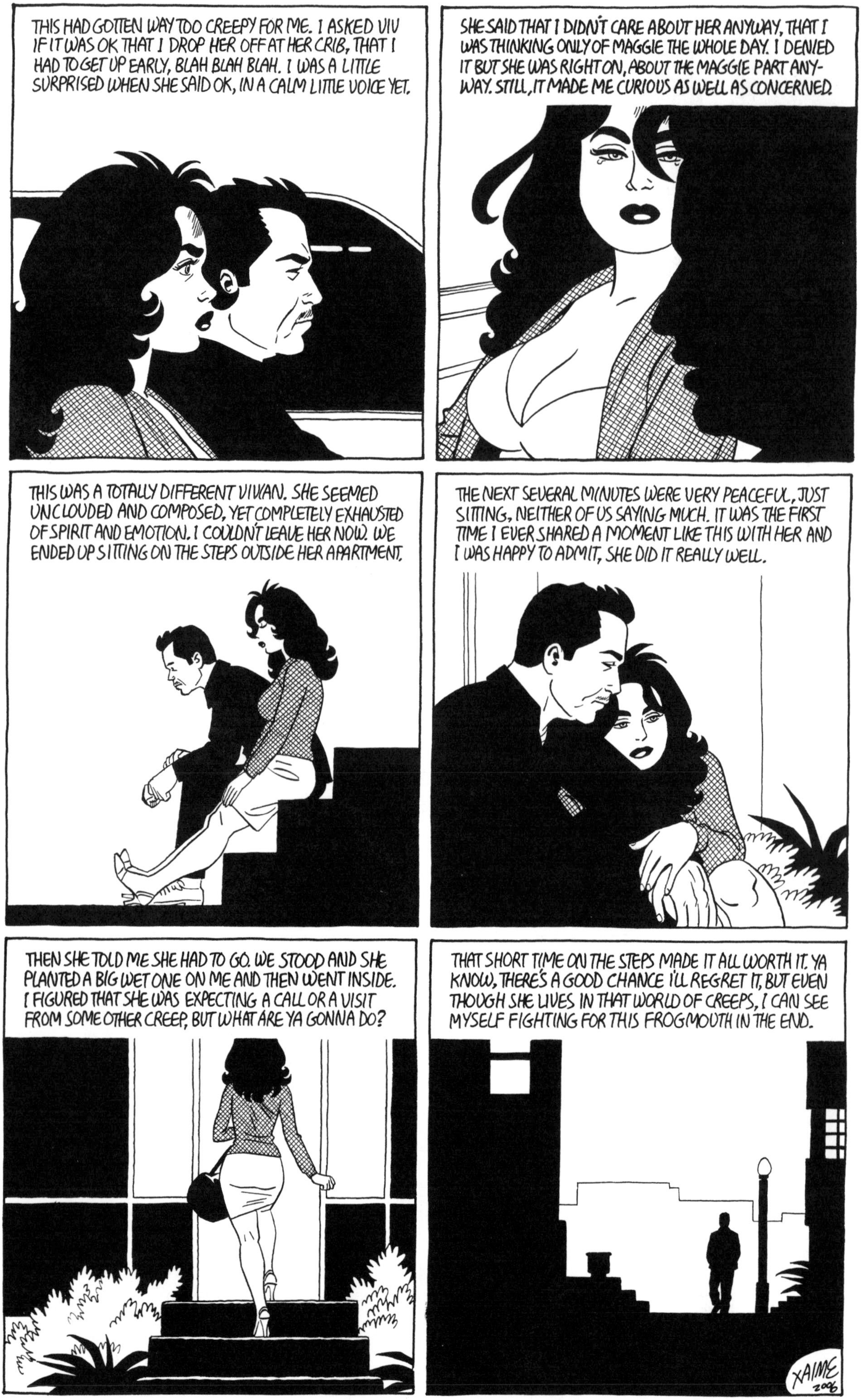
THIS HAD GOTTEN WAY TOO CREEPY FOR ME. I ASKED VIV IF IT WAS OK THAT I DROP HER OFF AT HER CRIB, THAT I HAD TO GET UP EARLY, BLAH BLAH BLAH. I WAS A LITTLE SURPRISED WHEN SHE SAID OK, IN A CALM LITTLE VOICE YET.
SHE SAID THAT I DIDN'T CARE ABOUT HER ANYWAY, THAT I WAS THINKING ONLY OF MAGGIE THE WHOLE DAY. I DENIED IT BUT SHE WAS RIGHT ON, ABOUT THE MAGGIE PART ANY-WAY. STILL, IT MADE ME CURIOUS AS WELL AS CONCERNED.
THIS WAS A TOTALLY DIFFERENT VIVIAN. SHE SEEMED UNCLOUDED AND COMPOSED, YET COMPLETELY EXHAUSTED OF SPIRIT AND EMOTION. I COULDN'T LEAVE HER NOW. WE ENDED UP SITTING ON THE STEPS OUTSIDE HER APARTMENT.
THE NEXT SEVERAL MINUTES WERE VERY PEACEFUL, JUST SITTING, NEITHER OF US SAYING MUCH. IT WAS THE FIRST TIME I EVER SHARED A MOMENT LIKE THIS WITH HER AND I WAS HAPPY TO ADMIT, SHE DID IT REALLY WELL.
THEN SHE TOLD ME SHE HAD TO GO. WE STOOD AND SHE PLANTED A BIG WET ONE ON ME AND THEN WENT INSIDE. I FIGURED THAT SHE WAS EXPECTING A CALL OR A VISIT FROM SOME OTHER CREEP, BUT WHAT ARE YA GONNA DO?
THAT SHORT TIME ON THE STEPS MADE IT ALL WORTH IT. YA KNOW, THERE'S A GOOD CHANCE I'LL REGRET IT, BUT EVEN THOUGH SHE LIVES IN THAT WORLD OF CREEPS, I CAN SEE MYSELF FIGHTING FOR THIS FROGMOUTH IN THE END.
XAIME 2006

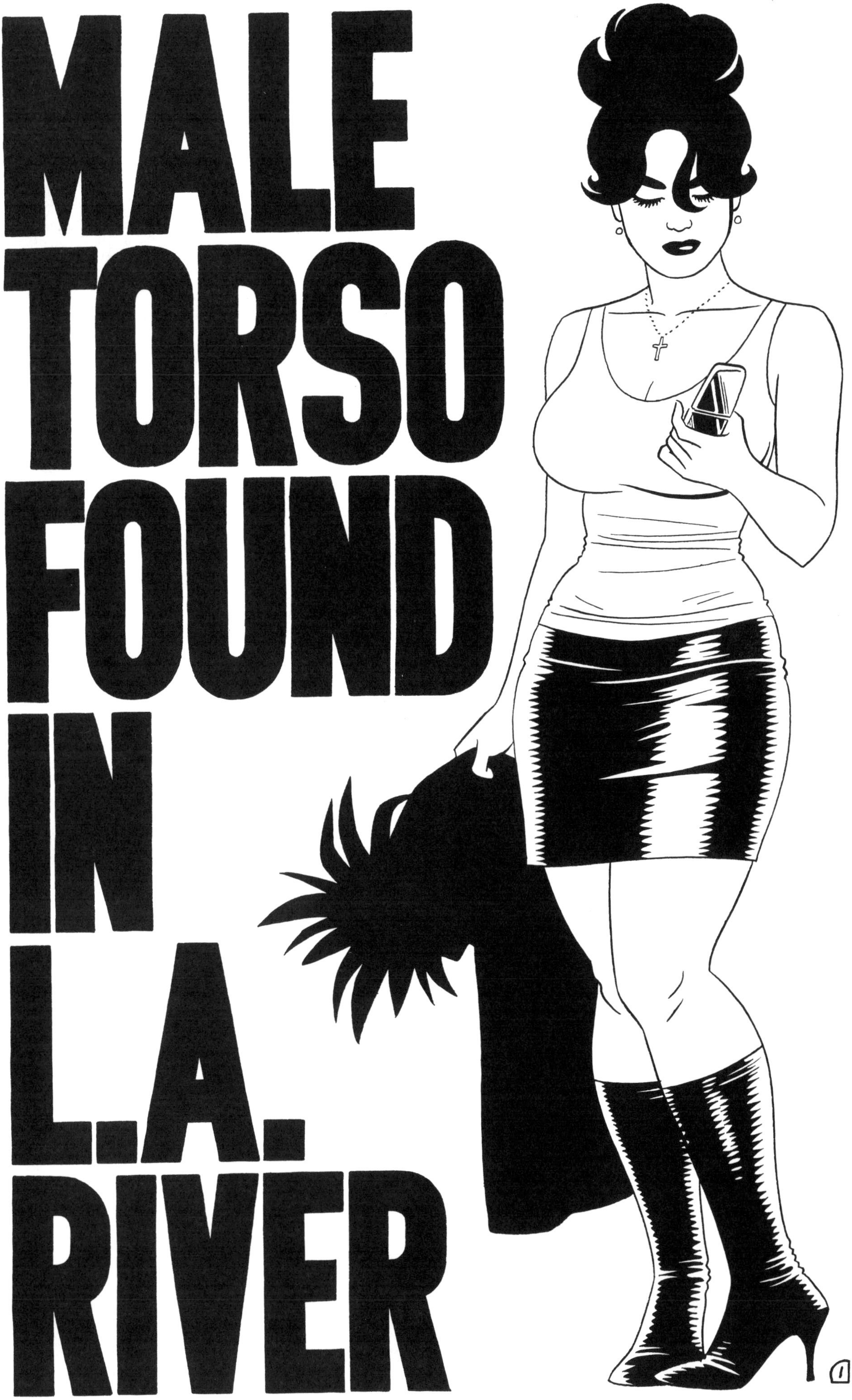
MALE
TORSO
FOUND
IN
L.A.
RIVER

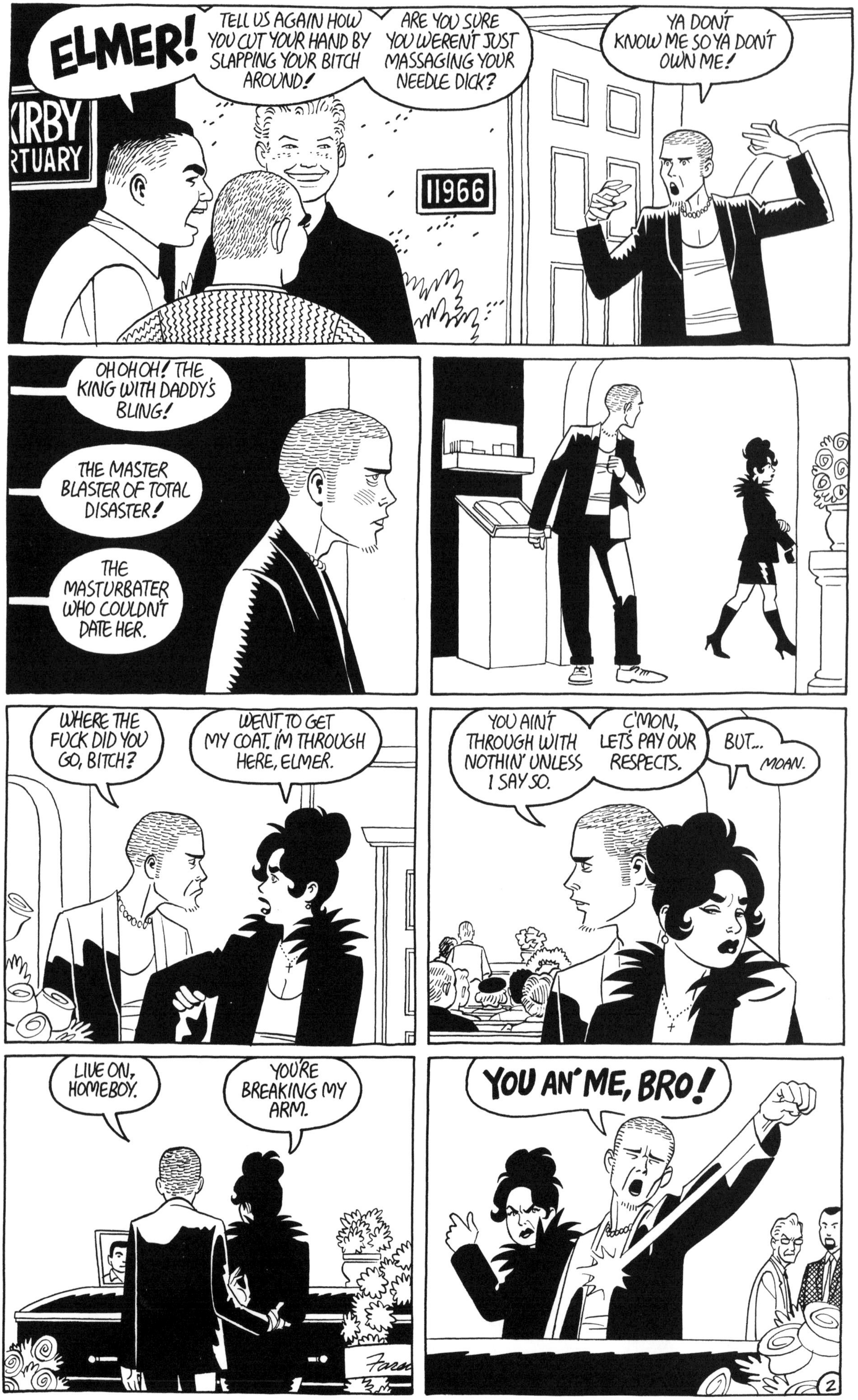
ELMER!
TELL US AGAIN HOW YOU CUT YOUR HAND BY SLAPPING YOUR BITCH AROUND!
ARE YOU SURE YOU WEREN'T JUST MASSAGING YOUR NEEDLE DICK?
KIRBY
RTUARY
11966
YA DON'T KNOW ME SO YA DON'T OWN ME!
OH OH OH! THE KING WITH DADDY'S BLING!
THE MASTER BLASTER OF TOTAL DISASTER!
THE MASTURBATER WHO COULDN'T DATE HER.
WHERE THE FUCK DID YOU GO, BITCH?
WENT TO GET MY COAT. I'M THROUGH HERE, ELMER.
YOU AIN'T THROUGH WITH NOTHIN' UNLESS I SAY SO.
C'MON, LET'S PAY OUR RESPECTS.
BUT... MOAN.
LIVE ON, HOMEBOY.
YOU'RE BREAKING MY ARM.
YOU AN' ME, BRO!
2

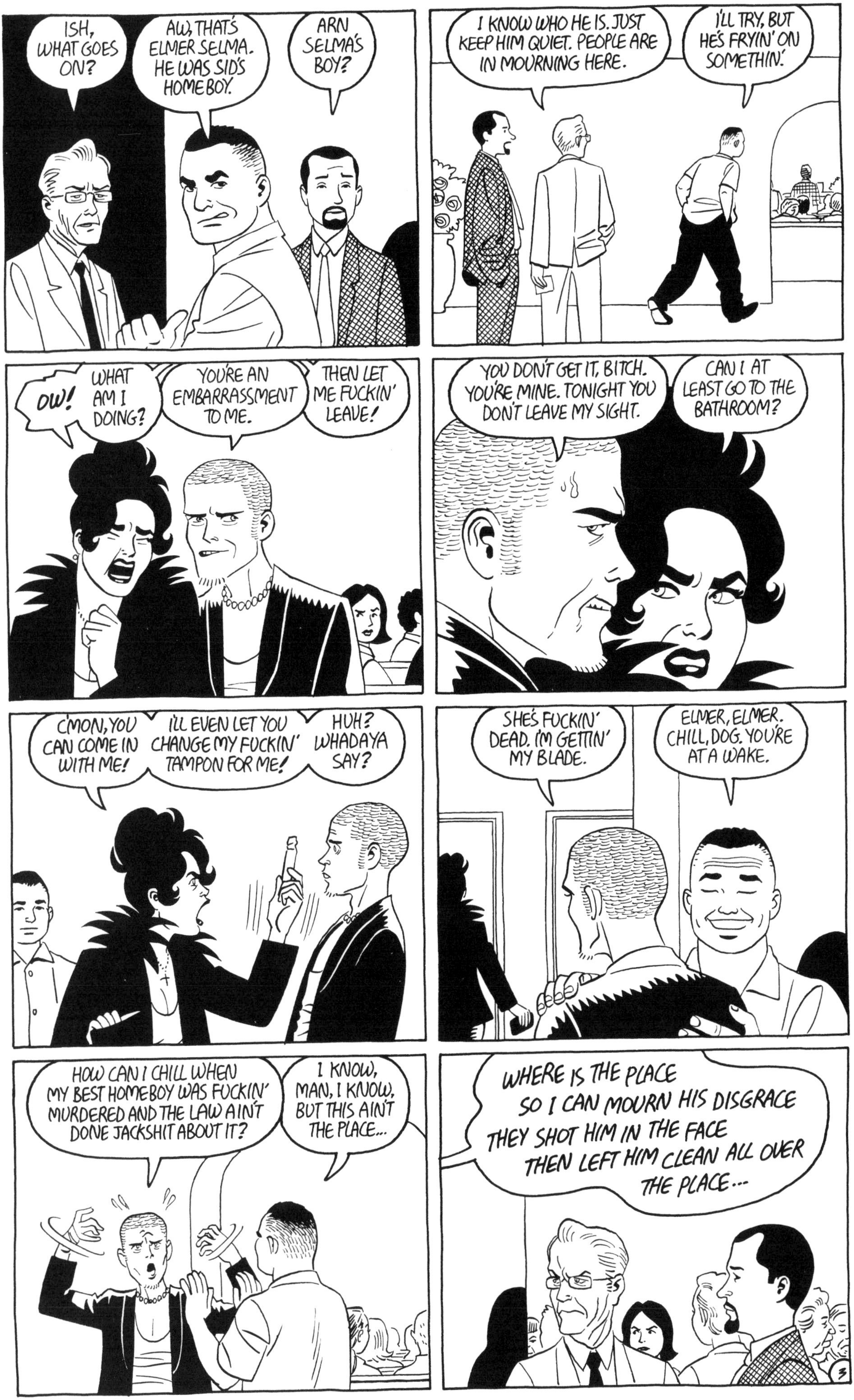
ISH, WHAT GOES ON?
AW, THAT'S ELMER SELMA. HE WAS SID'S HOMEBOY.
ARN SELMA'S BOY?
I KNOW WHO HE IS. JUST KEEP HIM QUIET. PEOPLE ARE IN MOURNING HERE.
I'LL TRY, BUT HE'S FRYIN' ON SOMETHIN'.
OW!
WHAT AM I DOING?
YOU'RE AN EMBARRASSMENT TO ME.
THEN LET ME FUCKIN' LEAVE!
YOU DON'T GET IT, BITCH. YOU'RE MINE. TONIGHT YOU DON'T LEAVE MY SIGHT.
CAN I AT LEAST GO TO THE BATHROOM?
C'MON, YOU CAN COME IN WITH ME!
I'LL EVEN LET YOU CHANGE MY FUCKIN' TAMPON FOR ME!
HUH? WHADAYA SAY?
SHE'S FUCKIN' DEAD. I'M GETTIN' MY BLADE.
ELMER, ELMER. CHILL, DOG. YOU'RE AT A WAKE.
HOW CAN I CHILL WHEN MY BEST HOMEBOY WAS FUCKIN' MURDERED AND THE LAW AIN'T DONE JACKSHIT ABOUT IT?
I KNOW, MAN, I KNOW, BUT THIS AIN'T THE PLACE...
WHERE IS THE PLACE
SO I CAN MOURN HIS DISGRACE
THEY SHOT HIM IN THE FACE
THEN LEFT HIM CLEAN ALL OVER
THE PLACE...
3

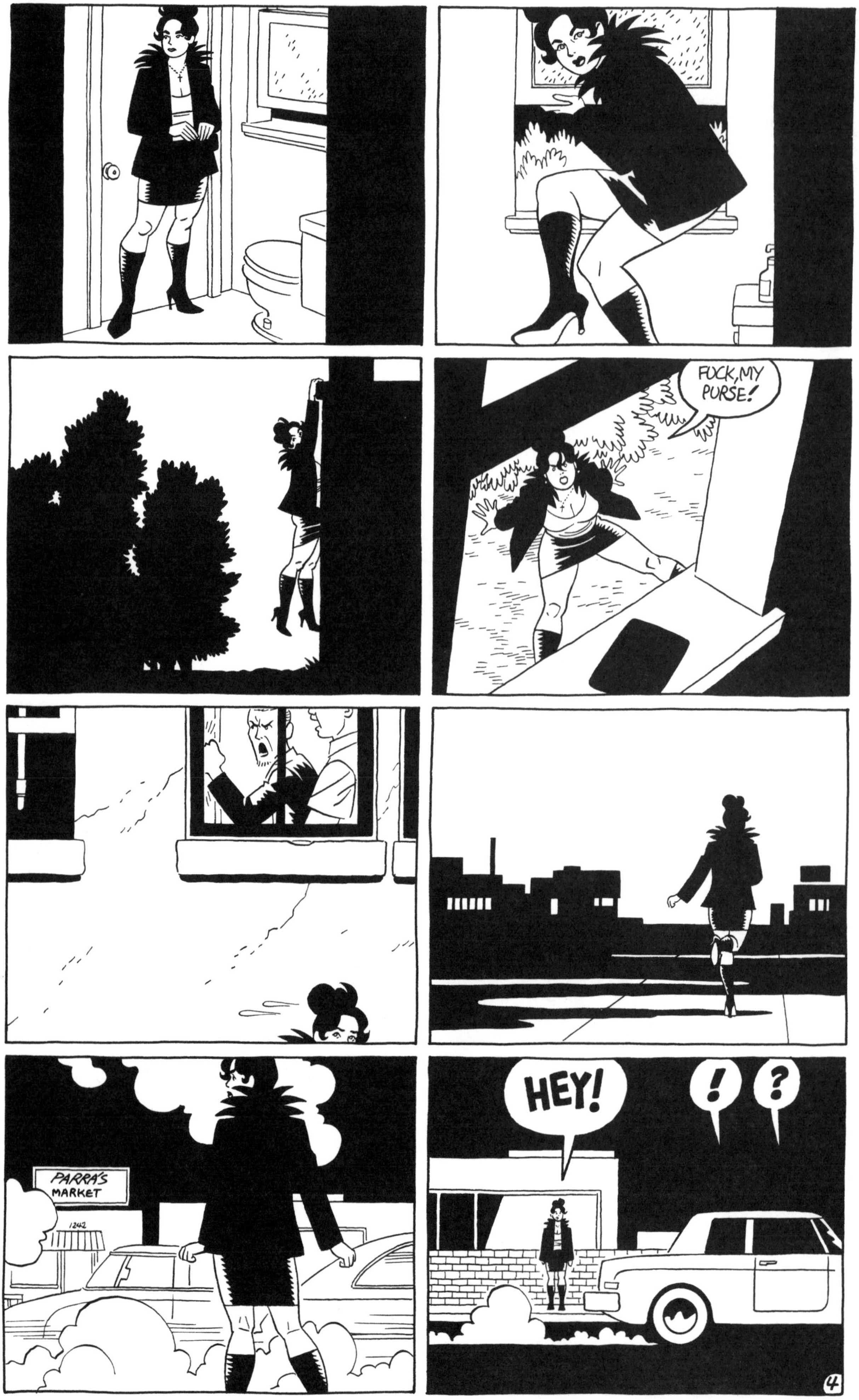
FUCK, MY PURSE!
PARRA'S MARKET
1242
HEY!
!
?

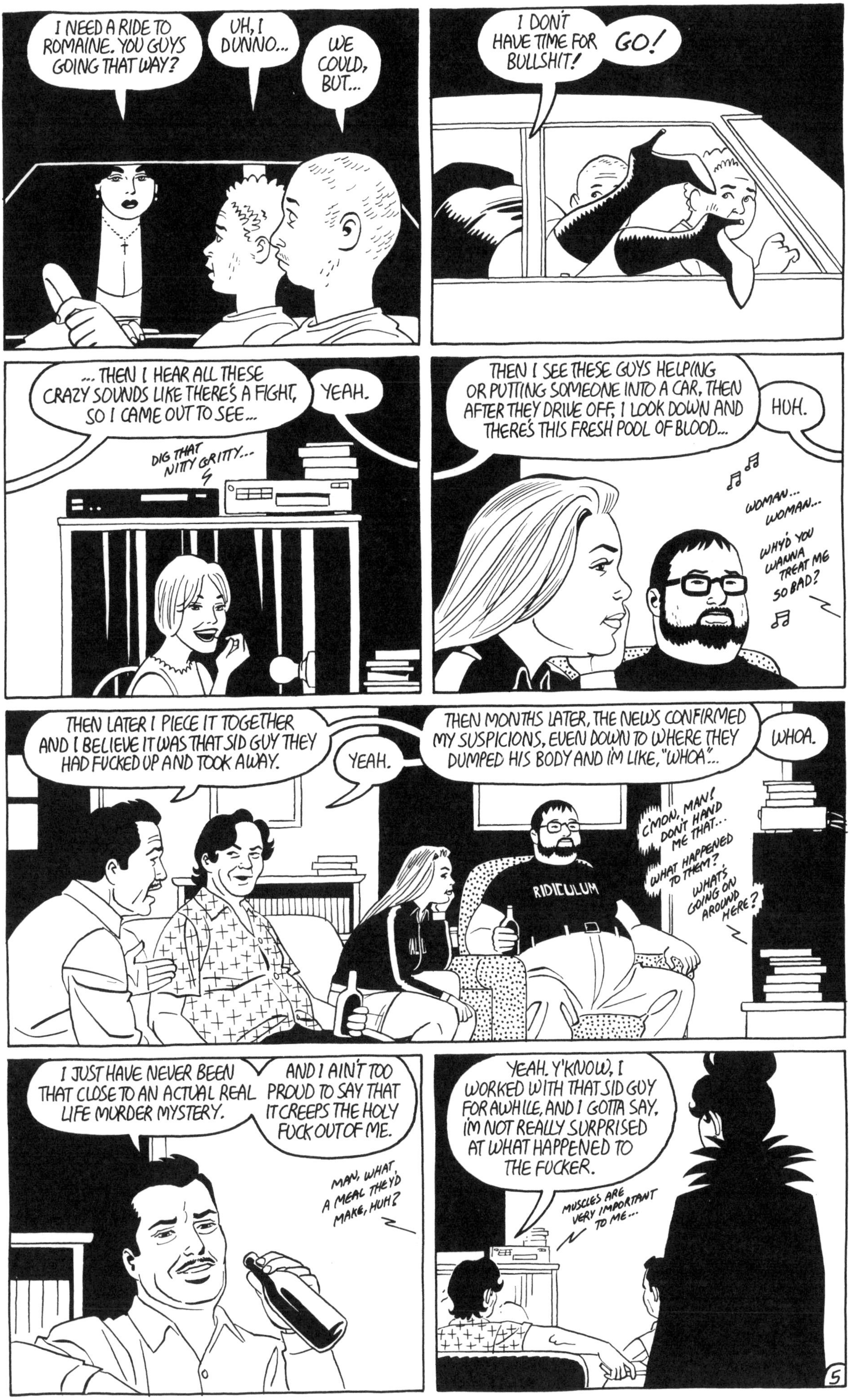
I NEED A RIDE TO ROMAINE. YOU GUYS GOING THAT WAY?
UH, I DUNNO...
WE COULD, BUT...
I DON'T HAVE TIME FOR BULLSHIT!
GO!
... THEN I HEAR ALL THESE CRAZY SOUNDS LIKE THERE'S A FIGHT, SO I CAME OUT TO SEE...
YEAH.
DIG THAT NITTY GRITTY...
THEN I SEE THESE GUYS HELPING OR PUTTING SOMEONE INTO A CAR, THEN AFTER THEY DRIVE OFF, I LOOK DOWN AND THERE'S THIS FRESH POOL OF BLOOD...
HUH.
WOMAN... WOMAN...
WHY'D YOU WANNA TREAT ME SO BAD?
THEN LATER I PIECE IT TOGETHER AND I BELIEVE IT WAS THAT SID GUY THEY HAD FUCKED UP AND TOOK AWAY.
YEAH.
THEN MONTHS LATER, THE NEWS CONFIRMED MY SUSPICIONS, EVEN DOWN TO WHERE THEY DUMPED HIS BODY AND I'M LIKE, "WHOA"...
WHOA.
C'MON, MAN! DON'T HAND ME THAT...
WHAT HAPPENED TO THEM?
WHAT'S GOING ON AROUND HERE?
RIDICULUM
I JUST HAVE NEVER BEEN THAT CLOSE TO AN ACTUAL REAL LIFE MURDER MYSTERY.
AND I AIN'T TOO PROUD TO SAY THAT IT CREEPS THE HOLY FUCK OUT OF ME.
MAN, WHAT A MEAL THEY'D MAKE, HUH?
YEAH. Y'KNOW, I WORKED WITH THAT SID GUY FOR AWHILE, AND I GOTTA SAY, I'M NOT REALLY SURPRISED AT WHAT HAPPENED TO THE FUCKER.
MUSCLES ARE VERY IMPORTANT TO ME...
5

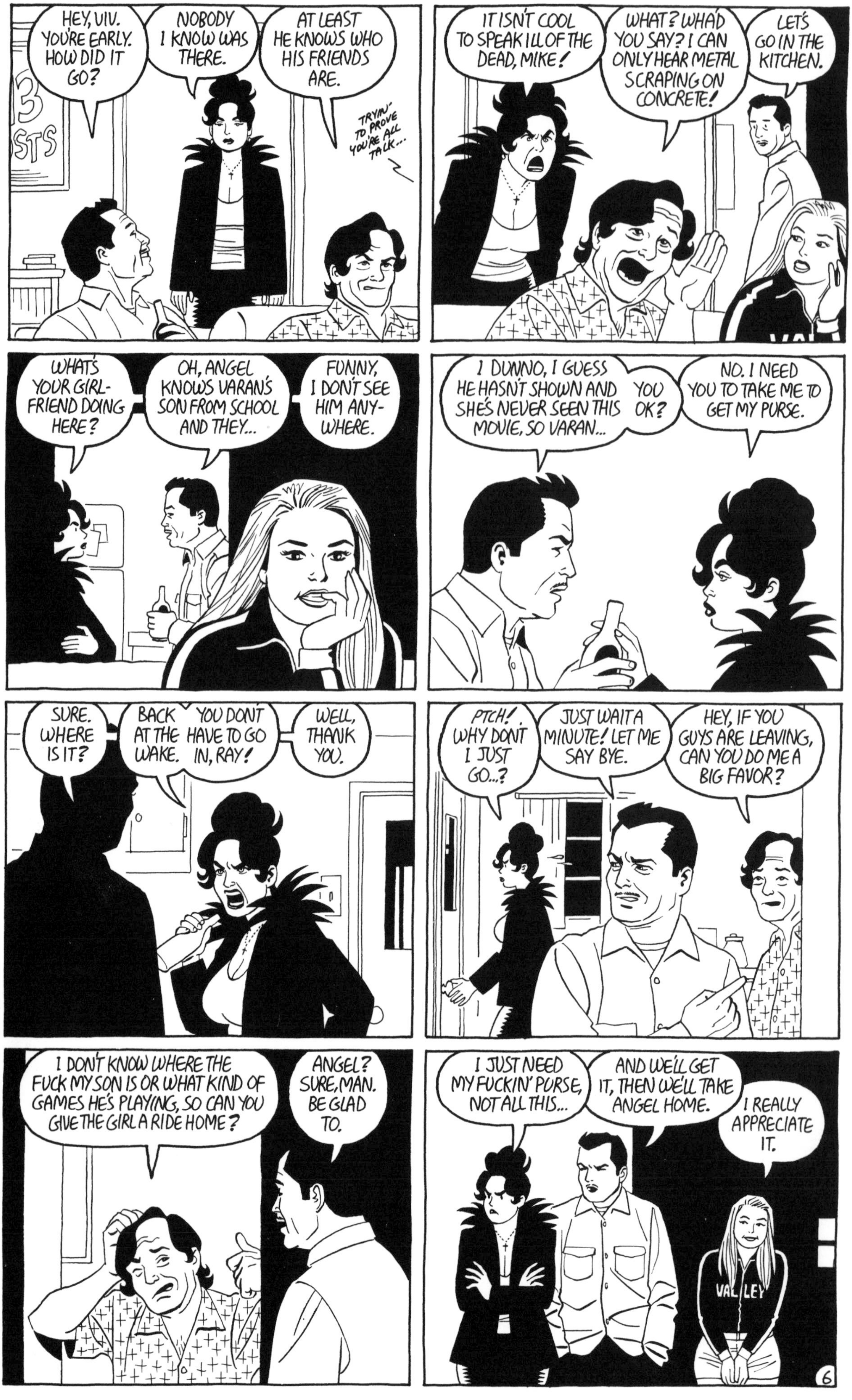
HEY, VIV. YOU'RE EARLY. HOW DID IT GO?
NOBODY I KNOW WAS THERE.
AT LEAST HE KNOWS WHO HIS FRIENDS ARE.
TRYIN' TO PROVE YOU'RE ALL TALK...
IT ISN'T COOL TO SPEAK ILL OF THE DEAD, MIKE!
WHAT? WHAD YOU SAY? I CAN ONLY HEAR METAL SCRAPING ON CONCRETE!
LET'S GO IN THE KITCHEN.
WHAT'S YOUR GIRLFRIEND DOING HERE?
OH, ANGEL KNOWS VARAN'S SON FROM SCHOOL AND THEY...
FUNNY, I DON'T SEE HIM ANYWHERE.
I DUNNO, I GUESS HE HASN'T SHOWN AND SHE'S NEVER SEEN THIS MOVIE, SO VARAN...
YOU OK?
NO. I NEED YOU TO TAKE ME TO GET MY PURSE.
SURE. WHERE IS IT?
BACK AT THE WAKE.
YOU DON'T HAVE TO GO IN, RAY!
WELL, THANK YOU.
PTCH! WHY DON'T I JUST GO...?
JUST WAIT A MINUTE! LET ME SAY BYE.
HEY, IF YOU GUYS ARE LEAVING, CAN YOU DO ME A BIG FAVOR?
I DON'T KNOW WHERE THE FUCK MY SON IS OR WHAT KIND OF GAMES HE'S PLAYING, SO CAN YOU GIVE THE GIRL A RIDE HOME?
ANGEL? SURE, MAN. BE GLAD TO.
I JUST NEED MY FUCKIN' PURSE, NOT ALL THIS...
AND WE'LL GET IT, THEN WE'LL TAKE ANGEL HOME.
I REALLY APPRECIATE IT.
VALLEY
6

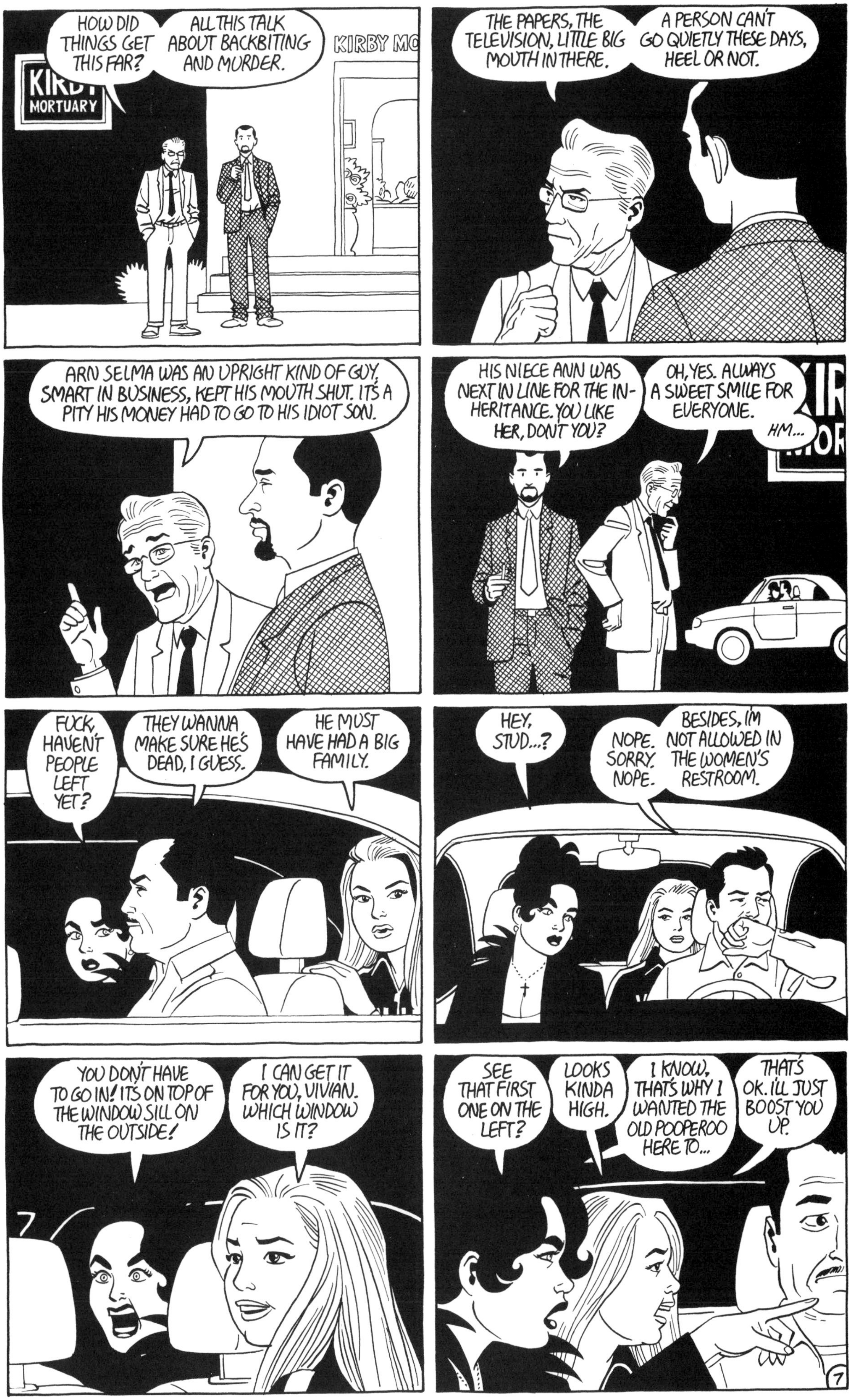
HOW DID THINGS GET THIS FAR?
ALL THIS TALK ABOUT BACKBITING AND MURDER.
KIRBY MO
MORTUARY
THE PAPERS, THE TELEVISION, LITTLE BIG MOUTH IN THERE.
A PERSON CAN'T GO QUIETLY THESE DAYS, HEEL OR NOT.
ARN SELMA WAS AN UPRIGHT KIND OF GUY, SMART IN BUSINESS, KEPT HIS MOUTH SHUT. IT'S A PITY HIS MONEY HAD TO GO TO HIS IDIOT SON.
HIS NIECE ANN WAS NEXT IN LINE FOR THE IN-HERITANCE. YOU LIKE HER, DON'T YOU?
OH, YES. ALWAYS A SWEET SMILE FOR EVERYONE.
HM...
FUCK, HAVEN'T PEOPLE LEFT YET?
THEY WANNA MAKE SURE HE'S DEAD, I GUESS.
HE MUST HAVE HAD A BIG FAMILY.
HEY, STUD...?
NOPE. SORRY. NOPE.
BESIDES, I'M NOT ALLOWED IN THE WOMEN'S RESTROOM.
YOU DON'T HAVE TO GO IN! IT'S ON TOP OF THE WINDOW SILL ON THE OUTSIDE!
I CAN GET IT FOR YOU, VIVIAN. WHICH WINDOW IS IT?
SEE THAT FIRST ONE ON THE LEFT?
LOOKS KINDA HIGH.
I KNOW, THAT'S WHY I WANTED THE OLD POOPEROO HERE TO...
THAT'S OK. I'LL JUST BOOST YOU UP.
7

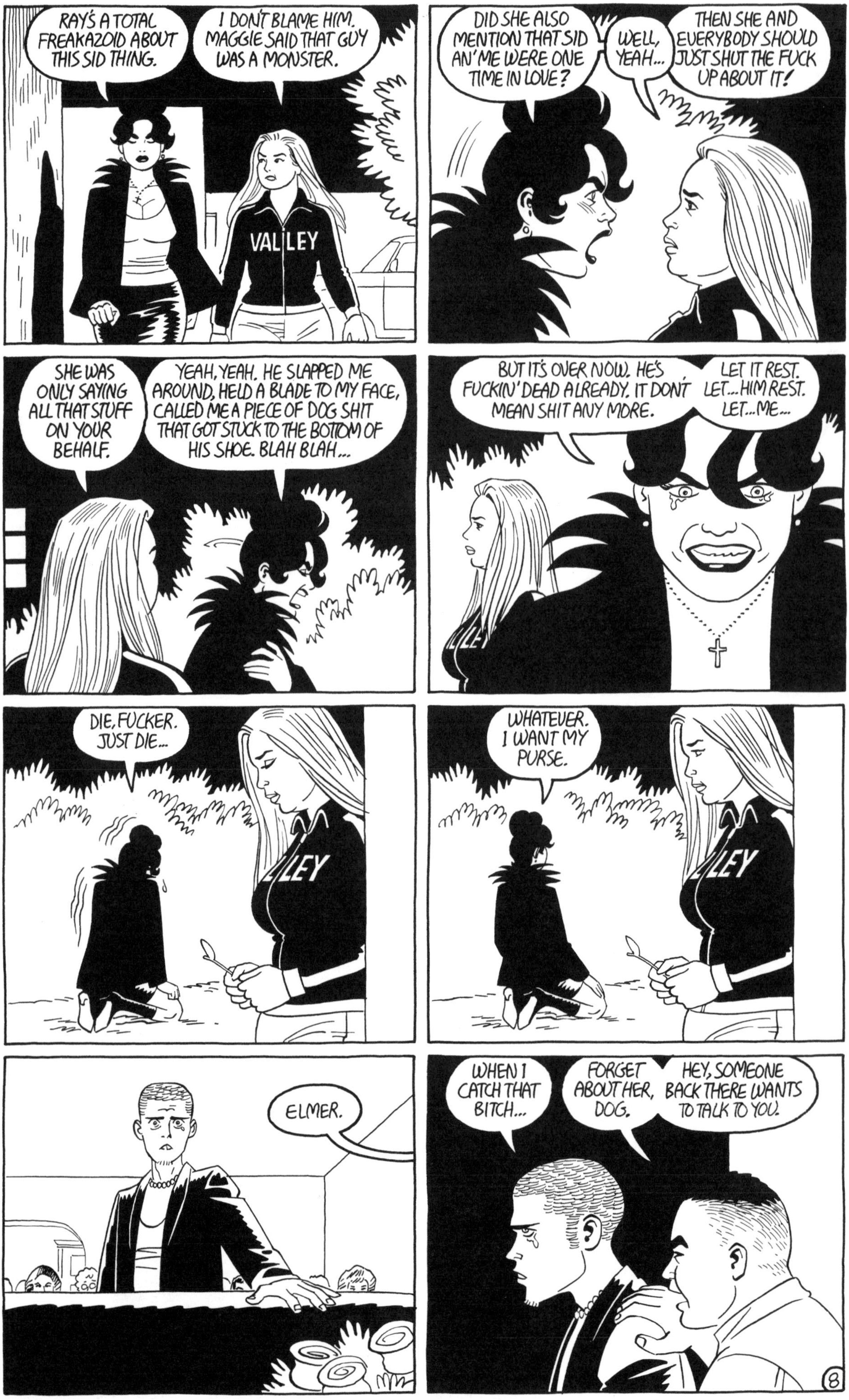
RAY'S A TOTAL FREAKAZOID ABOUT THIS SID THING.
I DON'T BLAME HIM. MAGGIE SAID THAT GUY WAS A MONSTER.
VALLEY
DID SHE ALSO MENTION THAT SID AN' ME WERE ONE TIME IN LOVE?
WELL, YEAH...
THEN SHE AND EVERYBODY SHOULD JUST SHUT THE FUCK UP ABOUT IT!
SHE WAS ONLY SAYING ALL THAT STUFF ON YOUR BEHALF.
YEAH, YEAH. HE SLAPPED ME AROUND, HELD A BLADE TO MY FACE, CALLED ME A PIECE OF DOG SHIT THAT GOT STUCK TO THE BOTTOM OF HIS SHOE. BLAH BLAH...
BUT IT'S OVER NOW. HE'S FUCKIN' DEAD ALREADY. IT DON'T MEAN SHIT ANY MORE.
LET IT REST. LET...HIM REST. LET...ME...
DIE, FUCKER. JUST DIE...
WHATEVER. I WANT MY PURSE.
ELMER.
WHEN I CATCH THAT BITCH...
FORGET ABOUT HER, DOG.
HEY, SOMEONE BACK THERE WANTS TO TALK TO YOU.
8

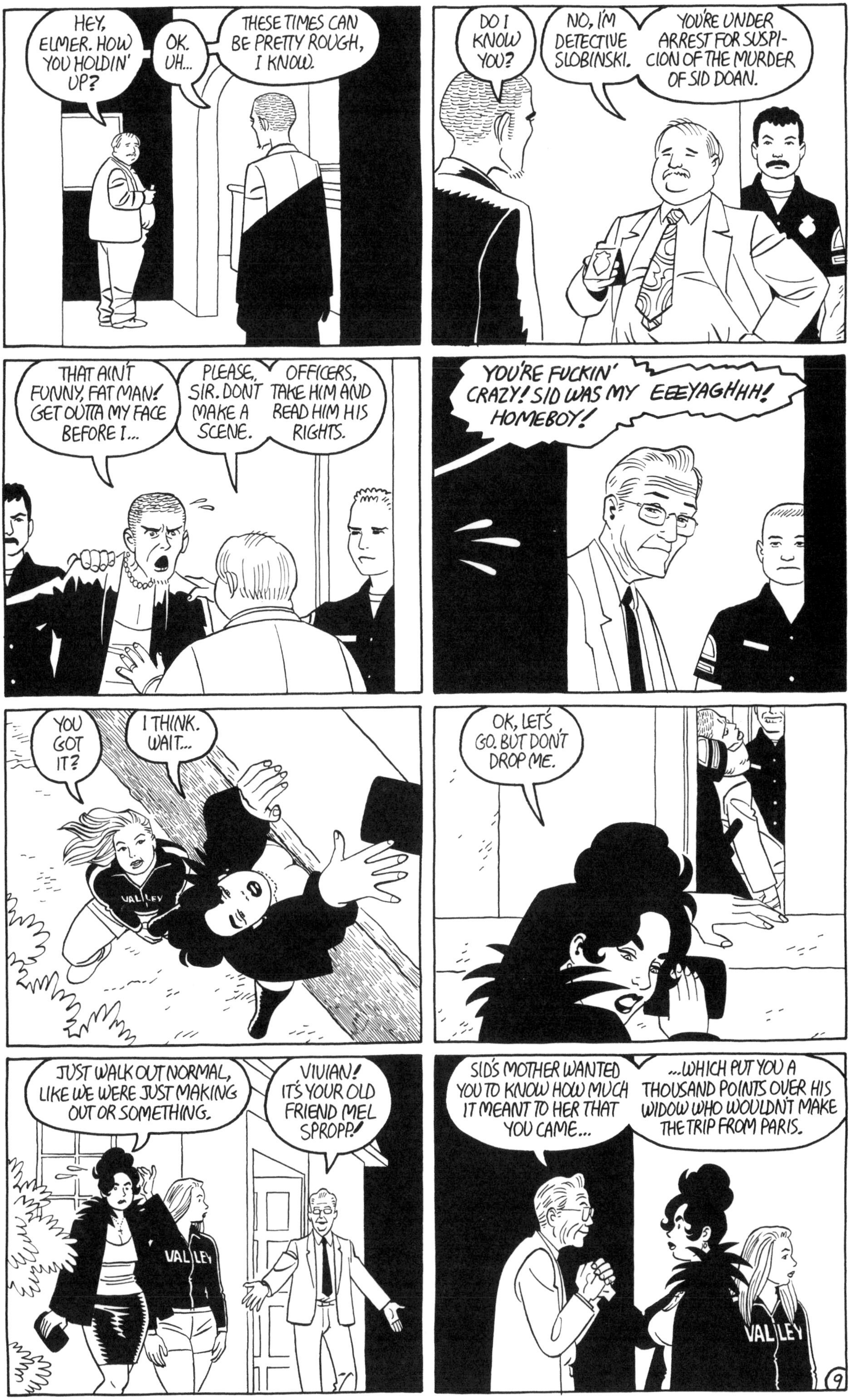
HEY, ELMER. HOW YOU HOLDIN' UP?
OK. UH...
THESE TIMES CAN BE PRETTY ROUGH, I KNOW.
DO I KNOW YOU?
NO, I'M DETECTIVE SLOBINSKI.
YOU'RE UNDER ARREST FOR SUSPICION OF THE MURDER OF SID DOAN.
THAT AIN'T FUNNY, FAT MAN! GET OUTTA MY FACE BEFORE I...
PLEASE, SIR. DON'T MAKE A SCENE.
OFFICERS, TAKE HIM AND READ HIM HIS RIGHTS.
YOU'RE FUCKIN' CRAZY! SID WAS MY HOMEBOY!
EEEYAGHHH!
YOU GOT IT?
I THINK. WAIT...
VALLEY
OK, LET'S GO. BUT DON'T DROP ME.
JUST WALK OUT NORMAL, LIKE WE WERE JUST MAKING OUT OR SOMETHING.
VIVIAN! IT'S YOUR OLD FRIEND MEL SPROPP!
VALLEY
SID'S MOTHER WANTED YOU TO KNOW HOW MUCH IT MEANT TO HER THAT YOU CAME...
...WHICH PUT YOU A THOUSAND POINTS OVER HIS WIDOW WHO WOULDN'T MAKE THE TRIP FROM PARIS.
VALLEY
9

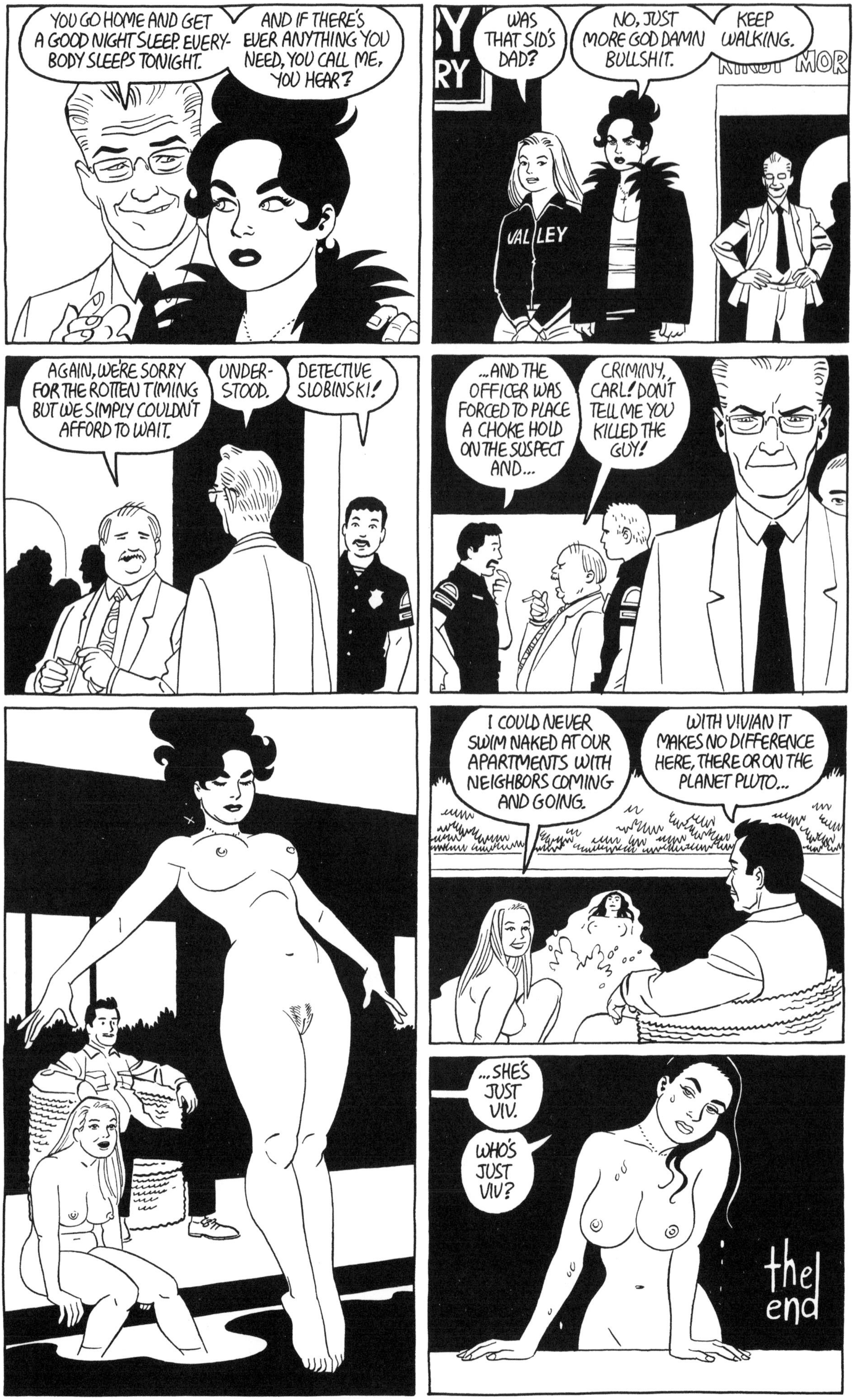
YOU GO HOME AND GET A GOOD NIGHT SLEEP. EVERYBODY SLEEPS TONIGHT.
AND IF THERE'S EVER ANYTHING YOU NEED, YOU CALL ME, YOU HEAR?
WAS THAT SID'S DAD?
NO, JUST MORE GOD DAMN BULLSHIT.
KEEP WALKING.
VALLEY
AGAIN, WE'RE SORRY FOR THE ROTTEN TIMING BUT WE SIMPLY COULDN'T AFFORD TO WAIT.
UNDERSTOOD.
DETECTIVE SLOBINSKI!
...AND THE OFFICER WAS FORCED TO PLACE A CHOKE HOLD ON THE SUSPECT AND...
CRIMINY, CARL! DON'T TELL ME YOU KILLED THE GUY!
I COULD NEVER SWIM NAKED AT OUR APARTMENTS WITH NEIGHBORS COMING AND GOING.
WITH VIVIAN IT MAKES NO DIFFERENCE HERE, THERE OR ON THE PLANET PLUTO...
...SHE'S JUST VIV.
WHO'S JUST VIV?
the end

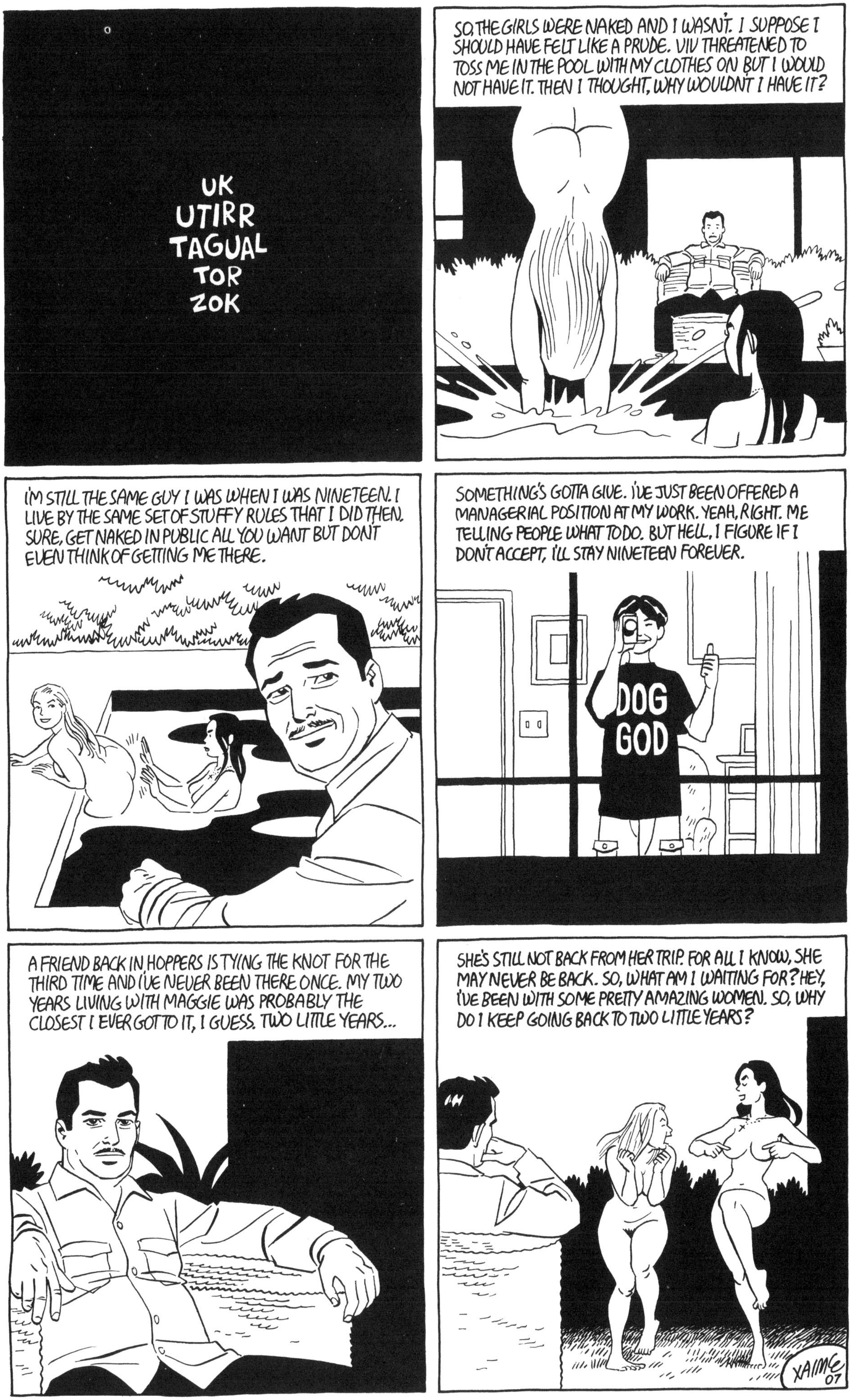
UK
UTIRR
TAGUAL
TOR
ZOK
SO, THE GIRLS WERE NAKED AND I WASN'T. I SUPPOSE I SHOULD HAVE FELT LIKE A PRUDE. VIV THREATENED TO TOSS ME IN THE POOL WITH MY CLOTHES ON BUT I WOULD NOT HAVE IT. THEN I THOUGHT, WHY WOULDN'T I HAVE IT?
I'M STILL THE SAME GUY I WAS WHEN I WAS NINETEEN. I LIVE BY THE SAME SET OF STUFFY RULES THAT I DID THEN. SURE, GET NAKED IN PUBLIC ALL YOU WANT BUT DON'T EVEN THINK OF GETTING ME THERE.
SOMETHING'S GOTTA GIVE. I'VE JUST BEEN OFFERED A MANAGERIAL POSITION AT MY WORK. YEAH, RIGHT. ME TELLING PEOPLE WHAT TO DO. BUT HELL, I FIGURE IF I DON'T ACCEPT, I'LL STAY NINETEEN FOREVER.
DOG
GOD
A FRIEND BACK IN HOPPERS IS TYING THE KNOT FOR THE THIRD TIME AND I'VE NEVER BEEN THERE ONCE. MY TWO YEARS LIVING WITH MAGGIE WAS PROBABLY THE CLOSEST I EVER GOT TO IT, I GUESS. TWO LITTLE YEARS...
SHE'S STILL NOT BACK FROM HER TRIP. FOR ALL I KNOW, SHE MAY NEVER BE BACK. SO, WHAT AM I WAITING FOR? HEY, I'VE BEEN WITH SOME PRETTY AMAZING WOMEN. SO, WHY DO I KEEP GOING BACK TO TWO LITTLE YEARS?
XAIME 07

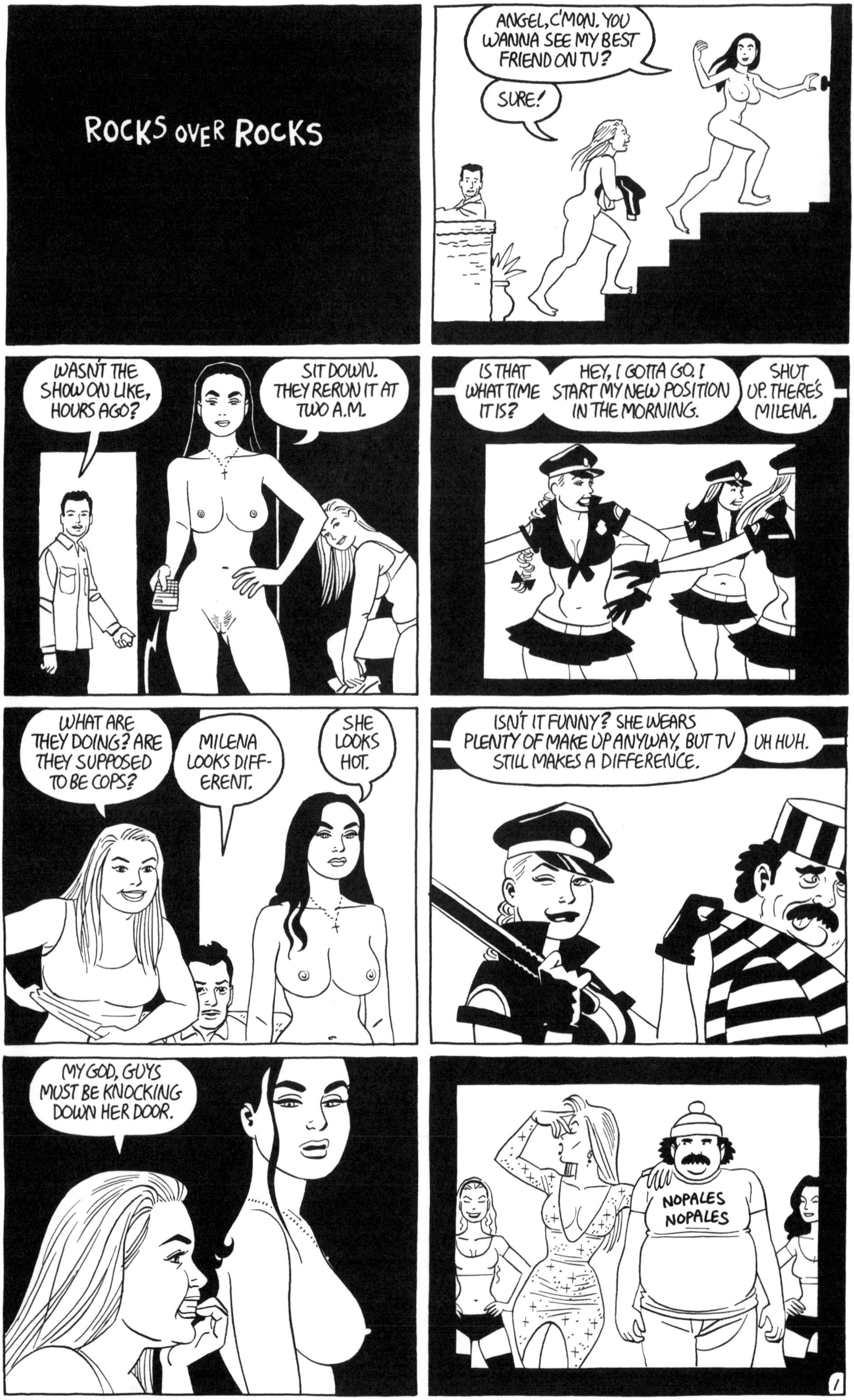
ROCKS OVER ROCKS
ANGEL, C'MON. YOU WANNA SEE MY BEST FRIEND ON TV?
SURE!
WASN'T THE SHOW ON LIKE, HOURS AGO?
SIT DOWN. THEY RERUN IT AT TWO A.M.
IS THAT WHAT TIME IT IS?
HEY, I GOTTA GO. I START MY NEW POSITION IN THE MORNING.
SHUT UP. THERE'S MILENA.
WHAT ARE THEY DOING? ARE THEY SUPPOSED TO BE COPS?
MILENA LOOKS DIFF- ERENT.
SHE LOOKS HOT.
ISN'T IT FUNNY? SHE WEARS PLENTY OF MAKE UP ANYWAY, BUT TV STILL MAKES A DIFFERENCE.
UH HUH.
MY GOD, GUYS MUST BE KNOCKING DOWN HER DOOR.
NOPALES NOPALES
1

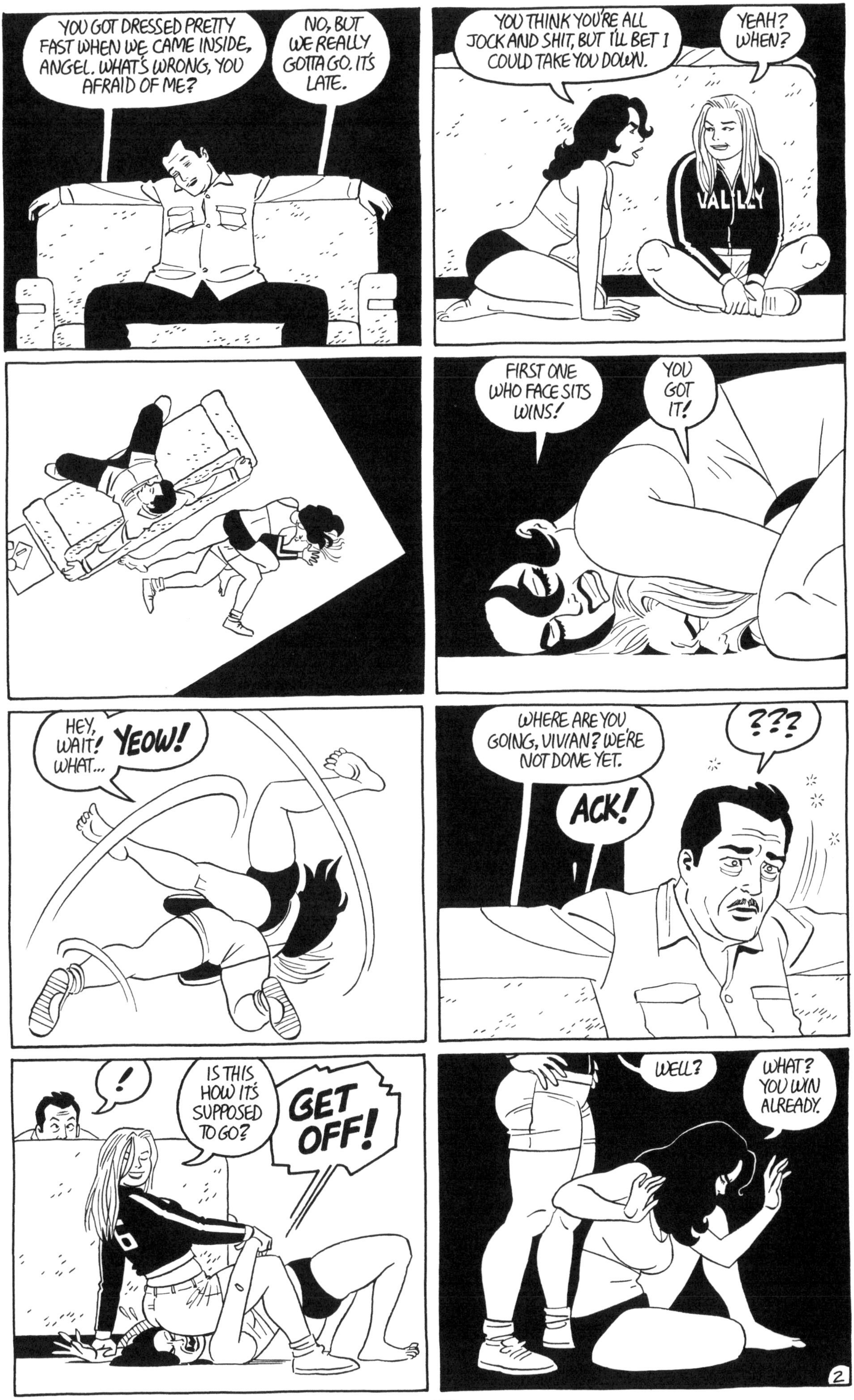

YOU GOT DRESSED PRETTY FAST WHEN WE CAME INSIDE, ANGEL. WHAT'S WRONG, YOU AFRAID OF ME?
NO, BUT WE REALLY GOTTA GO. IT'S LATE.
YOU THINK YOU'RE ALL JOCK AND SHIT, BUT I'LL BET I COULD TAKE YOU DOWN.
YEAH? WHEN?
VALLEY
FIRST ONE WHO FACE SITS WINS!
YOU GOT IT!
HEY, WAIT! WHAT...
YEOW!
WHERE ARE YOU GOING, VIVIAN? WE'RE NOT DONE YET.
???
ACK!
!
IS THIS HOW IT'S SUPPOSED TO GO?
GET OFF!
WELL?
WHAT? YOU WIN ALREADY.
2

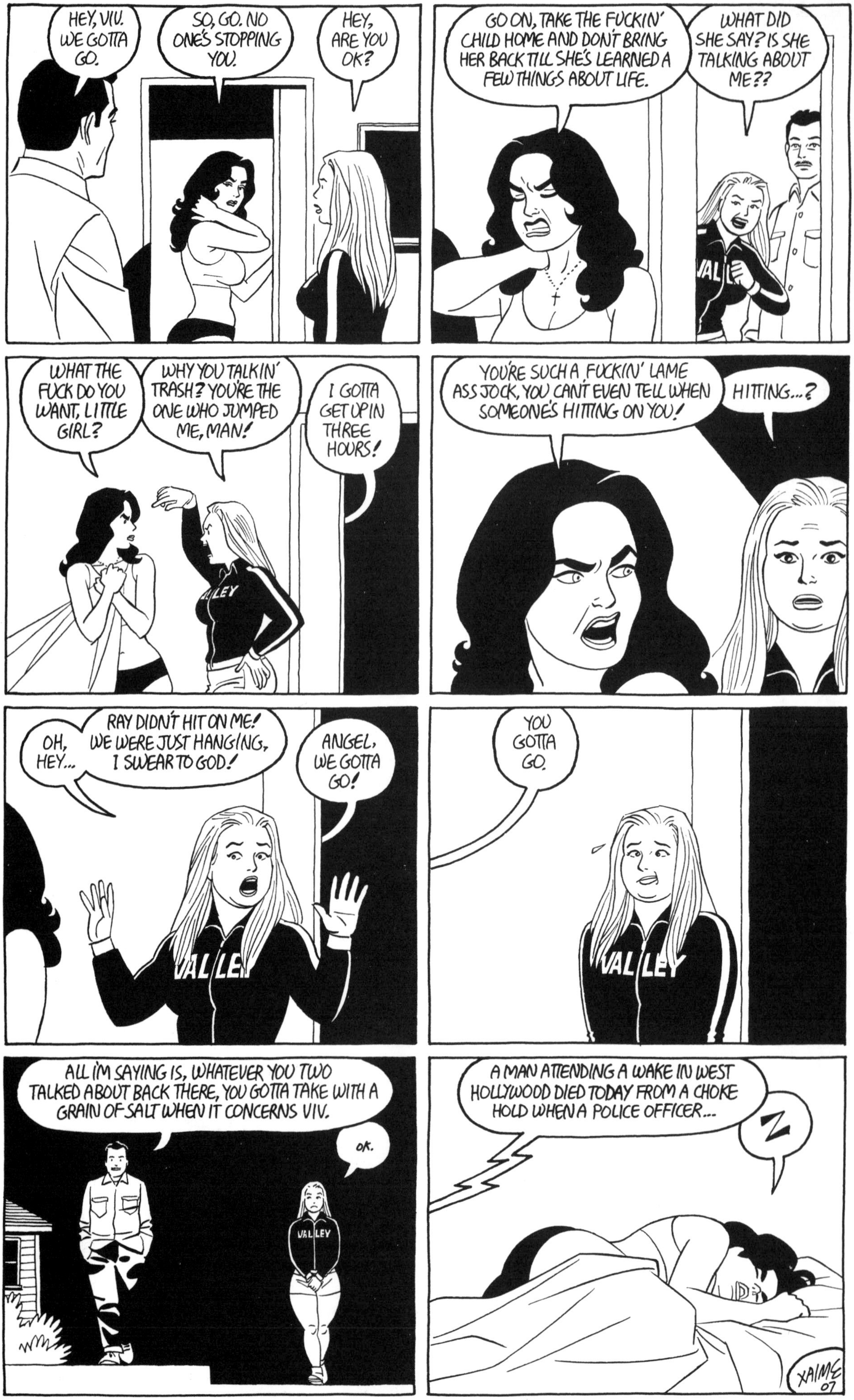
HEY, VIV. WE GOTTA GO.
SO, GO. NO ONE'S STOPPING YOU.
HEY, ARE YOU OK?
GO ON, TAKE THE FUCKIN' CHILD HOME AND DON'T BRING HER BACK TILL SHE'S LEARNED A FEW THINGS ABOUT LIFE.
WHAT DID SHE SAY? IS SHE TALKING ABOUT ME??
VALLEY
WHAT THE FUCK DO YOU WANT, LITTLE GIRL?
WHY YOU TALKIN' TRASH? YOU'RE THE ONE WHO JUMPED ME, MAN!
I GOTTA GET UP IN THREE HOURS!
VALLEY
YOU'RE SUCH A FUCKIN' LAME ASS JOCK, YOU CAN'T EVEN TELL WHEN SOMEONE'S HITTING ON YOU!
HITTING...?
OH, HEY...
RAY DIDN'T HIT ON ME! WE WERE JUST HANGING, I SWEAR TO GOD!
ANGEL, WE GOTTA GO!
VALLEY
YOU GOTTA GO.
VALLEY
ALL I'M SAYING IS, WHATEVER YOU TWO TALKED ABOUT BACK THERE, YOU GOTTA TAKE WITH A GRAIN OF SALT WHEN IT CONCERNS VIV.
OK.
VALLEY
A MAN ATTENDING A WAKE IN WEST HOLLYWOOD DIED TODAY FROM A CHOKE HOLD WHEN A POLICE OFFICER...
Z
XAIME 07

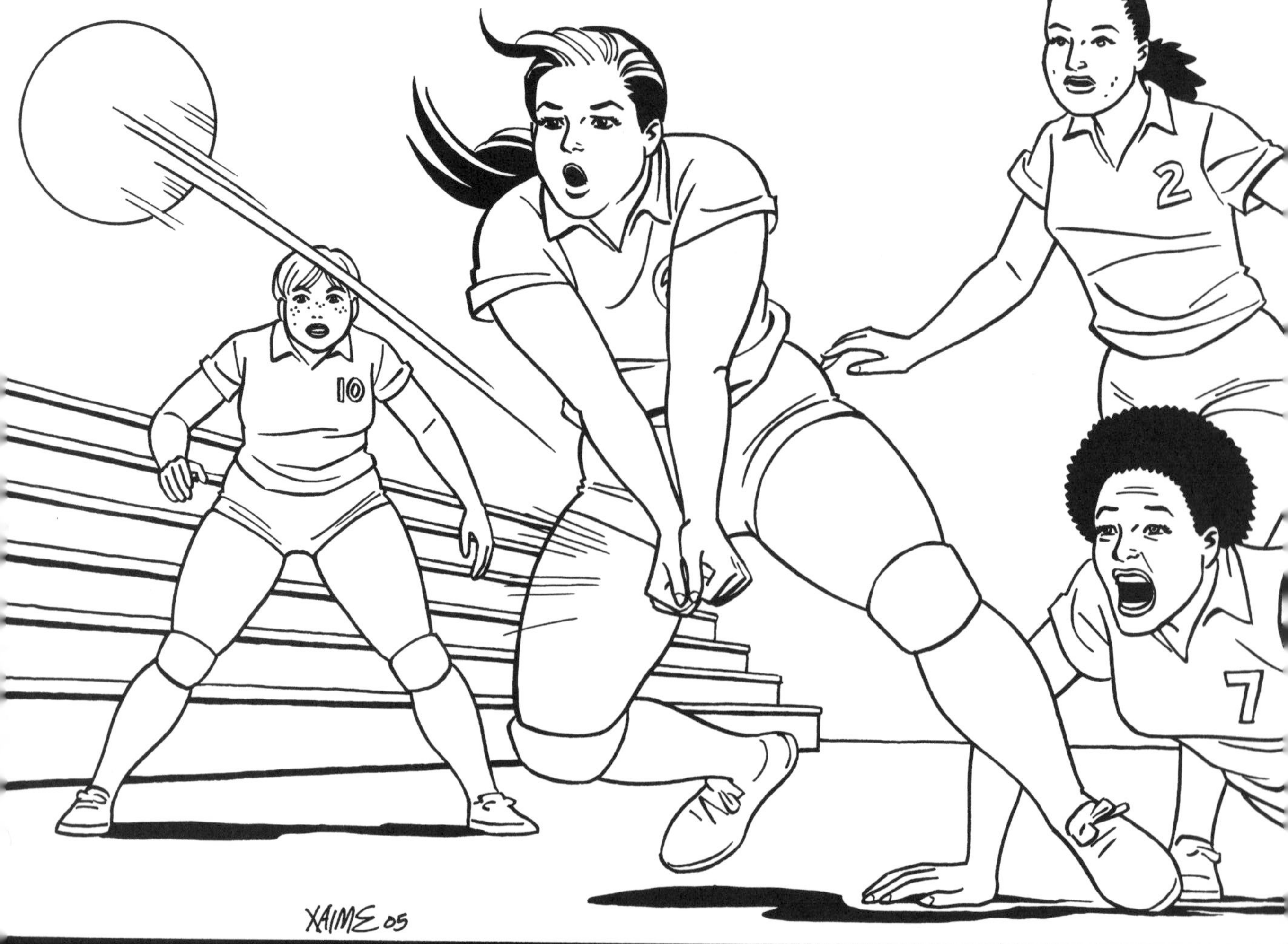
10
2
7
XAIME 05

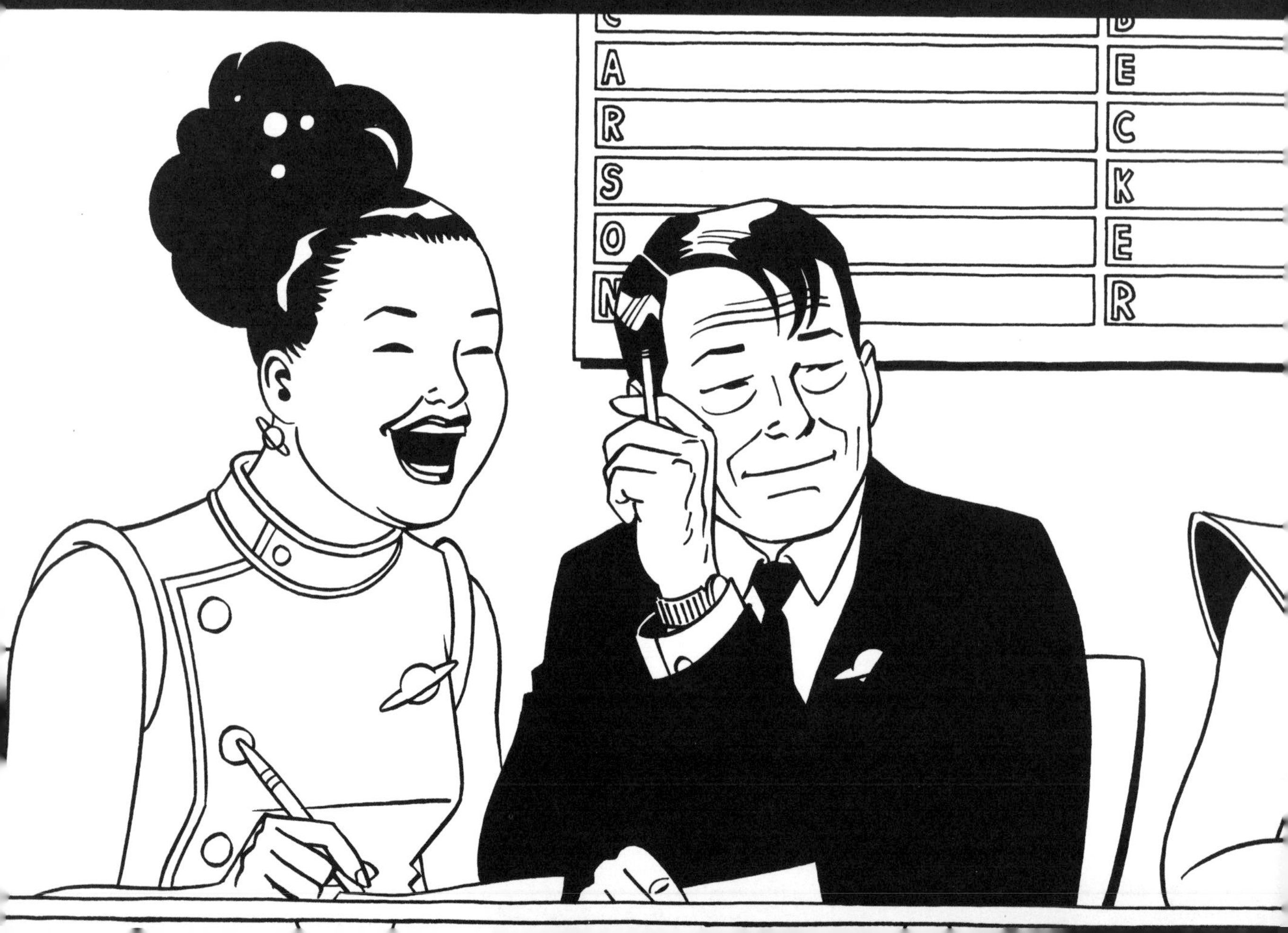
CARSON
BECKER

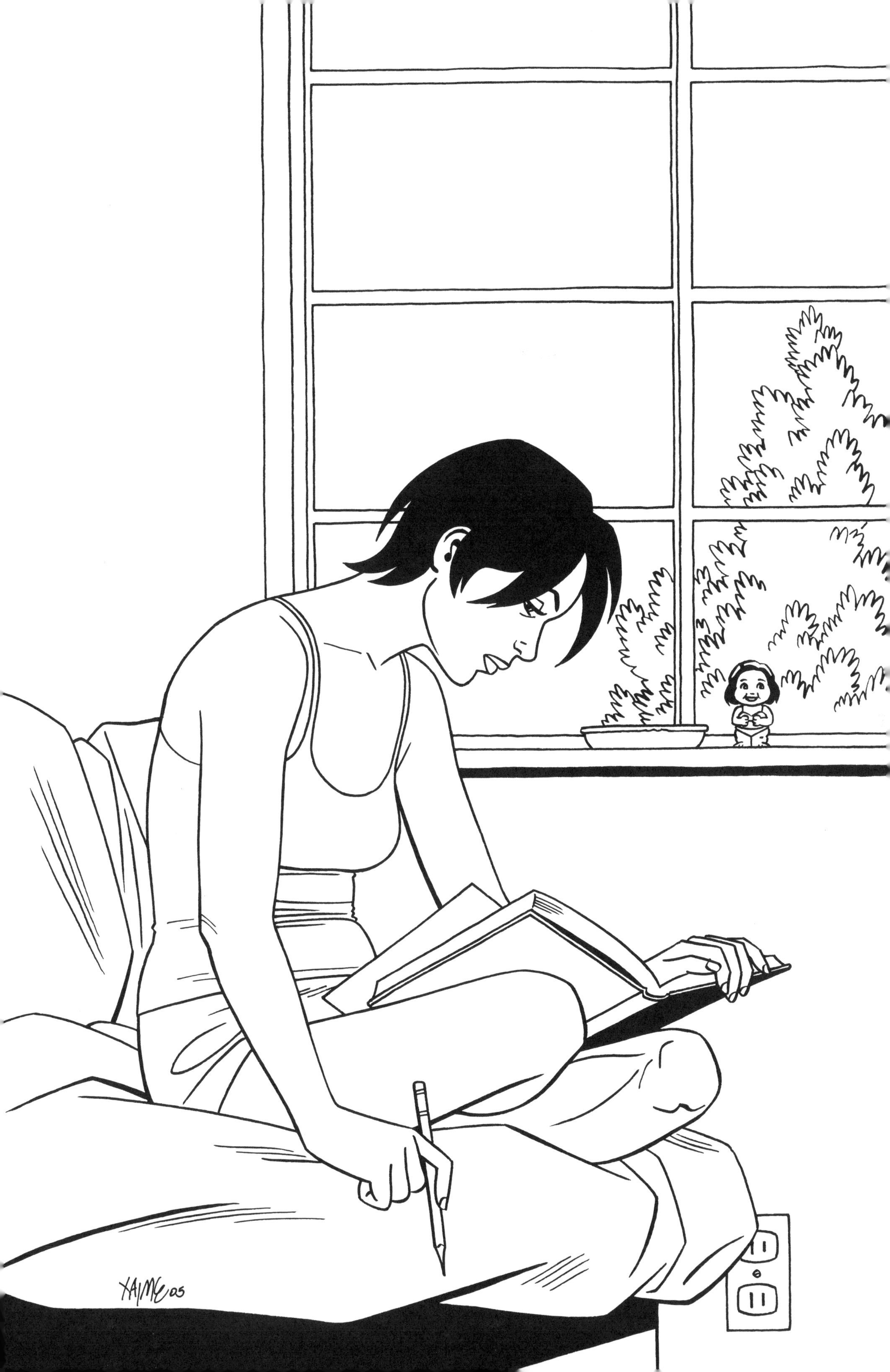

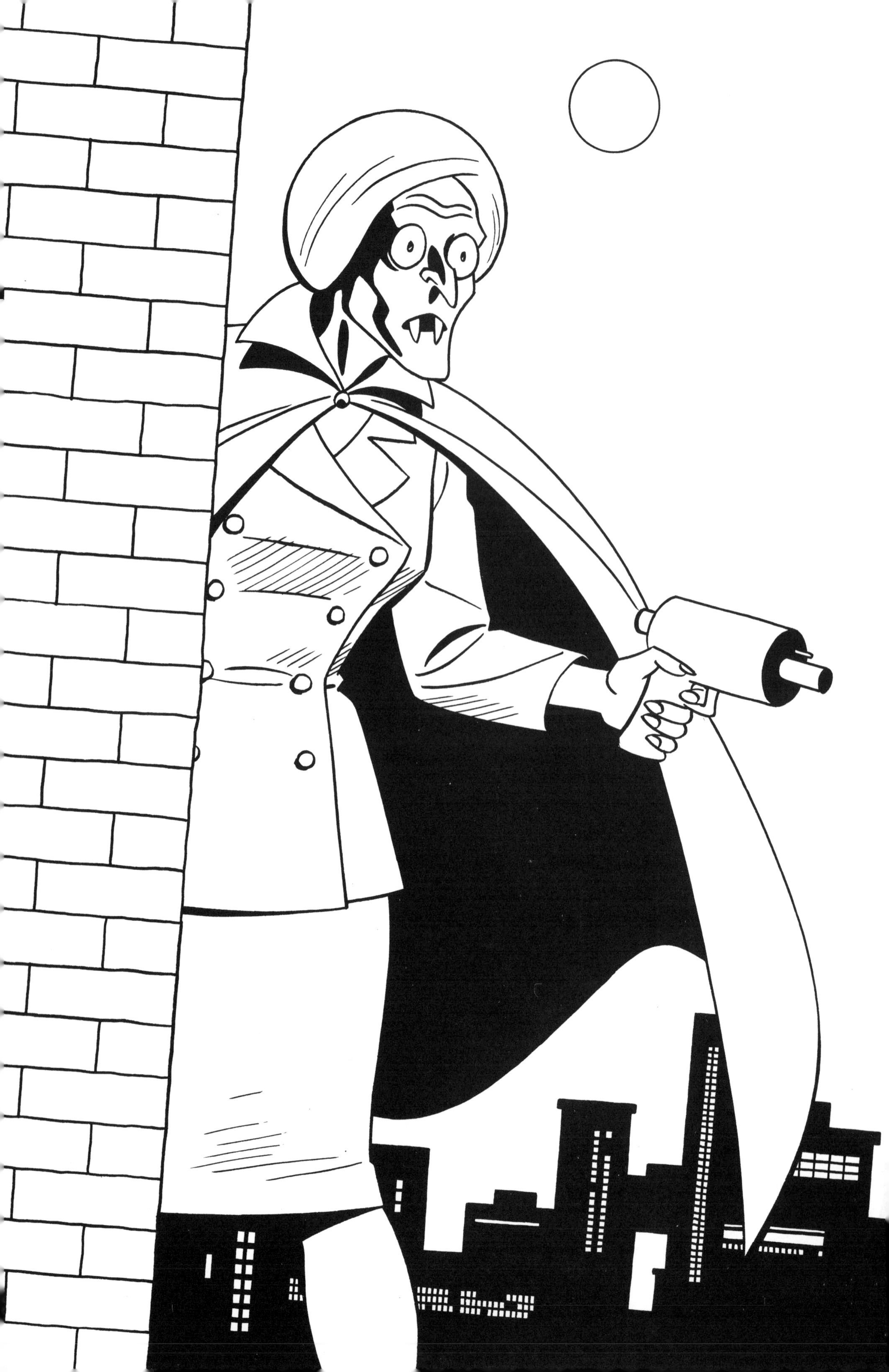

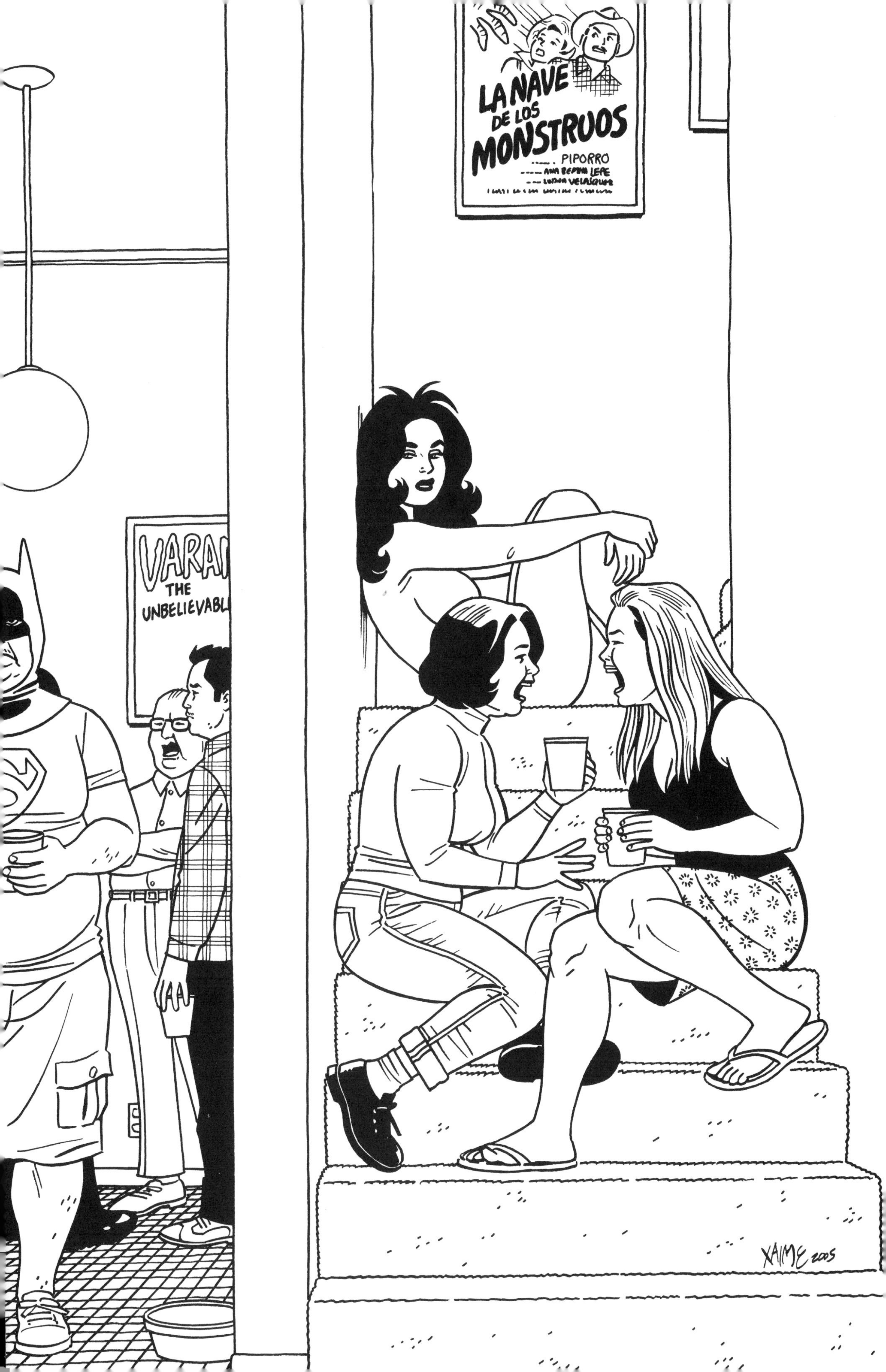
LA NAVE
DE LOS
MONSTRUOS
PIPORRO
ANA BERTHA LEPE
LORENA VELASQUEZ
VARAN
THE
UNBELIEVABL
XAIME 2005

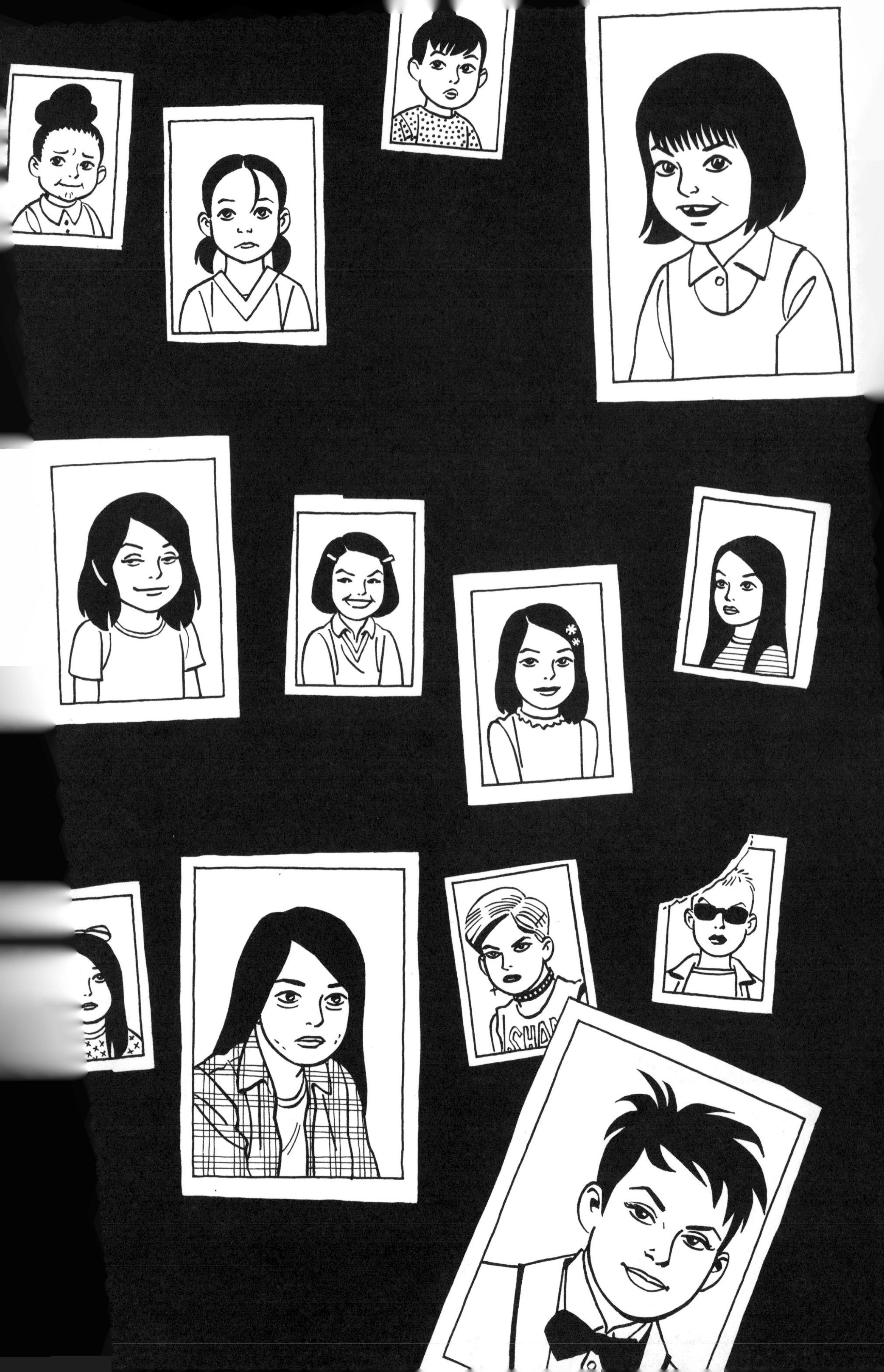

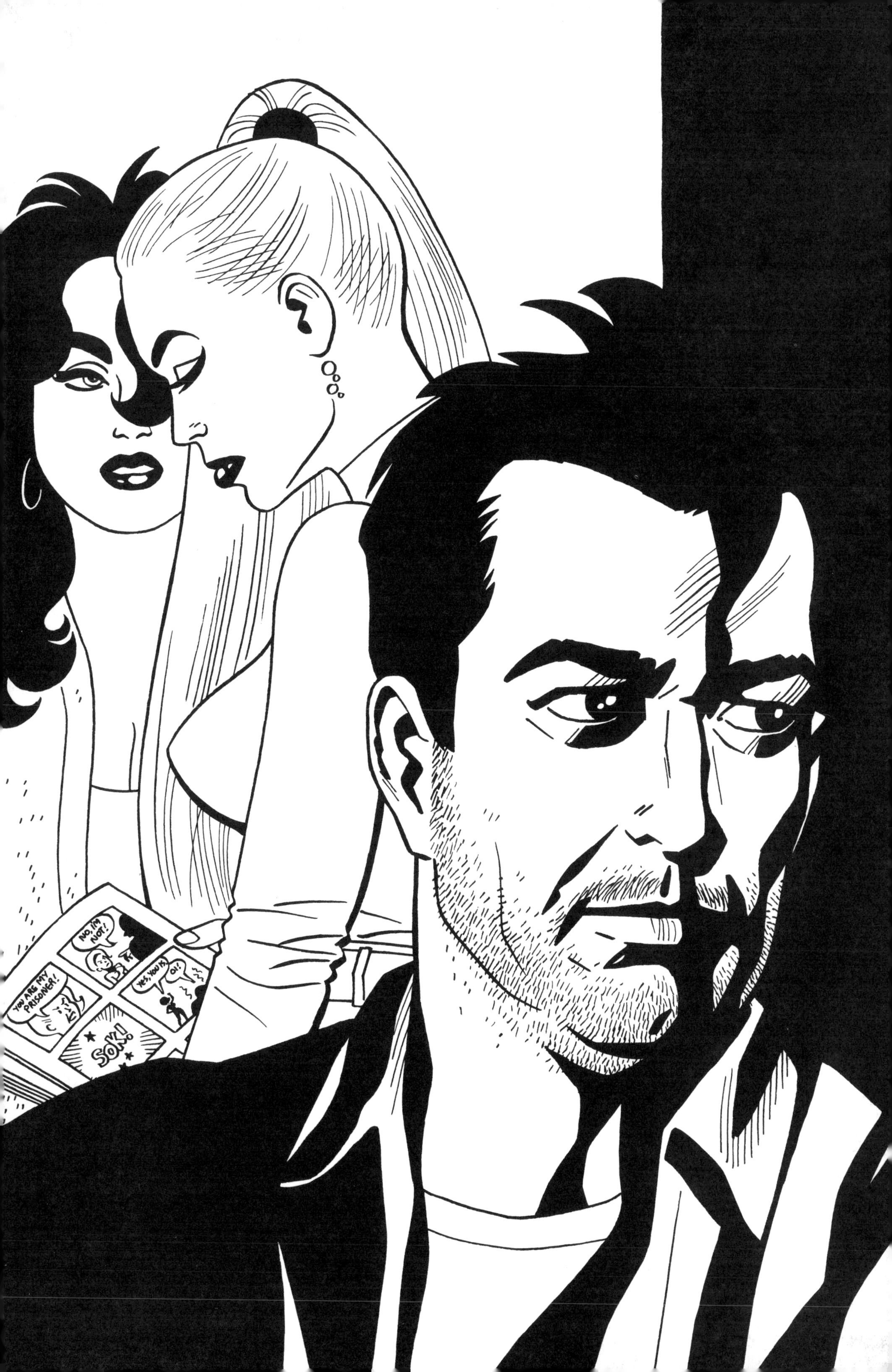
YOU ARE MY PRISONER!
NO, I'M NOT!
YES, YOU IS.
OI!
SOK!

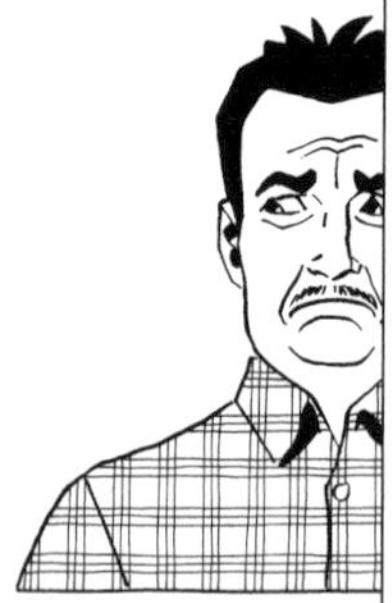

Love & Rockets Book 1
MUSIC FOR MECHANICS
Short stories by Los Bros.; collects L&R #1-2

Love & Rockets Book 2
CHELO'S BURDEN
Short stories by Los Bros.;
Collects L&R #3-4

Love & Rockets Book 3
LAS MUJERES PERDIDAS
Graphic novel by Jaime
plus short stories by Gilbert

Love & Rockets Book 4
TEARS FROM HEAVEN
Short stories by Gilbert & Jaime

Love & Rockets Book 5
HOUSE OF RAGING WOMEN
Short stories by Gilbert & Jaime

Love & Rockets Book 6
DUCK FEET
Short stories by Gilbert & Jaime

Love & Rockets Book 7
THE DEATH OF SPEEDY
Graphic novella and short stories by Jaime

Love & Rockets Book 8
BLOOD OF PALOMAR
Graphic novel by Gilbert

Love & Rockets Book 9
Flies on the Ceiling
Short stories by Gilbert & Jaime

Love & Rockets Book 10
Love & Rockets X
Graphic novel by Gilbert

Love & Rockets Book 11
Wigwam Bam
Graphic novel by Jaime

Love & Rockets Book 12
POISON RIVER
Graphic novel by Gilbert

Love & Rockets Book 13
CHESTER SQUARE
Graphic novel by Jaime

Love & Rockets Book 14
LUBA CONQUERS THE WORLD
Short stories by Gilbert

Love & Rockets Book 15
HERNANDEZ SATYRICON
Short stories by Los Bros.

Love & Rockets Book 16
WHOA, NELLIE!
Graphic novel by Jaime

Love & Rockets Book 17
FEAR OF COMICS
Short stories by Gilbert

Love & Rockets Book 18
LOCAS IN LOVE
Short stories by Jaime

Love & Rockets Book 19
LUBA IN AMERICA
Short stories by Gilbert

Love & Rockets Book 20
DICKS AND DEEDEES
Short stories by Jaime

LOVE & ROCKETS SKETCHBOOKS
Volume 1 and Volume 2
By Gilbert & Jaime

Love & Rockets Book 21
LUBA: THE BOOK OF OFELIA
Short stories by Gilbert

Love & Rockets Book 22
GHOST OF HOPPERS
Graphic novel by Jaime

Love & Rockets Book 23
LUBA: THREE DAUGHTERS
Short stories by Gilbert

Love & Rockets Book 24
THE EDUCATION OF HOPEY GLASS
Short stories by Jaime

www.fantagraphics.com